The Best is Yet to Be

The First 125 Years of a Law Firm

Published by Womble Carlyle Sandridge & Rice, PLLC, in association with John F. Blair, Publisher
WINSTON-SALEM, NORTH CAROLINA

The Best is Yet to Be

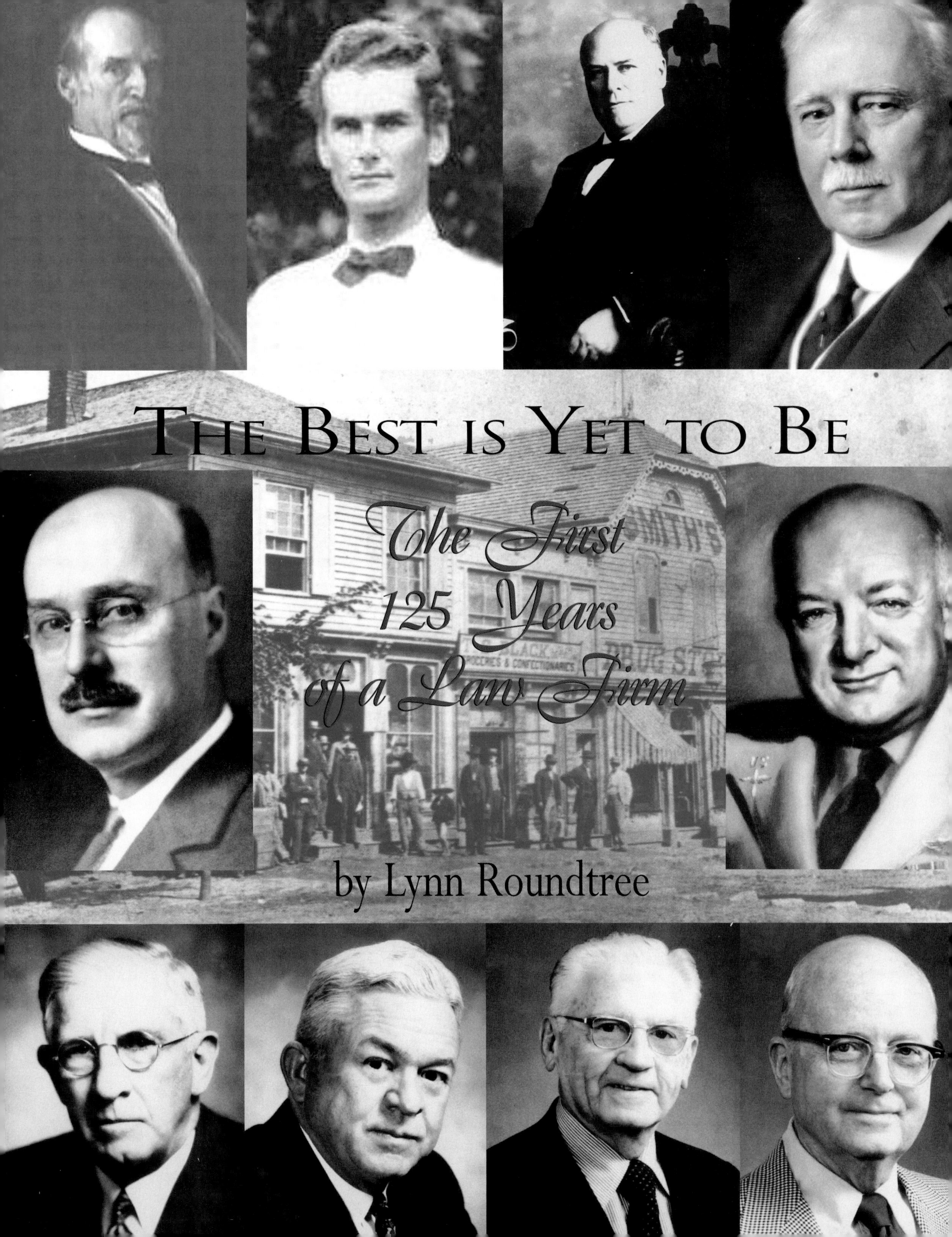

The First 125 Years of a Law Firm

by Lynn Roundtree

*The paper in this book meets the guidelines
for permanence and durability of the
Committee on Production Guidelines for
Book Longevity of the Council on Library Resources.*

Library of Congress Cataloging-in-Publication Data

Roundtree, Lynn Paul.
The best is yet to be: the first 125 years of a law firm / by Lynn P. Roundtree
p. cm.
Includes bibliographical references and index.
ISBN 0-89587-251-X (alk. paper)
1. Womble, Carlyle, Sandridge & Rice—History. 2. Law firms—North Carolina—
History. I. Title.

KF354.N65 R68 2001
338.7'6134'009756—dc21
2001037610

Text design by Debra Long Hampton

This book is

dedicated

to the staff of

Womble Carlyle Sandridge & Rice, PLLC.

You make it all possible.

CONTENTS

Foreword by William F. Womble ix
Preface by John L.W. Garrou xi
Acknowledgments xiii
Introduction: In the Early Days of Its Prosperity: Winston in 1876 xv

Chapter 1 Starting a Tradition: 1876–1885 3
Chapter 2 A Growing Practice: 1885–1890 15
Chapter 3 From East to West: 1890–1896 23
Chapter 4 Covering All the Bases: 1896–1905 33
Chapter 5 Arrivals and Departures: 1905–1910 41
Chapter 6 A Firm Consolidation: 1911–1920 51
Chapter 7 A Building Boom Town: 1920–1929 65
Chapter 8 The Habit of Success: 1930–1939 75
Chapter 9 Service in a Time of War: 1940–1945 85
Chapter 10 Returning to Responsibilities: 1946–1954 95
Chapter 11 Expanding Opportunities: 1954–1965 107
Chapter 12 Beginnings and Endings: 1966–1976 119
Chapter 13 Planning for the Future: 1976–1982 133
Chapter 14 Branching Out: 1982–1987 145
Chapter 15 Investing in the Future: 1987–1996 155
Chapter 16 Embracing Change: 1996– 165

Appendix A FirmLogic, LP 183
Appendix B Womble Carlyle Distinguished Service Awards Winners 185
Appendix C Predecessor Names of Womble Carlyle Sandridge & Rice 187
Bibliography 189
Index 198

Foreword
A GLIMPSE BACK—AS WE GO FORWARD

In my 84 years of living and nearly 62 years with our firm, it has been my happy privilege to be associated with some of the best and finest members of the legal profession, staff, and clients.

Clement Manly (known to all as Colonel Manly) was a highly esteemed member of our firm from 1891 until his death in 1928. When I was a small boy, I knew Colonel Manly as our beloved next-door neighbor on Summit Street. One of Colonel Manly's peers said of him, "To him, the law is a noble profession. The ethics of the profession are to him as sacred as the canons of his religious faith." Colonel Manly was an early builder of our firm and mentor to my father, B. S. Womble, who joined the firm in January 1911 and was a member from then until his death in 1976. Dad, an outstanding lawyer and citizen and a wonderful family man, led the firm's management and growth for a number of years following Colonel Manly's death.

William Mayhew Hendren, a member of our firm from 1896 until his death a month before I came with the firm in 1939, was a fine man, an eminent "lawyer's lawyer." Mr. Hendren's "Philosophy of Life," found among his papers after his death, read as follows:

A Philosophy of Life

> To measure life by the standard of love, to prize wealth as a potential service, reputation as a latent influence, learning for the light it can shed, power for the help it can give, station for the good it can do; to treat others as I would be treated, and myself as my best friend; to make no gain by another's pain, to harbor no thought of another which I would be unwilling that they should know; to say nothing unkind to amuse myself, and nothing false to please others; to take no pride in weaker men's failings and to bear no malice towards those who do no wrong; to pity the selfish no less than the poor, and the proud as much as the outcast, and the cruel even more than the oppressed, to worship God in all that is good and

> true and beautiful; to serve Christ whenever a sad heart can be made happy, or a wrong will set right; to recognize God's Kingdom in every institution and person that helps men to love one another.

Though one of a different faith might refer to the master of the universe differently, Mr. Hendren captured beautifully the basics upon which our firm was founded and has endured.

This is but a glimpse of the quality and strength of the precious heritage upon which we were privileged—and challenged—to build. Happily, the history of our first 125 years reflects the rewards of adhering to those solid principles upon which the firm was established.

As we move forward to meet today's challenges and opportunities, I have great optimism for, and faith in, the future of our firm. In John Garrou and others, I see an appreciation of the basics—the "core values," as John puts it—that have brought us to this good day, as well as a strong determination to continue to build the firm upon them.

William F. Womble

Preface

> *"You can never plan the future by the past."*
>
> Edmund Burke

We cherish our past; that is why we commissioned this history on the occasion of the 125th anniversary of our founding.

There is not much in these pages that we can use to predict the future of our firm; certainly, no one could have foreseen more than a few years ago where we would be today.

However, there are a few characteristics of our firm as it will exist years from now that we can safely predict, because they formed the bedrock of the firm's past success.

One of those easy predictions is that the firm's core values will remain: devotion to clients, integrity, and respect for the individual. These are the enduring tenets of our firm, and they will remain unchanged because they are the essence of our firm's success..

A second safe prediction is that we will remain flexible and open-minded about change. Our firm has always been open to change, willing to adapt to changing conditions and new developments.

The future of the law as a learned profession is very much in doubt. There is a fine line between protecting the values of the profession—independence, integrity, assuring equality before the law—on the one hand and protecting the pocketbooks of practitioners on the other. When we use our traditions and our standards for the public good, we gain plaudits; when we use them as shields against honest competition, we earn cynicism.

Our firm has always maintained professional standards higher than those imposed upon us by law and canon; therefore, we need not apologize for entering the marketplace with vigor and enthusiasm. So long as we maintain our core values and act with the honor and compassion that we have always upheld, we should not hesitate to compete vigorously with other law firms and other businesses that compete with us or with which we choose to compete.

Our path will not be easy. Reading the following pages gives one a sense of serenity and stability that will not be felt in our firm again. Was it better then? Perhaps, but for those who love challenges and welcome change, the best is yet to be.

John L. W. Garrou
Chairman

Acknowledgments

Winston Churchill famously observed that history is "just one damned thing after another." In writing the history of Womble Carlyle Sandridge & Rice, I have tried to make the story more than just a dull chronology. With the support and encouragement of the firm's History Book Committee, I have tried to craft a chronicle that is inclusive and at the same time interesting. I hope that this narrative is a compelling tale of the dynamic growth and development of a law firm ever striving to better serve its clients and communities.

In writing about an organization as large and diverse as Womble Carlyle, it is at times difficult to know where to draw the line as to whom to include in the story. During a busy year of research and writing, I heard many remarkable stories and compelling anecdotes about the life and labors of those involved in the firm over the last 125 years. Obviously, I could not recount every story in this history. Historians have to make some judgment calls and hard choices, just like lawyers. I have tried to capture the essence of the firm and faithfully represent its core values and most significant moments.

While Womble Carlyle is now a regional law firm with eight offices from Atlanta to northern Virginia, the firm existed in Winston-Salem alone for 106 of its 125 years. The narrative thus focuses initially on the Winston-Salem experience, then takes up the story of each new office and each merger partner as the chronology unfolds.

A published history of an organization as venerable and distinguished as Womble Carlyle requires the collective effort of many people and organizations. The following list of contributors is by no means exhaustive of the hundreds of people who answered the call in a variety of ways.

My thanks go to John L. W. Garrou, chairman of the Firm Management Committee, for his steadfast support and guidance throughout the project. I also owe a large debt of gratitude to William F. Womble for his unwavering encouragement and willingness to answer any question that arose about the firm's history. Without him, this book would not have been possible.

Members of the firm's History Book Committee took time from their regular duties to give yeoman service to this project. Cynthia Pruitt was instrumental in finding contemporary photographs and securing permissions from a variety of sources. Paula Blanchat's thematic suggestions and editorial corrections proved invaluable. Our committee chair, Donald H. Adamick, was indispensable from start to finish, holding us to our deadlines, coordinating the editing and permissions work, and negotiating contracts with vendors.

It would be a serious omission if I did not acknowledge the work of Robin Jackson, who spent hundreds of hours in the bowels of the Forsyth County Public Library, poring over newspaper articles on microfilm and ferreting out photographs relating to the firm's history. This book would be the poorer without her work. I hasten to thank Ms. Molly Rawls of the North Carolina Room of the Forsyth County Public Library for going beyond the call of duty in identifying photographs for use in the text. I thank Frank V. Tursi for permission to adapt certain passages from his book *Winston-Salem: A History*.

My thanks also go to Jane E. Hixon, executive assistant to the chairman of the Firm Management Committee. With efficiency and good humor, Jane did the countless little things necessary to make this project a success—from scheduling dozens of interviews to keeping everyone involved in the project regularly informed—while all the time holding down her regular job of supporting John Garrou in the management of the firm. As Jimmy H. Barnhill has noted, much of the secret of Womble Carlyle's success over the years is due to the dedicated contributions of loyal staff members, a category to which Jane most certainly belongs.

And to my wife, Kathy—thank you for your love and enduring support.

—*Lynn Roundtree*

The law firm that would become Womble Carlyle Sandridge & Rice was founded in 1876, just as Southern industry was beginning to recover from the economic devastation of the Civil War.

FORSYTH COUNTY PUBLIC LIBRARY PHOTOGRAPH COLLECTION

Introduction
IN THE EARLY DAYS OF ITS PROSPERITY: WINSTON IN 1876

The year 1876 witnessed a number of memorable events in the history of America. Alexander Graham Bell received a patent for the telephone on March 7 and three days later, in Salem, Massachusetts, made the first telephone call. Mark Twain published *The Adventures of Tom Sawyer*. Major-league baseball began with the first National League game. A patent for the first cigarette-rolling machine was issued. Kudzu was imported from Japan as an ornamental plant for the first time. And perhaps most memorably, on June 25, Colonel George Armstrong Custer and 212 troops were surrounded and defeated by some 2,000 Sioux, Cheyenne, and Arapaho warriors under Sitting Bull and Crazy Horse at the Battle of the Little Bighorn in Montana—the worst military defeat in the history of the United States.

For most of North Carolina, the year 1876 was quite difficult. The Civil War had wiped out most invested funds, money was scarce, and prices for most farm products were low. The unsettling era of Reconstruction, during which federal troops remained garrisoned in the state, was just ending. In a region still

The nation marked its first 100 years and celebrated its industrial progress at the United States International Exposition in Philadelphia in 1876.

THE GRANGER COLLECTION, NEW YORK

haunted by the palpable presence of maimed veterans and the ghosts of the Confederate dead, there was little sentiment for reconciliation with the states of the North and little capital available from Northern banks and manufacturers for industrial development.

One North Carolina chronicler predicted that "the year 1876 will long be remembered by the people of the State as a year of ruinous financial embarrassment." The state debt totaled nearly $42 million. There was virtually no money in the budget for public schools. And the University of North Carolina—closed for five years during Reconstruction—had just reopened with a tiny appropriation from the state. North Carolina could not even afford to resume work on the bankrupt Western North Carolina Railroad—save for work by convicts from the state penitentiary—until some Wilmington businessmen contributed $10,000 for the laying of new track.

Although there was little to celebrate, the year 1876 marked something of a turning point for the state. For the first time since the Civil War, the Fourth of July was generally celebrated by the people of North Carolina, particularly at the State Capitol in Raleigh. The year also marked the centennial of American independence. While the General Assembly refused to appropriate any money toward an official representation at the Centennial Exposition in Philadelphia in mid-July, the women of North Carolina did commission the painting of a North Carolina Centennial Banner celebrating historic Revolutionary War battles fought in the state. These events, almost insignificant in themselves, proved to be the first notable attempt by the state to reunify with the nation and the first public effort to collect, preserve, and publicize North Carolina's history.

In 1876, Winston and Salem were two quite small neighboring towns just beginning to recover from the ravages of the Civil War and Reconstruction. Winston was established in 1849 as the seat of justice in the new county of Forsyth; the Moravian brethren of Salem sold 51 acres of woods east of town for that purpose at a cost of five dollars an acre. The town grew slowly at first; by 1870, Winston numbered about 400 inhabitants. But in 1872, Major T. J. Brown relocated to Winston from Davie County and established the first warehouse for the sale of leaf tobacco. Brown hired the young James A. Gray as his bookkeeper. That same year, a connection to the Richmond & Danville Railroad was built. Winston was off and running.

A young lawyer from Yadkin County, William Bynum Glenn, looked to the east and saw the possibilities available in the new tobacco town of Winston. He moved to Forsyth and teamed up with an established lawyer, a native of the county by the name of Cyrus Barksdale Watson. On Fourth Street opposite the courthouse, they opened a law office under the name of Watson & Glenn, the beginning of a 125-year heritage of service to clients and the community.

Cyrus Barksdale Watson, a respected lawyer in Winston, partnered with William Bynum Glenn in 1876 to form the firm of Watson & Glenn, the predecessor of Womble Carlyle.

THE NORTH CAROLINA DIVISION OF ARCHIVES AND HISTORY

The Best is Yet to Be

The First 125 Years of a Law Firm

The Edward Belo House, completed in 1860, was the finest home in Forsyth County in 1876.
Wachovia Corporation

STARTING A TRADITION *1876 – 1885*

"The past year opened with a heavy cloud overhanging the national sky. The Presidential election of the previous year had led to a disputed result, and there was a danger of anarchy. In the good Providence of God, the solid sense of the nation triumphed over the passions of politicians, and a peaceable outcome was secured, whereby the two great sections of our country have been brought nearer to each other in interests and in sympathies than had been the case for many years."

Bishop Edward Rondthaler,
The Memorabilia (1877)

The Moravians of Salem long had a custom, inherited from the founders of the Wachovia settlement in North Carolina, of writing an annual "Memorabilia" of the noteworthy events of the year. In his review of 1877 in Salem and environs, Moravian bishop Edward Rondthaler spoke of the election of 1876, one of the most bitterly contested and most controversial presidential elections in the nation's history, highlighted by charges of fraud, voter intimidation, and manipulation of the black vote. In the contest between Democrat Samuel J. Tilden and Republican Rutherford B. Hayes, Tilden won the popular tally by 250,000 votes. Yet neither candidate held a clear majority in the electoral count. Bickering intensified after the election, and the disputed states of Oregon, Louisiana, South Carolina, and Florida submitted two sets of electoral returns to Congress, each showing a different result.

Confronted with an astounding mess, Congress debated for weeks about the proper outcome. The year 1876 ended, and still the president-elect had not been chosen. Finally, in late January 1877, Congress appointed a bipartisan, 15-member electoral commission to rule on the electoral counts. In a series of strict party-line votes, each of the disputed states went to the G.O.P., and Hayes won the presidency by a single electoral vote.

Incensed Democrats threatened violent retaliation and obstruction of the election. As Bishop Rondthaler noted, there was real fear in the nation that war might break out. But bloodshed was averted, most likely due to a compromise that historians believe was struck between the two parties. The deal stipulated that if the Democrats would allow Hayes to become president, the Republicans would allow the removal of the remaining federal troops stationed in the South, effectively ending Reconstruction—a matter of great importance to Southern Democrats. In early March, the Senate certified the electoral vote, and Rutherford Hayes was inaugurated as the 19th president of the United States. Within a few months, no federal troops remained garrisoned south of the Mason-Dixon line.

Winston weathered the electoral crisis of the winter of 1876-77 without violence or bloodshed, as did Salem. The two small communities, and especially the relatively new town of Winston, were showing signs of growth in the mid-1870s.

There had been little to alter the rhythms of small-town life in Winston prior to 1870, the year in which census takers counted a population of 470 citizens. Blackberries, not tobacco, were Winston's leading export. Local merchants bartered goods with rural residents or sold dry goods and groceries wholesale to country merchants. The outstanding occasions in the social life of the community were the regular sessions of court, complete with noisy and good-natured crowds that blocked the muddy streets, talked politics, swapped horses, and crowded stores. During court week, everybody came to town, and everybody

This photograph of the corner of Fourth and Liberty in Winston in the 1870s suggests both the spirit of industry and the frontier conditions in the growing town.

Forsyth County Public Library Photograph Collection

in town descended on the courthouse square, not so much for the purpose of attending to legal affairs as to mingle and generally have a good time. They came on horseback, on foot, and in covered wagons bearing the trademarks of the Nissen and Spach wagon works of Forsyth County. They brought fresh eggs, kegs of butter, beeswax, and dried fruit to barter at town stores for such goods as shoes, dishpans, and dress materials. If they lived some distance from town, families in wagons would come prepared to stay overnight at the town camping ground. Patchwork quilts, frying pans, tin coffee pots, and lanterns could be seen hung about all the wagons. Wood fires burned brightly. The music of fiddles and banjos was often heard until late at night.

The establishment of a tobacco warehouse in 1872 and the completion of the railroad from Greensboro in 1873 changed everything in the little town of Winston. Before that time, the nearest tobacco market was in Danville, Virginia. Local growers had to carry their tobacco by wagon to Danville or sell it to small local manufacturers or speculators at a lower price. Major T. J. Brown's idea of establishing a large warehouse for the sale of leaf tobacco quickly caught on, as local growers obtained good prices for their product. Soon, more acreage began to be devoted to the cultivation

Inspired by the Italianate facades of buildings constructed for the United States International Exposition in Philadelphia in 1876, the firm of Pfohl and Stockton built Winston's first modern high-rise for its general store.

Forsyth County Public Library Photograph Collection

of tobacco, and buyers began to relocate from Danville to Winston. By 1875, five tobacco manufacturers were operating in the town, including R. J. Reynolds, who immigrated that year from Patrick County, Virginia. Business was so prosperous that Winston's leading general-store owner, E. A. Pfohl, was one of the few North Carolinians able to attend the Centennial Exposition in Philadelphia in the summer of 1876.

Growth became the watchword as builders and contractors flocked to the community to erect stores, factories, and houses. Busy streets bustling with trade and commerce stretched east and west from the courthouse, replacing land that had only recently been field and forest. By 1879, some 3,500 people lived in Winston, triple the population of adjoining Salem. More than a dozen tobacco factories, seven ready-made clothing factories, two marble yards, and two wagon shops were located there. Winston boasted three hotels, two banks, four newspapers, and six churches. One immigrant to the town reported that he had been told that in Winston, times were so prosperous that roast pigs were running around the streets with a knife and fork sticking in their backs with a placard attached, inviting the hungry to come and eat!

Lawyers held prominent places in the newly bustling town. The country lawyer—who may not have known everything about anything, but knew something about everything—was beginning to pass from the scene. In his memoirs of the town, Henry W. Foltz, a longtime real-estate and insurance man, recalled the legal scene in 1875:

> The leading lawyers were D. H. Starbuck, T. J. Wilson, Joe Masten, Cyrus B. Watson and Daniel P. Mast, with J. C. Buxton and W. B. Glenn as the young members of the bar. Lawyers of adjoining counties always attended our courts, and our attorneys attended theirs. John R. Cloud was judge of this district, and courts were held about once in three months. . . . In a part of the space on the west, south and east sides of the courthouse square there were erected hitching posts and horse troughs for the accommodation of people coming to town. Around the square there was a dilapidated paling fence, with the gates always standing open. Cattle, hogs and sheep roamed at large, and the sheep spent their nights under the cover of the large portico at the south end of the courthouse building.

William Bynum Glenn was born on the family plantation in Yadkin County in 1847, the son of Tyre Glenn and Margaret Bynum Glenn. The Glenns were wealthy planters and slaveholders in Yadkin County before the Civil War. Margaret Glenn's brother, John Gray Bynum, was a prominent Lincoln County officeholder, and her sister-in-law, Mary Bynum McDowell, was the wife of Richmond Pearson, chief justice of the State Supreme Court. Frequent visitors to the Glenn home included Governor Zebulon B. Vance, Justice Pearson, and Judge Thomas Settle, William B. Glenn's brother-in-law.

Schooled in Yadkin County as a youth, W. B. Glenn attended the Virginia Military Institute for six months at the end of the Civil War. He enrolled at Princeton University in the fall of 1867. A fine student throughout his four years at the college, he was selected to deliver the Library Oration by the senior class. He also played on Princeton's Ivy League-champion baseball team of 1870. After graduation, he studied law with Justice Pearson at his famous law school, Richmond Hill, located in Yadkin County. He was admitted to the bar in 1872. While practicing law in Yadkin County, he was elected as a Republican to the General Assembly in 1875, where he upset many of the state's Grand Old Party members by voting his conscience and opposing the ratification of the federal civil-rights amendments. The issue was so divisive for Glenn that he went over to the Democratic Party, in

The Princeton College baseball team of 1870. W. B. Glenn is in the center of the back row.

UNIVERSITY ARCHIVES, DEPARTMENT OF RARE BOOKS AND SPECIAL COLLECTIONS, PRINCETON UNIVERSITY LIBRARY

which he was chosen as a presidential elector for Tilden in 1876.

At least in part because of his political troubles in Yadkin County, Glenn and his family moved to the prosperous town of Winston sometime in 1876. He quickly gained respect in his new town's legal community, so much so that when Chief Justice Richmond Pearson died in 1878, W. B. Glenn was chosen by the North Carolina Bar as one of the five attorneys to accompany the body to Raleigh for the funeral.

Cyrus Barksdale Watson was born in 1844 in a part of Stokes County that was soon added to Forsyth County. He was the son of John and Marie Folger Watson. John Watson was a prominent citizen of Forsyth County who served as a justice of the peace and chairman of the Warden's Court for many years.

In the spring of 1862, after a year at school in Kernersville, Cyrus Watson enlisted in Company K of the 45th North Carolina Regiment and reported to Camp Mangum. Sergeant Watson served with courage, valor, and distinction in General Robert E. Lee's Army of Northern Virginia in the epic battles of the Wilderness, Petersburg, and Spotsylvania Court House. In the latter battle, he was gravely wounded in the shoulder and left to die. But he proved the surgeons wrong and went on to serve another year with a bandaged arm. He was with Lee's army at the time of the surrender at Appomattox Court House.

A jaunty-looking Cyrus B. Watson

FORSYTH COUNTY PUBLIC LIBRARY PHOTOGRAPH COLLECTION

Cyrus Watson returned to Forsyth County after the war. His arm still useless for manual labor, he obtained a clerkship in a store at Kernersville and later in High Point. But after a little more than a year, he became restless and decided to move to Lexington, Virginia, where he studied law under James Madison Leach, a prominent member of the Virginia Bar. In 1869, Watson was admitted to the North Carolina Bar and relocated to Winston.

Active in the town's public affairs from his arrival to the end of his life, he was elected first in 1874 as a town commissioner, then in 1882 to the first of two terms in the State Senate. From the start of his career, he was successful in his professional practice, giving time and care to every case. "No other attorney had a better reputation for ability in examining witnesses and in forcibly presenting his case to the jury," wrote Colonel W. A. Blair of Winston. Watson was widely regarded as one of the finest criminal lawyers of his generation.

The Forsyth County Courthouse, built in 1850, was the first public building in the new county seat of Winston.

North Carolina Collection, University of North Carolina at Chapel Hill Library

The offices of Watson & Glenn were on Liberty Street, on the north side of the courthouse square. Cyrus Watson's residence was located on the southwest corner of Old Town and Sixth Streets, while William B. Glenn's family lived on the northwest corner of Fourth and Spring Streets. Both the established attorney, Watson, and the younger partner, Glenn, were recognized as public-spirited, civic-minded gentlemen and active Democrats.

The earliest mention of the Watson & Glenn firm appeared in the Salem *People's Press* edition of June 1, 1876. W. B. Glenn and C. B. Watson represented the "Hicks boys" on a charge of larceny in a case brought over from Yadkin County. After a two-day trial, the jury returned a verdict of not guilty, which came as a relief to the indicted, "who had been incarcerated a long time, and are men of families," according to the article. But the glow of victory for the firm quickly faded, as Revenue Officer John White quickly rearrested one of the Hicks brothers, John, on the charge of illegal operation of a distillery. Bond was set at $400, which Cyrus Watson paid, according to the newspaper.

The second mention of Watson & Glenn was a notice in the *People's Press* of August 10, 1876, showing that the firm had defended at trial a certain Will Hughes, who was released "due to a defect or informality in the drawing of the warrant."

At the county courthouse less than a year later, in March 1877, W. B. Glenn and C. B. Watson addressed "the colored citizens of Salem and Winston" on the subject of education. "It was well handled by the gentlemen," according to the *People's Press*.

Such was the growth of Winston that by 1879, four more attorneys had established practices in town, including the respected Colonel John W. Alspaugh, who allied with the formidable J. C. Buxton in the firm of "Alspaugh & Buxton, Attorneys-at-Law and Insurance." Other newcomers to the law were Bartlett Y. Rayle, who served as solicitor of the District Court; Eugene E. Gray, who allied with Register of Deeds D. P. Mast in the firm of Mast & Gray;

Left: The railroads were the lifeblood of Winston business and industry from the latter half of the 19th century to well into the next century.
FORSYTH COUNTY PUBLIC LIBRARY PHOTOGRAPH COLLECTION

Facing page: George Brooks, James A. Gray, Sr., and R. J. Reynolds outside the offices of Wachovia National Bank at Main and Third Streets in Winston in 1889
FORSYTH COUNTY PUBLIC LIBRARY PHOTOGRAPH COLLECTION

WACHOVIA
NATIONAL
BANK.

Wachovia National Bank in 1888
W. A. Lemly, president, is in the center window, and James A. Gray, Sr., head cashier, is in the second window.
Founded in 1879, Wachovia was an early client of the firm.
FORSYTH COUNTY PUBLIC LIBRARY PHOTOGRAPH COLLECTION

Justin Field, who joined with D. H. Starbuck in the firm of Starbuck & Field; and George P. Everett.

Within a few years of its founding, Watson & Glenn was an established and highly respected firm. By 1879, the 32-year-old William Glenn had already been elected a commissioner of the town of Winston and was serving on the Standing Committee on Fires. A year later, he was elected by Forsyth County to the State Senate. No doubt, his government service made W. B. Glenn familiar with town officers, for records show that by 1884 (and perhaps earlier), Watson & Glenn were chosen as city attorneys. Thus began the firm's long tradition of representing the corporate interests of the city of Winston.

In the 1870s, the firm of Watson & Glenn also began to represent other units of local government—including Forsyth, Stokes, and Stanly Counties—in court proceedings. In one case, *Belo v. Commissioners of Forsyth County*, the firm successfully defended Forsyth County in a suit brought by Edward Belo against the ad valorem tax levied by the county on certain railroad bonds alleged to have been issued by the county.

While Watson & Glenn would soon come to be seen as a business and corporate law firm representing banks, railroads, and the like, it had in its first years a broader practice of civil and criminal law, including the occasional capital case. In 1877-78, Watson & Glenn even represented an individual in a suit for damages against the Richmond & Danville Railroad, a future client and one of the entities most responsible for Winston's prosperity. In *Crutchfield v. Railroad*, the attorneys represented one of the railroad's brakemen, whose arm was crushed while he was attempting to uncouple two rail cars.

Following the financial depression of the late 1870s, the 1880s began a period of even greater expansion for the towns of Winston and Salem. In his chronicle of the events of 1882, Bishop Rondthaler noted, "Winston and Salem are so situated that their prosperity is inseparable; as much so as is the sunlight which shines on them both. We are reminded of this fact by the freight returns of the joint Railroad Depot; by the building operations of Messrs. Fogle [the Fogle Bros. planing mills] and Messrs. Miller, which have to a great extent built the newer parts of both places; and by the successful business undertakings of Salem people across the almost imaginary line dividing the two places."

The Rondthaler report for the year 1884 was even more positive: "We may regard 1884 as the most marked year in the phenomenal growth of this new town of Winston. Six new tobacco factories have been erected; two very large tobacco warehouses have been opened; the Iron Repair Works of Messrs. Vance & Co. are already doing a thriving business; the Gray block of store buildings is one of the finest in our State; [and] the Graded School has been put into successful operation."

Watson & Glenn's business increased accordingly in the early 1880s. New governmental clients included Davie and Yadkin Counties, while new corporate clients included a furniture company, the Lexington Manufacturing Company, and the Richmond & Danville Railroad (the firm's first railroad client). One case in 1881 involved two longstanding clients of the firm. In *Lemly v. Commissioners*, Watson & Glenn represented the Board of Commissioners of Forsyth County in a suit brought by W. A. Lemly, one of the founding officers of the Wachovia Bank and Trust Company. The plaintiff was seeking relief against an assessment of taxes by Forsyth County on shares of stock in the First National Bank of Salem, owned by Israel G. Lash. Lemly had been cashier for Lash until the bank's closing, when he became founding president of Wachovia Bank.

Cyrus B. Watson left the partnership with William B. Glenn in 1885 to join with Colonel J. C. Buxton, another prominent Winston lawyer and frequent opponent in court. Soon, W. B. Glenn formed a new partnership with Robert Broadnax Glenn of Rockingham County under the firm name of Glenn & Glenn. The new firm would continue to grow in the prosperous Twin City. Indeed, as publisher Charles Emerson proclaimed, "Winston will continue to grow and become the most important inland town in the State. . . . The climate is highly salubrious and healthy, and the people are industrious, honest, economical, intelligent and refined. The sale of spirituous liquors has long been strictly forbidden, and the salutary effect of such a policy is seen and felt in the high moral tone of the community."

Brown's Warehouse on Main Street was completed in 1884.
It was the most successful of the many tobacco auction houses in Winston.
FORSYTH COUNTY PUBLIC LIBRARY PHOTOGRAPH COLLECTION

A GROWING PRACTICE *1885 – 1890*

"The ground so sparsely settled a hundred years ago is now occupied by two prosperous and growing towns. A Chamber of Commerce now amicably and usefully binds the two towns together. The Railroad depot which they share together has again borne its witness to our growing prosperity, having received and shipped about three million pounds of freight. . . . We note with congratulations the increase of stores, factories and private residences in Winston, and also the interesting fact that direct shipments of the main staple, tobacco, are now being made to Europe. . . . A kind Providence has given us good public health and good harvests. There has been widespread prosperity. It has been a golden year of peace."

Bishop Edward Rondthaler,
The Memorabilia (1885)

The year 1885 was indeed a time of peace and prosperity in the towns of Winston and Salem, and the next five years would bring more growth and improvements. Between 1880 and 1885, the population of Winston more than doubled. By 1885, the town boasted the largest tobacco warehouse in the world—Colonel A. B. Gorrell's Farmers' Warehouse on Liberty Street—as well as one of the largest tobacco manufacturers—P. H. Hanes and Company. R. J. Reynolds's tobacco manufactory had grown to occupy a three-story brick building on Chestnut Street. In October of that year, tobacco men such as Dick Reynolds and P. H. Hanes joined with Charles A. Fogle, Henry E. Fries, and others to form the Winston Board of Trade

The Winston Graded School was recognized as one of the model public schools in the South when it opened in 1884.

Forsyth County Public Library Photograph Collection

(Chamber of Commerce), an organization that would become one of the prime engines of growth for the Twin City. And by 1885, Winston boasted a brand-new graded public school with an enrollment of 275 students, one of the first in the state and a national model for cooperative efforts between public officials and businessmen and industrialists. The five elected school commissioners—James A. Gray, Pleasant Hanes, Calvin H. Wiley, James Martin, and W. A. Whitaker—had worked night after night for months crafting a workable plan for the new town school system.

There were, of course, problems in Winston, this town of "astounding prosperity," in R. J. Reynolds's phrase. The streets of the town raised clouds of dust in the dry season. Some became mud ponds when the rains came. The public roads into town—rutted by the booming wagon trade—remained to be graded and macadamized. Outdoor privies of downtown homes fouled Winston's creeks. Public drunkenness became more prevalent as newcomers streamed into the town's tobacco factories. And a newspaper editorial in May 1887 complained of the storage of fertilizer downtown: "Who ever heard of any decent town tolerating such a thing as a great pile of guano heaped up in aromatic massiveness right in the most public part of town? It would be about as reasonable to build a hog pen right in the middle of the city."

In the boom town that was Winston in 1885, it appears that there was plenty enough business for lawyers old and new. By all accounts, the parting of Cyrus Watson from the firm of Watson & Glenn was a peaceable one. In January, the local newspapers reported the formation of "a spanking team of lawyers" in the partnership of Watson & Buxton. By April, news came forth of the move of Robert Broadnax Glenn from Danbury in Stokes County to form another new partnership in the town. "Winston congratulates herself upon the acquisition of so worthy a gentleman as a citizen," said editor Edward A. Oldham of Winston's *Western Sentinel*. "Glenn & Glenn stands individually in the front ranks of the legal profession of the State, and this union will, if anything, add additional strength." W. B. Glenn had worked with R. B. Glenn in state Democratic Party activities.

Robert Broadnax Glenn was born in Yadkin County in 1854, the son of Chalmers and Annie Dodge Glenn. After his father's death at the Battle of South Mountain in 1862, the family moved to the Dan River Meadows area of Rockingham County, where young Robert received his education. After graduation from Davidson College and a brief stint at the University of Virginia, R. B. Glenn entered Judge Pearson's famed Richmond Hill School of Law in Yadkin County in 1876. The following year, he was licensed by the State Supreme Court. In 1878, he moved his new wife, Nina Deaderick Glenn of Jonesborough, Tennessee, to Danbury in Stokes County to begin the practice of law.

Such was the boom in Winston that there was no suitable house for the Glenns to rent. While the rest of his family remained in Danbury for most of the year as Fogle Bros. built a nine-room frame residence on Fourth Street, R. B. Glenn began the practice of law in Winston in the spring of 1885. An advertisement appearing in local newspapers throughout the year announced the new partnership:

W. B. Glenn R. B. Glenn
GLENN & GLENN
Attorneys and Counselors at Law
Winston, N. C.

Practice in all the State and Federal Courts. Collections made in any part of the State. Loans negotiated on best security. Real Estate sold on commission. Abstract titles made & conveyances and contracts of all kinds carefully prepared.

Robert Broadnax Glenn quickly set about establishing himself in the community, just as William Bynum Glenn had done after arriving in Winston in

W. B. GLENN. R. B. GLENN.

GLENN & GLENN,

Attorneys-at-Law,

FOURTH STREET, BETWEEN MAIN AND LIBERTY,

WINSTON, N. C.

PRACTICE IN ALL THE COURTS, STATE & FEDERAL.
CLAIMS PROMPTLY COLLECTED.

W. B. Ellis & Co.,

Tobacco Manufacturers,

And Proprietors North State Cigar Works,

WINSTON, N. C.

R. R. CRAWFORD,

DEALER IN

WAGONS,

BUGGIES,

And Carriages

4th between Liberty and Old Town Streets.

WINSTON, N. C.

C. B. CASH,

Tonsorial Palace,

Fourth Street, Next to Crawford's Hardware Store,

WINSTON, N. C.

Shaving, Hair Cutting, Shampooing and Dying in the latest styles. Workman Experienced, Polite, and Attentive. A share of your trade solicited.

A late-1880s advertisement for Glenn & Glenn in a Winston city directory

FORSYTH COUNTY PUBLIC LIBRARY PHOTOGRAPH COLLECTION

1876. In September 1885, both Glenns were among the prominent citizens who chartered the Chamber of Commerce. Soon after arriving, Robert B. Glenn joined the Twin-City Club, described in its charter as "a literary, social and fraternal organization of business and professional men." The club had been founded in February of that year by James A. Gray, J. C. Buxton, and others. Like his law partner, Robert B. Glenn became sought after as a speaker by local literary societies and academies. And even more so than W. B. Glenn, he became involved in Democratic Party politics. In 1887, for example, he joined Cyrus Watson on a stump tour of Wilkes County, where "ringing speeches were given at five voting precincts, along with sweet music from the Twin-City Cornet Band," according to the Winston *Union Republican*.

Young R. B. Glenn was held in such high regard that by November 1885, he was being put forward by prominent Democrats as the leading candidate for solicitor of the Ninth Judicial District. He won the post and served with distinction during the spring and fall terms of Forsyth Superior Court in 1886, winning praise from a local editor for the "rapid manner in which [he] transacts business, pushing matters with vigor and zeal; by doing so he saves a great deal of costs to the county."

As prominent local businessmen, the two Glenns were ardent supporters of increased railway facilities for the Twin City during the 1880s. At a citizens' mass meeting held at the Opera House on February 23, 1887, the new partners were among the leading attorneys who delivered "rousing & ringing" speeches in favor of a public subscription of $60,000 to extend the Northwestern North Carolina Railroad to Wilkesboro. News accounts state that W. B. Glenn hailed the resolutions as wise and judicious investments for the town, after which R. B. Glenn followed with a more stark response: "To adopt this proposition means Winston's welfare—to reject it means Winston's doom." The resolutions were soon ratified by the Chamber of Commerce. Within a few months, Robert B. Glenn was elected as an officer of the Northwestern line.

Glenn & Glenn built a flourishing practice in the mid- to late 1880s in the state and federal courts. Like Watson & Glenn, the new firm's practice extended to the surrounding counties of Surry, Stokes, Yadkin, Davidson, Davie, and Rockingham, in addition to Forsyth. In court, the firm defended clients in actions on a wide variety of matters, including fraud and collusion, recovery of land, wills and legacies, estates and conveyances, contracts, judgments, violation of municipal ordinances, willful trespass, recovery of real property, indigent apprentices, land disputes, and damages for right

THE GLENNS OF YADKIN

The earliest known description of the firm appeared in David Peter Robbins's *Descriptive Sketch of Winston-Salem* (1888), one of the early guidebooks to businesses and industry in the Twin City:

GLENN & GLENN
Fourth Street, Opp. Courthouse

W. B. Glenn, the senior partner of the above firm, is a native of Yadkin County, graduated from Princeton, N.J., read law under Chief Justice Pearson, and was admitted to the bar in 1872. He practiced in Yadkin for a time, and was for many years a partner in the firm of Watson & Glenn. He was a member of the Legislature in 1874, Democratic elector in '76 and in '81 served again in the General Assembly.

R. B. Glenn is from Rockingham County, attended Davidson College, the University of Virginia, subsequently read law under the instructions of Chief Justice Pearson, and was admitted to practice ten years ago. He was sent to the Legislature from Stokes County in 1881, was Democratic elector in '84, and was Solicitor for the 9th Judicial district in 1886-87. The alliance of Glenn & Glenn was formed in 1885, and the firm practices in all the adjacent Courts.

of way. Glenn & Glenn also represented clients in various cases on leases of tobacco land. In 1889, William Bynum Glenn even became a prime investor in a tobacco warehouse to be built in Germanton, just up the road from Winston.

The new firm continued to represent the town of Winston and the county of Forsyth in questions of governmental law, just as Watson & Glenn had done. In 1888, in *Board of Commissioners of Winston v. Taylor*, Robert B. Glenn defended the right of the town of Winston to collect a special license tax on W. B. Taylor and Bros., manufacturers of plug tobacco in Salem, who purchased leaf tobacco in the warehouses of Winston. And in February 1889, William B. Glenn and R. B. Glenn allied with C. B. Watson and J. C. Buxton in the defense of the Forsyth County sheriff, M. E. Teague, concerning the disputed election of 1888. Teague's challenger, John Boyer, protested that a number of the votes cast were fraudulent, and the case became the talk of Forsyth Superior Court during 1889. In the landmark 1890 case of *Boyer v. Teague,* the North Carolina Supreme Court set important precedents on the procedures and standards of evidence needed to substantiate legal and qualified votes.

But not every case handled by Glenn & Glenn was a conventional one, and not every client was an established member of the community. In 1887, Robert B. Glenn agreed to represent one S. J. Morrell. "Professor" Morrell arrived in Winston in the summer of 1887, rented a house, and set up a patent-medicine business. He bought alcohol, chloroform, capsicum, and other ingredients from local druggists, boiled them together, bottled them, and called the compound "Herbs of Life." Leasing vacant lots in different parts of town, he held open-air concerts featuring music, dancing, and minstrel performances. At intervals, Morrell would address the crowd, extract teeth, and "cure" the headaches of audience members, while associates passed through the crowd selling bottles of Herbs of Life. According to the newspaper, the professor's shows were well attended and highly

The patent medicine sold by "Professor" Morrell was a blood purifier similar to this concoction.

Courtesy of Ruben Negron

enjoyed. Over 500 bottles of the medicine sold on one Saturday night. But after several nights' performances, Morrell was arrested by the sheriff for refusing to pay the peddler's tax and take out a peddler's license. Although the medicine man claimed that his Herbs of Life was not produced by "a process of manufacturing" and thus was exempt from taxation under state law, the court ruled that Herbs of Life was indeed a "nostrum or medicine," as defined in statute.

Tragedy struck young William Bynum Glenn in the prime of his professional life. Late in 1889 or early in 1890, his health broke unexpectedly as a mental illness claimed his faculties. A man vigorous enough to be active in civic and business affairs and carry an extensive case load was suddenly removed from the activities of bench and bar.

A mention of W. B. Glenn in the press came in October 1889. On October 5, William Bynum Glenn helped his team, the "Lawyers Nine," to a 16-14 win over the "Tobacco Nine" in a baseball game at the Winston Athletic Grounds. Robert B. Glenn had an impressive 16 strikeouts in the charity affair for the benefit of the Twin-City Hospital. "The Lawyers Nine are not only a brainy and muscular company of gentlemen," wrote the editor of the Winston *Union Republican*, "but good looking we heard a lady say, as well."

In late October, W. B. Glenn traveled to Davidson County Court to prosecute the defendants in the sensational case of the "Lexington Lynchers," a mob that had hanged a black man, Robert Berrier, for allegedly raping a white woman. Glenn's petition to the governor to "maintain the law at all hazards" by issuing bench warrants for the arrest of the lynchers was said to be the first proceeding of its kind in the North Carolina courts.

He spent his last two years away from his beloved wife and children, at the North Carolina Asylum in Morganton, where he died on May 4, 1892. The *Union Republican* eulogized him as "a gentleman of fine appearance, a fluent speaker, and an able expounder of the law [who] had an extended acquaintance throughout the State." At a memorial service held at Forsyth Superior Court in June, members of the Winston Bar hailed their colleague as "a beloved friend and brother, one of the State's most able and useful sons, and one of the Bar's most eloquent and brightest members." His body rests in Salem Cemetery within sight of the offices of the law firm he founded.

Tobacco wagons clogged Main Street in front of Brown's Warehouse at harvest time in the 1890s.

NORTH CAROLINA COLLECTION, UNIVERSITY OF NORTH CAROLINA AT CHAPEL HILL LIBRARY

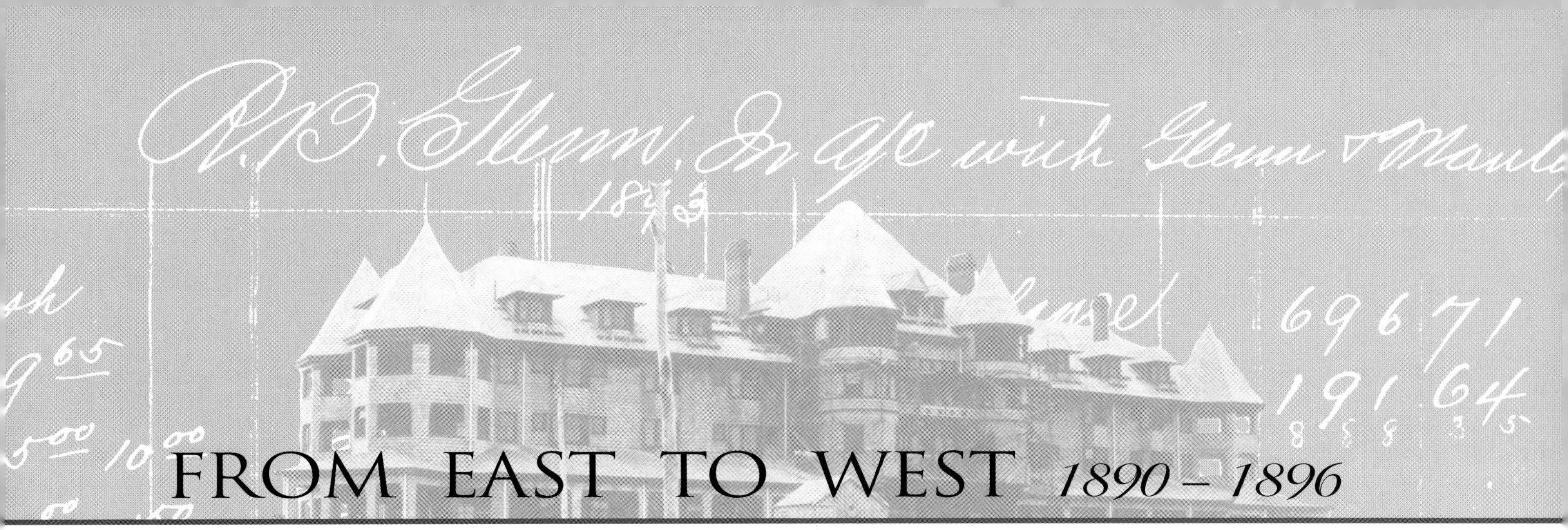

FROM EAST TO WEST *1890 – 1896*

> *"Salem—representing the sturdy old civilization of years of toil and care, with a refinement of taste in all its surroundings, coupled with the common-sense durability of the works of the early Moravian settlers—contrasted with the fresh enterprise, modern buildings and general air of the life of Winston today . . . The two towns recognize in each other the help-meet of the other. Winstonians invariably drive visitors to the places of historic interest in Salem, and Salemites, in turn, show their guests through the large tobacco factories of Winston, and explain the immense business that throbs and pulsates through the marts of trade. They are proud also of showing its elegant stores; handsome churches and fine private residences—a town with Macadamized streets, a courthouse square paved with square blocks of granite, and business houses built up compactly around the temple of justice, and stretching to the adjoining streets."*
>
> Angelina Winkler,
> *Souvenir of the Twin Cities* (1890)

In her historical sketch of Winston and Salem in 1890, Angelina Winkler described what visitors often noted: the unique spirit of enterprise in the adjoining towns. George Washington—who had visited the Wachovia settlement during his Southern tour of the new nation 100 years before—would have scarcely recognized the place. What had been a small village in a remote, red-clay part of North Carolina in 1791 was now called by boosters "the Bee Hive City," a place of unparalleled progress and prosperity. Only the "remarkable industry of the people there," which President Washington famously spoke of, remained as the hallmark of the place.

By 1890, almost 14,000 people lived in Winston and Salem. Twenty-nine plug tobacco factories, two smoking tobacco factories, two cigar factories, and 12 leaf factories employed some 5,000 workers. New cotton and wool factories joined established businesses such as the Fogle Brothers Iron Works and J. A. Vance Machine Shops. In the basement of the Vance shops, William Cyrus Briggs was perfecting a cigarette-rolling machine that would soon revolutionize the tobacco business.

Factories, stores, and residences were being completed at the rate of three a week, but even that pace did not meet the demand. Four banks served the Twin City, including the Wachovia Bank Company, which was said to be "as solid, financially, as the stone that composes its vaults." And city fathers rejoiced in 1890 when the Northwestern North Carolina Railroad was completed from Winston to Wilkesboro, assuring even greater access to raw materials and finished goods.

The towns now boasted electric lights, telephone and telegraph services, a waterworks, fire companies, and a new electric street railway, only the fourth in the nation. The sidewalks around the courthouse and along Main Street were made of granite blocks. A market house and a splendid new 100-room hotel, the Zinzendorf, were rising in Winston's West End. Roller skating was beginning to gain a considerable following among the young; cycling fanatics were beginning to appear on the streets of Winston and Salem; and the chewing-gum craze had arrived in Winston. "Even young ladies and young gentleman have fallen victim to the habit," grumbled one editorialist in January 1890.

The Winston *Union Republican* of November 6, 1890, carried this news item: "Mr. Clement Manly, of New Bern, goes the way of the world and comes to Winston-Salem. He will associate himself with Hon. F. M. Simmons, in the practice of law." With this simple notice began Clement Manly's 38 years of practice of the law and service to his profession and the state.

Clement B. Manly came from a distinguished eastern North Carolina family. He was born in New Bern in 1853, the son of Sarah Simpson Manly and Matthias E. Manly, an associate justice of the North Carolina Supreme Court. He attended Hillsboro Military Academy in Orange County as a young man but later followed in the footsteps of fellow New Bernian William Gaston by matriculating at Georgetown University. After graduating from Georgetown in 1876—the year the firm Watson & Glenn began—he read law in his father's office. Manly was admitted to the North Carolina Bar in 1878. In 1885, he married Emily Buford of Richmond, Virginia, the daughter of Colonel A. S. Buford, president of the Richmond & Danville Railroad.

In 1879, Manly began a practice in his hometown with Furnifold M. Simmons, a prominent young attorney active in Democratic politics. When Simmons was elected to Congress from North Carolina's Second District in 1886, Manly began a practice in New Bern with Owen H. Guion; that practice lasted until 1890. That same year, Simmons lost the Democratic nomination for Congress because of opposition from the Farmer's Alliance.

News reports indicate that the firm of Simmons & Manly reestablished itself and relocated from eastern North Carolina to the western Piedmont in the fall of 1890. Sharp lawyers and shrewd businessmen both, the two men no doubt recognized the commercial opportunities available in Winston. And as prominent members of the North Carolina Democratic Party, they surely welcomed the prospect of working with a fellow Democratic attorney and good friend of Manly, Cyrus B. Watson. For his part, Clement Manly had another important reason for moving: his wife's health. Doctors believed that the risk of contracting malaria was far less in Winston than on the coastal plain, and that the general climate of the hill country would be better for Emily Manly's frail condition.

Simmons appears to have been attracted to Winston primarily for its business prospects. Within a week

Inspired by a visit from inventor Thomas A. Edison in 1889, local investors formed the Winston-Salem Railway and Electric Company. Opened on July 14, 1890, the towns' electric streetcar line was the fourth in the nation to begin operations.

Forsyth County Public Library Photograph Collection

In his 1896 run as the Democratic candidate for governor of North Carolina, Cyrus B. Watson introduced the whistle-stop campaign tour to the state. At right is his longtime friend and fellow Democrat Clement Manly, chairman of the North Carolina Democratic Executive Committee.

FORSYTH COUNTY PUBLIC LIBRARY PHOTOGRAPH COLLECTION

An advertisement for the firm of Glenn & Manly in an 1892 Winston city directory

FORSYTH COUNTY PUBLIC LIBRARY PHOTOGRAPH COLLECTION

of arriving in October 1890, he was elected president and manager of the West End Land and Improvement Company, one of several real-estate development companies in town during that era. A Winston newspaper reported in December that "Hon. F. M. Simmons and other down East capitalists have just completed negotiations with Mr. H. R. Starbuck for some 300 acres of land some two miles south of the towns."

Congressman Simmons purchased a stately house in south Salem and quickly set about becoming a member of the Winston-Salem business establishment. He was active in the Chamber of Commerce and was one of the founding officers of the Sunny Side Club in 1891. But in May 1892, the Winston press carried news of the return of the Simmons family to New Bern. "They have made many warm friends during their sojourn," noted the editor of the *Union Republican*. Two months later, F. M. Simmons was selected as chairman of the State Democratic Executive Committee. He would go on to serve five terms as a United States senator.

Although Clement Manly came to Winston-Salem on December 17, 1890, intending to continue the practice of law with Furnifold Simmons, Robert B. Glenn convinced him within less than a month to join in establishing a new firm under the name Glenn & Manly. It seems likely that Colonel Simmons chose to focus on his commercial and business prospects in Winston, for city directories show no listings for the Simmons & Manly law firm in 1890 and 1891. Certainly, the prospect of working with a highly respected lawyer and fellow Democratic activist was of interest to Manly, and Robert B. Glenn no doubt made an attractive offer, having recently lost his partner and friend, William Bynum Glenn. By January 1891, Clement Manly had set up shop in the old Glenn & Glenn offices in the Harris Building at 7 West Fourth Street in Winston.

Soon after arriving, Colonel Manly became an active member of the Chamber of Commerce and joined the Twin-City Club; he became president of the club in 1894. He was one of the cofounders of the Sunny Side Club in 1891.

By the spring of 1890, Manly was already sought after as an orator and commencement speaker, a duty he performed throughout his life. Clement Manly's lifelong interest in extending opportunities to young people was chronicled in this news story from June 1896: "J. C. Banks, colored, goes to Philadelphia to take a special scientific and commercial course, with a view of becoming a member of the Slater Industrial Academy faculty. For several years he has been diligently applying himself in the office of Hon. Clement Manly, this city."

Robert Broadnax Glenn's career continued its rapid rise during these years. Having served as solicitor for the Ninth Judicial District, R. B. Glenn was appointed by President Grover Cleveland in 1892 to serve a four-year term as United States attorney for the Western District of North Carolina. "He discharged with ability and fidelity the delicate and responsible duties of the office of U.S. Attorney," wrote his partner, Clement Manly.

In the 1890s, R. B. Glenn served as director of the state YMCA and remained a speaker much in demand on public occasions. In 1891, he was appointed to a Chamber of Commerce committee charged with "locating at this place [Winston] a State Agricultural and Mechanical School for colored people." And for several years in the early 1890s, Captain Glenn could be found on the courthouse square in the evenings (weather permitting), drilling his Forsyth Riflemen under the glare of the town's new electric lights.

Both Glenn and Manly were very active in the Democratic Party. When the Forsyth County Democratic Club was organized in 1890, R. B. Glenn was elected its president. In 1892, Clement Manly was a delegate to the Forsyth County Democratic Convention. Two years later, he was a candidate for the General Assembly. Manly even accepted the chairmanship of the State Democratic Executive Committee in 1896, the year that his close friend Cy Watson lost the gubernatorial campaign to Populist Daniel Russell's "fusion" ticket.

In its first five years, the new partnership of Glenn & Manly continued and expanded the work begun by Glenn & Glenn. Clement Manly's connections throughout the state brought new clients to the firm, and Robert B. Glenn's position as district attorney for western North Carolina carried the new firm's name to clients in the mountains and the western Piedmont.

Glenn & Manly continued the work begun by William Bynum Glenn in representing the town of Winston and the county of Forsyth. When in 1893 the county commissioners sought to build a new courthouse, they consulted the firm on whether the county had a right to mortgage county land to secure bonds issued to build the new courthouse. A year later, Glenn & Manly successfully defended the county's right to tax certain real estate owned by the "Congregation of United Brethren of Salem," otherwise known as the Moravians.

During these years, the Northwestern North Carolina Railroad and its parent company, the Southern Railway Company, became clients of the firm, no doubt through the auspices of Clement Manly's father-in-law, Colonel A. S. Buford. In a number of cases, Glenn & Manly represented the railroads in various actions for damages, whether for damage to private property adjacent to rail lines or for injuries alleged to have been caused by negligence on the company's part.

In the early 1890s, the new partnership began to represent insurance companies—many of them based outside North Carolina—in actions in state courts. Clients such as the Home Insurance Company of New Orleans, the Niagara Fire Insurance Company, and the New York Bowery Fire Insurance Company appeared

Winston's grand Zinzendorf Hotel, built in 1890, burned to the ground just two years later.

Forsyth County Public Library Photograph Collection

A view of the hotel during the fire

Forsyth County Public Library Photograph Collection

in the files of the firm for the first time. Yet in the most famous insurance case of the period, the Zinzendorf Hotel fire case, Glenn & Manly represented the claimant, the West End Hotel and Land Company. Winston's grand hotel, built almost entirely of wood with cedar-shake shingles, had burned to the ground on November 24, 1892.

But it was in an entirely new field of practice that Clement Manly gained for the firm its greatest fame. In a number of protracted patent infringement cases, such as *Bonsack Machine Company v. National Cigarette & Tobacco Company* and *Carter Machine Company v. P. H. Hanes and Company*, Colonel Manly won a series of stunning victories against the American Tobacco Company for local clients such as William Cyrus Briggs and Pleasant Hanes. James Crawford Biggs, a noted member of the North Carolina Bar, described one of Manly's triumphs in these terms: "In one of the most gigantic legal struggles that our State has witnessed in many years, Mr. Manly entitled himself to almost any degree of praise. The defendants were fighting great foes, backed by enormous wealth. They were not able to employ eminent patent lawyers to conduct the technical examinations of witnesses and argue the technical points. They employed Mr. Manly. He became an assiduous student of patent law, and met and measured lances with the most eminent patent lawyers in America, and won."

The impressive new Forsyth County Courthouse, completed in 1897, symbolized the pride of local citizens in the community's economic progress and their aspirations for the future.

North Carolina Collection, University of North Carolina at Chapel Hill Library

COVERING ALL THE BASES *1896 – 1905*

> *"Our own towns have shared in the general experiences of the entire country. The new and handsome Court House, the tower of which is conspicuous far and near, is a fair indication of the spirit of our citizens in one of the busiest towns in the South. Several factory interests have settled on the South-side, among them the Chair Factory, which seems to have a very prosperous future before it. Other manufacturing establishments are preparing to build there. In a few years South-side will doubtless be a very busy suburb, and will contribute greatly both to the population and wealth of our Twin City."*
>
> Bishop Edward Rondthaler,
> *The Memorabilia* (1896)

In his review of the year 1896, Bishop Rondthaler wrote of "quiet prosperity and municipal improvement" in Winston and Salem. By that year, there were 62 tobacco factories in the county, 50 in Winston alone. William Cyrus Briggs had patented a new cigarette-rolling machine. Machinists at the J. A. Vance Company were fashioning them as quickly as possible. Cigarette manufacturers from Japan and China were visiting Winston to purchase the machinery for turning out "those little smokers."

By 1896, Richard Joshua Reynolds was tooling around town in his "knobby" new $375 Spider phaeton and enjoying fox hunts with friends on the outskirts of town. Cycling was becoming so popular that townsmen were organizing races at the Athletic Grounds and the aldermen were passing ordinances

Cycling had become a popular pastime for young ladies and gentlemen of Winston and Salem by the 1890s.
NORTH CAROLINA COLLECTION, UNIVERSITY OF NORTH CAROLINA AT CHAPEL HILL LIBRARY

to restrict riding on the sidewalks. "The bicycle mania is getting fair hold upon the Twin City, regardless of sex," reported the *Union Republican*, "but happily, bloomers are yet omitted by the feminine cyclists."

The new courthouse, where R. B. Glenn and Clement Manly would spend so many hours, was impressive indeed, as a correspondent for the *Charlotte Observer* had to admit: "Charlotte surpasses Winston in many respects, but it is hard to believe that she will have a better Court House. The Charlotte Court House grounds are not half so roomy and beautifully located as the ones here. Winston can certainly boast of the prettiest Court House." A local writer noted that the clock tower with its arc light served as "a beacon light of our triple city, Winston-Salem-South Side."

Not that there weren't problems. Civic leaders railed against the degree of public drunkenness in Winston, noting that "the men on Saturday swarm about the saloons like bees about a hive." Mayor Eugene E. Gray struggled to stop the traffic in illegal liquor in Winston, and the aldermen went back and forth on the need to ban the sale of "spirituous, vinous and malt liquors" in city barrooms. And on a less serious note, some complained that the floors of the new courthouse were already being littered not just with peanut shells, but with tobacco juice expectorated by lawyers and laymen alike.

William Mayhew Hendren entered the practice of law in Winston in 1894. He was born in New Bern in 1871 to Linville and Mary Elizabeth Hendren. His Methodist minister father held pastorates in a number of North Carolina towns, including Winston, where the Hendrens kept a permanent home and the Reverend Hendren maintained a small real estate firm in his later years. W. M. Hendren received his preparatory education in several public schools and at the Hill School in Statesville. He was licensed by the State Supreme Court at the September term in 1894, after graduating from the University of North Carolina School of Law.

Upon returning to Winston, W. M. Hendren ini-

William M. Hendren in the firm's law offices, circa 1920. Mr. Hendren had joined Glenn & Manly in 1896.
WOMBLE CARLYLE COLLECTION

tially established an office and set up a general practice of law. With his father in failing health back in New Bern, he also ran the Reverend Hendren's property and loan office until his father's death in 1896. That year, he joined the firm of Glenn & Manly, having known R. B. Glenn from growing up in Winston and the Manly family both in New Bern and Winston.

The middle years of the last decade of the 19th century were busy ones for Glenn & Manly. The firm continued as counsel for Western Union and Wachovia National Bank, as well as division counsel for the Southern Railway Company and counsel for the city of Winston. During the presidential campaign of 1896, Clement Manly served as chairman of the State Democratic Executive Committee. The next year, he was honored by his appointment as "master of equity" of the United States Court for the Western District of North Carolina. Robert B. Glenn was elected to the State Senate in 1899. When prominent attorneys from around the state gathered that summer to form the North Carolina Bar Association, each of the firm's partners became a charter member of the new organization.

Given the two men's busy professional lives, their deep involvement in Democratic politics, and the early acumen shown by William Hendren, it came as no surprise to the members of the bar when in 1897 Robert Glenn and Clement Manly invited W. M. Hendren into the partnership. Hendren had, as one of his later partners wrote, "a brilliant legal mind and great mental energy, and was a thorough student of the law." For the next seven years, the firm would be known as Glenn, Manly & Hendren.

W. M. Hendren quickly became involved in civic and social affairs in Winston, just as R. B. Glenn and Clement Manly had done upon arriving. When an Anti-Saloon League was formed in 1897, the 25-year-old Hendren was elected president. He became a member of the local branch of the YMCA and was elected that organization's state president in 1900. A candidate for county solicitor in 1900, he continued the firm's tradition of active involvement in the Forsyth County Democratic Party, serving as party chairman in 1905. Hendren was a sought-after orator and commencement speaker and even served as manager of Winston's football team in 1897. He married Miss Annie J. Rawley of Winston on March 28, 1899.

The firm continued to represent the city and county in a number of important cases at the turn of the century. When a smallpox epidemic broke out in June 1898, Clement Manly played a leading public role, advising local government leaders and even drawing up the ordinance giving the mayor and the Board of Health the power to require vaccinations and establish quarantines. Colonel Manly also represented the county commissioners at an inquiry involving the most sensational news event of 1901, the beating death of prisoner Rand Hart by one Pink Fulton, a guard at the county's convict camp. Hart, who had been sentenced to work on the county roads for stealing a pistol, was flogged by Fulton for three straight hours, allegedly for not working fast enough. The scourging and death of Rand Hart led to Fulton's conviction and the resignation of the supervisor of the prison camp.

At a time of intense racial animosity in the state, Colonel Manly was a voice of moderation among Democrats, urging whites to "work in harmony and good will with the more considerate and enlightened of the colored race." He continued his association with the Slater Industrial School, delivering speeches at school functions and encouraging his young office assistant, J. C. Banks, who would soon join the Slater faculty. Manly, a devout Roman Catholic, also received widespread acclaim for a meditation, "The Trial of Christ From a Judicial Standpoint," delivered to over 200 men gathered at Home Moravian Church in March 1903. In introducing the speech, the editor of the *Winston-Salem Journal* noted that since the speaker had "served as a scholar, speaker and representative citizen, Mr. Manly needs no introduction."

During these same years, Robert B. Glenn's political career continued its steady rise. In February

Colonel Manly was a supporter of the Slater Industrial and Normal School, opened in 1892 by Dr. Simon Green Atkins (foreground). The city's first educational center for African-Americans, Slater became Winston-Salem Teacher's College in 1925 and subsequently Winston-Salem State University.

FORSYTH COUNTY PUBLIC LIBRARY PHOTOGRAPH COLLECTION

1902, he was a candidate for the Democratic nomination to the United States Senate, but lost to Cyrus Watson. When leading citizens of Forsyth sought a new federal building and post office from the treasurer of the United States, it was R. B. Glenn whom they sent to Washington to argue the case for the Twin City.

In 1897 and 1898, the firm was involved in a high-profile case for an old friend, Judge Thomas J. Wilson, against one of the city's newer businesses, the Winston-Salem Railway and Electric Company. The Wilsons' young son, Richard, had been run over and killed in 1896 by one of the company's streetcars near the Winston Graded School in the West End. At trial in Forsyth Superior Court in January 1897, Glenn & Manly won a $3,000 verdict from the jury on behalf of Judge Wilson. After an appeal by the defendant, the North Carolina Supreme Court returned the case for a new trial, scheduled for the January term in 1898. But before the case could be heard, one of the witnesses, Paul Stockton, a former resident of Salem in town to testify, was shot and killed on the same streetcar line near the place where Richard Wilson had died. The gunman, J. W. Harrison, a salesman at Rosenbacher and Brothers Department Store, drove directly to the downtown offices of Glenn, Manly & Hendren, where he told Colonel Manly what had happened and surrendered to the police. At trial in Forsyth Superior Court in March, Clement Manly defended Harrison and won acquittal on the grounds of self-defense.

Late in 1902, Glenn, Manly & Hendren was employed to help settle the question of who owned Pilot Mountain. The Surry County landmark—which looms in the distance over the Twin City—had been purchased several years earlier by the firm's clients. However, another group of investors claimed that it was entitled to an interest in "the Pilot," as well as some 8,000 acres of land surrounding it. The firm's principal client, J. W. Beasley, prevailed. He soon developed the site as a popular park, picnic site, and local tourist attraction.

In 1904, the firm used its expertise in municipal

Forsyth County residents at the turn of the 20th century often trekked northwest to Pilot Mountain for daylong outings.

FORSYTH COUNTY PUBLIC LIBRARY PHOTOGRAPH COLLECTION

law and taxation matters on behalf of the local office of the Sperry and Hutchinson Company—the S & H Green Stamp people. In an appeal to the North Carolina Supreme Court, Manly & Hendren won a reversal of a ban by the Winston Board of Aldermen on the use of the stamps; the aldermen considered the stamps to be "an illegal advertising scheme." But the city soon passed a new ordinance requiring merchants who offered the stamps to pay a privilege tax of $25 a year.

The firm continued to handle its share of estate cases in Forsyth and the surrounding counties at the start of the new century. One case, tried in Surry County in 1905 and appealed to the State Supreme Court, stands out. In *Bunker v. Bunker*, Clement Manly and W. M. Hendren represented Adelaide Bunker, widow of Chang, one of the "Original Siamese Twins," in a suit filed by her son, C. W. Bunker, for certain rents and profits produced from lands received from Chang's estate. The state's high court ruled in Adelaide Bunker's favor, noting that the earlier judgment in the case in Surry County Superior Court was final and the former decision conclusive between the parties.

Chang and Eng had first traveled to the United States in 1829 as part of a world lecture tour organized by a British merchant and entrepreneur. At a lecture in New York in 1836, the twins became acquainted with Dr. James Calloway, a Wilkes County physician, who invited his new friends on a hunting and fishing trip to North Carolina. The two accepted his invitation and liked the secluded, peaceful landscape of rural Wilkes so much that they decided to settle there. Not long after arriving, they met two sis-

In 1905, the firm defended Adelaide Bunker, widow of Chang Bunker (left), one of the "Original Siamese Twins," who spent the last 30 years of their lives in Surry County, North Carolina.

North Carolina Collection, University of North Carolina at Chapel Hill Library

ters from Wilkesboro, Adelaide and Sarah Yates. Chang fell in love with Adelaide, the younger sister. Eng, with less enthusiasm, developed a relationship with Sarah, partly in deference to his brother's passions and to the necessity of "balancing" the relationship. When the foursome proposed a double wedding, the Yates family, its friends, and the townspeople were aghast at such an unconventional alliance. But despite these concerns, a double marriage ceremony was held at the Yates homestead in April 1843. Together, the four moved into the twins' farmhouse in nearby Trap Hill. Chang and Adelaide had 12 children over the next 22 years, while Eng and Sarah had 10. Chang Bunker died in his sleep on the evening of January 17, 1875. One of Eng's sons discovered his uncle's death when he tried to wake him. Stirred from his sleep, Eng was distraught to learn of his brother's passing. A doctor was summoned to attend to Eng but did not arrive in time to save him. Autopsies showed that Chang had died of a stroke and Eng of shock.

BASE BALL!!!

LAWYERS VS. DOCTORS.

South Side Park, Monday, May 30th, 1904.

BENEFIT TWIN-CITY HOSPITAL.

The Lawyers and Doctors will play a match game of Ball at South Side Park, May 30th the proceeds will be applied to the Twin-City Hospital. It will prove an event and be worth coming miles to see. A reasonable admission fee will be charged. The game will be called at 3 P. M., and will be lined up as follows:

LAWYERS.

Lindsay Patterson,	Catcher
C. B. Watson,	Short stop
Clement Manly,	Pitcher
J. C. Buxton,	1st Base
Bob Glenn,	2nd Base
J. S. Grogan,	3rd Base
A. E. Holton,	L. Field
E. E. Gray,	C. Field
H. L. Beckerdite,	R. Field

Substitutes.—George Pell, Louis Swink, G. H. Hasten, H. O. Sapp, J. T. Benbow, S. E. Hall, J. E. Alexander, H. R. Starbuck, D. H. Blair, W. O. Cox, F. T. Baldwin, D. P. Mast, A. E. Griffith, H. Montague, Walter Swink, W. M. Hendren, Thomas Watson, A. H. Eller, A. B. Harold, W. A. Blair, D. H. Blair.

DOCTORS.

D. N. Dalton,	Catcher
H. T. Bahnson,	Pitcher
Dr. Kerner,	1st Base
E. Fulp,	2nd Base
E. F. Strickland,	3rd Base
A. Y. Linville,	Short Stop
J. P. Farrington,	L. Field.
H. J. Thomas,	C. Field
C. S. Summers,	R. Field

Substitutes.—H. J. Montague, J. W. Davis, John Bynum, S. F. Pfohl, J. T. Wright, Dr. Spainhour, J. L. Hanes, F. L. Locket, H. H. Kapp, J. F. Shaffner, W. C. Linville, W. C. Ashworth, Dr. Dicks, J. P. Williams, A. P. Davis, J. C. Hammock, H. S. Lott,

UMPIRE—Judge Allen.

Each of the firm's partners at the turn of the 20th century—Robert B. Glenn, Clement Manly, and William M. Hendren—was an avid baseball fan and a regular participant in charity baseball games.

THE *WINSTON-SALEM JOURNAL*

As busy as Glenn, Manly & Hendren was during these years, the firm was not "all work and no play." Clement Manly, R. B. Glenn, and W. M. Hendren were all avid baseball fans. Glenn, Hendren, and David H. Blair led the Winston-Salem Athletic Association early in the century. When in 1904 the Forsyth County Bar Association challenged the physicians of Forsyth to a charity game of baseball for the benefit of the Twin-City Hospital, the firm's lawyers led the effort, just as W. B. Glenn and R. B. Glenn had done 13 years earlier.

Bob Glenn was the captain of the team and its starting pitcher, Clement Manly was the center fielder, and W. M. Hendren was one of the five attorneys in reserve on the bench. Captain Glenn played well, but Manly attracted the attention of reporters for "his apparent ignorance of the use of a bat." In the end, the younger doctors' team prevailed by a score of 18-10. The Ladies' Auxiliary of the hospital thanked both groups of "busy professional gentlemen for the time and interest taken in the game."

Glenn, Manly & Hendren may not have harbored the best trio of baseball players in North Carolina, but it was already recognized as one of the strongest legal firms in the state.

By 1897—just 20 years after arriving from Virginia—R. J. Reynolds was the most prominent businessman in Winston and one of the richest men in the South.

Forsyth County Public Library Photograph Collection

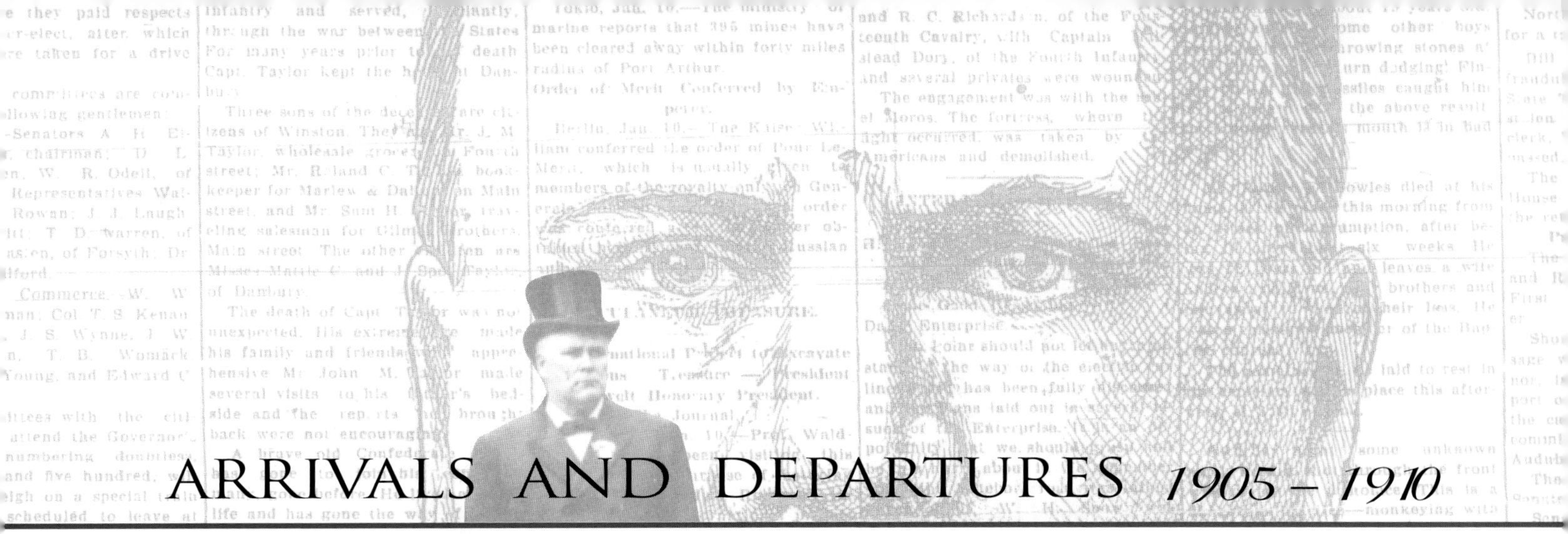

ARRIVALS AND DEPARTURES *1905 – 1910*

"I live in a town which is the greatest seat of the plug-tobacco industry in the world. Last year there was a production of 32 million pounds of this tobacco in the factories of Winston-Salem, and the output is constantly increasing. Winston and Salem are two separate and independent municipalities, and yet are practically but one town. Salem is by long odds the older, as it was founded by Moravians from Pennsylvania in 1753, while its partner is a giddy young thing, whose record goes back only half a century. These Moravians were a fine race of people, thrifty, pious and orderly, and the same good traits are exemplified in their descendants. The most striking personality in our community is that of R. J. Reynolds, the tobacco magnate and head of a company which has 400 traveling salesmen and 6,000 people in its employ. Mr. Reynolds came to Winston-Salem thirty years ago with a little capital. Today he is several times a millionaire, and so strongly entrenched that the tobacco trust had to be content with taking stock in his company. North Carolina can boast the two greatest tobacco kings in the world—R. J. Reynolds and J. B. Duke."

Colonel J. C. Buxton
in the *Washington Post* (1905)

The year 1905 was a banner time for the community and for the firm of Glenn, Manly & Hendren. Winston and Salem continued to prosper almost without interruption. Winston's leading citizen, R. J. Reynolds, was the wealthiest man in the state, having bought out a number of his competitors. His brother, William N. Reynolds, could be seen tooling around town in his Cadillac Model H touring car, its 30-horsepower engine capable of producing a speed of 60 miles an hour. The leading manufacturing community in the state, Winston was growing fast, and hustle and bustle were everywhere.

By 1905, Winston and Salem comprised the second-largest city in the state, with a population of almost 30,000. The Twin City boasted over 100 factories producing more than 200 types of products. The two towns were shipping tobacco, knit goods, furniture, cigarette machines, sawmill machinery, and even ice by the carload to domestic markets and foreign customers in Latin America, Europe, and eastern Asia. The new P. H. Hanes Knitting Company was into its third year of production of men's and women's underwear, and the Chatham Manufacturing Company was about to open a large woolen blanket factory in the city. One of Glenn, Manly & Hendren's oldest clients, the Wachovia National Bank, had become the largest bank in the state and one of the largest and strongest in the entire South, its assets having grown tenfold in just a decade.

There were nearly 1,000 telephones in Winston and Salem by 1905, up from just 75 in 1890. Automobiles were beginning to appear on town streets and county roads in significant numbers, so much so that the county commissioners felt compelled to pass a speed limit of 10 miles an hour for the horseless carriage and to supply town policemen with stopwatches. But the Twin City also had more serious problems. Downtown pool halls were becoming more rowdy and were often the scenes of violence. Cocaine use and the carrying of concealed weapons were both on the increase. Saloons were so popular and plentiful in the "wet" city of Winston that the aldermen felt it necessary to pass an ordinance forbidding them from providing liquor to women and minors. The new railway between Winston and Greensboro, a "dry" city, was so popular with the drinking crowd that it came to be called "the Booze Line."

In 1905, the firm's senior members were some of the most respected men in the community and among the handful of leading orators in the Twin City. Each stood at the pinnacle of his profession. That July, Clement Manly, in his 27th year as a lawyer, was elected as

The saloon at the elegant, new Zinzendorf Hotel (erected on Main Street in 1906) was the city's finest drinking establishment.

FORSYTH COUNTY PUBLIC LIBRARY PHOTOGRAPH COLLECTION

In 1905, the firm's offices were located on the courthouse square near the corner of Fourth and Liberty, depicted in this postcard view.
FORSYTH COUNTY PUBLIC LIBRARY PHOTOGRAPH COLLECTION

the seventh president of the North Carolina Bar Association. The *North Carolina Journal of Law* hailed Manly as "one of the most popular and successful lawyers in the State." But it was in the realm of politics that the firm reached its greatest heights in 1905.

Robert B. Glenn had long been the most politically active member of the firm. Even before coming to Winston in 1885, he had served in the General Assembly as a 26-year-old legislator from Danbury. A power in the Forsyth County Democratic Party from the moment of his arrival, Glenn had served as solicitor and as United States attorney for the Western District of North Carolina. After playing a prominent role statewide in the effort by the Furnifold Simmons "machine" to defeat the "fusion" ticket of Populists and Republicans in 1898, Glenn won election to the State Senate the next year. An early candidate for his party's nomination for the United States Senate in 1902, he was not chosen but was nonetheless the most forceful and eloquent speaker in the campaign for the Democratic ticket around the state.

By the spring of the next year, Bob Glenn was being mentioned as a likely candidate for governor in the election of 1904. His loyalty to the party's candidates and his prowess as an orator had won him recognition; indeed, the name Bob Glenn had become something of a household word in the state. When he announced his candidacy for governor on September 24, 1903, his hometown Democratic newspaper backed him to the hilt: "In R. B. Glenn are blended all those qualities which could be demanded by a Democratic constituency. His ability and culture is of the highest order. His life is that of a pure Christian gentleman. His services to the State for the past fifteen years have furnished an opportunity for him to make an enviable reputation for courage and pure Jeffersonian democracy. He is a lawyer of unusual ability and force and is gifted in executive power. Yet, withal, there is a modesty about Mr. Glenn which distinguishes him from the politician and at once stamps him as a statesman whose highest ideal is found in the honor and satisfaction that flows from an earnest, honest effort in the uplift of humanity, and the maintaining of pure and honest government."

In the general election held on November 8, 1904,

Robert B. Glenn headlined a strong Democratic ticket. He won the governor's office by a margin of 50,000 votes.

The proud citizens of Winston and Salem organized a large official delegation to escort their favorite son to the swearing-in ceremony in Raleigh on January 11, 1905. The Forsyth Riflemen would make the trip, as would the regimental band from Reidsville in Glenn's native county of Rockingham. When the Inaugural Committee arrived at Winston's Union Station on the train from Raleigh, it was to the offices of Glenn, Manly & Hendren on West Fourth Street that its members came to pay their respects to the governor-elect. After a driving tour of the community, they were hosted by the Twin-City Club. The reception and "smoker" there, attended by the most prominent citizens of Forsyth, were described by one writer as "perhaps the most notable social event in the long history of the club."

Nearly 300 of the county's citizens—including prominent businessmen, public officials, and grizzled veterans of the Civil War—boarded the special Raleigh-bound train. After a brief reception and a military parade up Fayetteville Street, Governor-elect Glenn, accompanied by the popular outgoing governor, Charles B. Aycock, arrived by carriage at the inaugural stage, set up in the Academy of Music on Martin Street. A steady rain had driven the proceedings inside. The large crowd greeting the governor-elect included members of the legislature and the state judiciary and other public officials.

When Governor Aycock rose to introduce Robert B. Glenn, the wild cheers of the crowd drowned out his words and compelled him to be seated for a time, until the storm of applause subsided. With order restored, R. B. Glenn was duly introduced, took the oath of office from Chief Justice Walter Clark, signed a copy of the State Constitution, and took the podium to deliver his inaugural address. In it, he sought to continue Aycock's popular programs of improved roads, better schools, industrial development, and low taxes. And while Glenn hewed to the party line on the treatment of the state's African-Americans—he felt that "the Negro should have the most practical method of education and training suited to his needs"—he did oppose a school-funding formula based on the amount of taxes paid by each race, arguing for an equitable and just distribution that would not "close the door of hope in the Negro's face."

Governor Glenn hosted an elaborate reception in the rotunda of the State Capitol after the speech. That event was followed by an equally elaborate inaugural ball at Raleigh's Olivia Raney Library. "The splendor of the occasion was greatly enhanced by the beautiful and fashionable ladies of the city and state who graced the occasion," wrote the Raleigh correspondent for the *Winston-Salem Journal*.

The ball gown worn by Mrs. Nina Glenn at the inauguration of her husband, Governor Robert B. Glenn, in January 1905

THE NORTH CAROLINA MUSEUM OF HISTORY

THE WINSTON-SALEM JOURNAL

VOL. XI. NO. 9. WINSTON-SALEM, N. C., WEDNESDAY MORNING, JANUARY 11, 1905 PRICE 5 CENTS.

OFF TO RALEIGH

OUR GOVERNOR WILL HAVE BIG ESCORT TO CAPITAL.

WILL LEAVE THIS MORNING

The Legislative Committee and Chamber of Commerce Committee From Raleigh Met and Entertained—The Impression They Created—The "Smoker" by the Twin-City Club Brim Full of Pleasure.

The committees from the Legislature and chamber of commerce, Raleigh, arrived in the city yesterday and were met at the union station by the local committee on appointed at the Twin-City Club meeting on Saturday night. The visitors were taken to the hotel in carriages, and after being assigned to rooms, visited the office of Glenn, Manly & Hendren, where they paid respects to the Governor-elect, after which the visitors were taken for a drive over the city.

The Raleigh committees are composed of the following gentlemen:

Legislature—Senators A. H. Eller, of Forsyth, chairman; D. L. Ward, of Craven; W. R. Odell, of Cabarrus; and Representatives Walter Murphy, of Rowan; J. J. Laughinghouse, of Pitt; T. D. Warren, of Jones; G. H. Hastings, of Forsyth; Dr. Gordon, of Guilford.

Chamber of Commerce—W. W. Robards, chairman; Col. T. S. Kenan, R. M. Phillips, J. S. Wynne, J. W. Thompson, Hon. T. B. Womack, Hon. J. R. Y. Young, and Edward C. Smith.

These committees with the citizens who will attend the Governor's inauguration, numbering doubtless, between four and five hundred, will return to Raleigh on a special train this morning scheduled to leave at 8 o'clock. The inauguration ceremonies are to take place at noon.

JAPS LIFT MINES

NOGI REINFORCES OYAMA WITH 15,000 MEN.

KAISER HONORING RUSSIANS

TWO WERE KILLED

ENGAGEMENT BETWEEN REBELS AND AMERICAN FORCES.

FEW AMERICANS WOUNDED

ITEMS FROM WILKESBORO.

Major W. W. Vannoy Dead—Was 72 Years Old and Confederate Soldier.

FIGHT ON JUG LAW

CONSIDERING THE ENLARGEMENT OF CAPITOL BUILDING

HONORING EX-SENATORS

Northampton Petitions for a Dog Tax Bill to Repay Treasurer Lacy the Money That Clerk Martin Embezzled—Bill to Reduce Hours in Factories—Other Bills.

CONFEDERATE VETERAN DEAD.

GREENSBORO'S BIG FIRE.

The Winston-Salem Journal *proudly proclaimed the election of the city's native son.*

The *Winston-Salem Journal*

When the National Auto Tour visited Winston in 1909 to promote road and highway construction in the state, Colonel Manly was one of the leaders of the welcoming delegation.

FORSYTH COUNTY PUBLIC LIBRARY PHOTOGRAPH COLLECTION

During the Glenn administration, the state's debt was satisfactorily settled, education and public-health services were expanded, and low passenger rates on railroads were maintained against strong opposition. While Bob Glenn shared the white supremacist beliefs of the state's elite and supported the passage of Jim Crow laws and ordinances, he vigorously enforced state laws designed to prosecute and bring to justice the perpetrators of lynchings.

But Glenn is chiefly remembered as "the Prohibition Governor" for his successful 1908 campaign to ban liquor statewide. An advocate of temperance from his youth, he saw prohibition as a great moral question for the state and its citizens, and accordingly threw himself body and soul into the effort, leading the opposition to the state's powerful liquor interests. In a famous speech at Selma extensively covered in the press and widely reprinted, he said, "What wreck and ruin strong drink produces! If it is true that it brings mourning instead of rejoicing, tears instead of health, ruin instead of up building, death instead of life, damnation instead of salvation, you men of North Carolina, how dare you to vote for this monster curse?"

Upon Glenn's departure from the Executive Mansion in 1909, the *Winston-Salem Journal* summed up the governor's term with these words: "Robert B. Glenn has administered the functions of his office with remarkable tact, good judgment and firmness, and he has displayed a high order of executive ability in dealing with important questions of state and public affairs."

Even with Bob Glenn away in Raleigh, the firm continued to enjoy a reputation as one of the finest in the state. Clement Manly and W. M. Hendren remained among a handful of the city's top public men, looked to for leadership and called upon at public occasions.

Mr. Hendren was in greater demand as a public speaker, and Colonel Manly became the favorite master of ceremonies and toastmaster in the western Piedmont. When the National Auto Highway Tour, a "good roads" organization, came to Winston-Salem in 1909, for instance, it was Colonel Manly who was invited to introduce the organization's featured speaker, baseball great Ty Cobb. He was also a charter member of the Cosmos Club, a gentlemen's literary club founded in Winston in March 1909.

Clement Manly and W. M. Hendren continued to serve as counsel for prominent community organizations such as the Board of Aldermen and the Winston-Salem Board of Trade and to represent leading companies such as the Southern Railway, the Wachovia Bank and Trust Company, the P. H. Hanes Knitting Company, the Chatham Manufacturing Company, and the Fries Manufacturing and Power Company, owner of the city's street railway. During these years, the firm's attorneys also began to serve as corporate directors of area firms; Clement Manly served on the boards of the People's National Bank, the Union Guano Company, and the Winston-Salem Power Company.

The R. J. Reynolds Tobacco Company had long been one of the firm's most important clients, particularly in the realm of personal injury and negligence claims. Although Reynolds hired Burton Craige in 1905 as in-house counsel, Manly, Hendren & Womble continued as general counsel. When young Willie Rolin, a Reynolds employee, lost his hand in an industrial accident in one of the company's tobacco factories in 1905, he sued the company for damages. The firm handled the case. Rolin was under 12 years of age at the time. The case allowed the State Supreme Court to construe for the first time a statute enacted by the legislature in 1903 prohibiting child labor in mills and factories. The decision revolved around whether the R. J. Reynolds Tobacco Company "knowingly and willfully"

By the second decade of the 20th century, the P. H. Hanes Knitting Company had its own railroad station, mill village, school, and ballpark.

Forsyth County Public Library Photograph Collection

employed the child. Justice Henry Groves Connor, writing for the court, ruled that "the act is the result of the well considered, and, we think, wise conclusion of the General Assembly, reflecting and crystalizing into law the will of the people of the State. It is a matter of importance, too, to employers of labor in mills and factories, to know the standard of their rights and liabilities. The industrial life and development of the State are not only consistent with, but promoted by, the exclusion of young children from mills and factories. The child, educated and developed before beginning work of this kind, becomes not only more useful and efficient, but in all respects a better citizen." The case was returned to Forsyth Superior Court, which granted a nonsuit on the motion of the attorneys.

In 1906, Clement Manly revisited one of his greatest legal triumphs when he again represented William Cyrus Briggs and his Winston Cigarette Machine Company in an action against the Wells-Whitehead Tobacco Company. The cigarette company had signed a contract to exhibit the famous Briggs cigarette machine at the Louisiana Purchase Exposition in St. Louis in 1904. Briggs alleged that he had prepared the machine for exhibition and delivered it to St. Louis at considerable expense, but that Wells-Whitehead had refused to exhibit the machine as it had promised to do, denying the Winston Cigarette Machine Company considerable public exposure and sales. The North Carolina Supreme Court upheld the lower court's ruling in Briggs's favor, noting the "learned and able counsel for the plaintiff in their excellent brief." It returned the case for trial on the issue of damages for the company's failure to exhibit the machine.

As leading members of the community, Clement Manly and W. M. Hendren continued to be called upon to assist with controversial cases.

In the sensational 1905 case of J. W. Hammons, who was sentenced to death for murdering his wife, W. M. Hendren was appointed by the court to assist Hammons in seeking a commutation of his life sentence from Governor Glenn. The governor refused the request of his law partners. Hammons was hanged on a gallows erected on the third floor of the county jail, the third execution in Forsyth County in the new century.

When Henry Kobre, a Jewish saloon owner, was robbed and brutally murdered in March 1906, Manly and Hendren were asked to represent the defendant, Sam Kobre, half-brother of the owner. They helped secure a verdict of not guilty from the jury. Judge R. B. Peebles remarked that he would not have convicted "a yaller dog" on the evidence presented by the state's star witness, Miss Sallie Stewart, who was described in the Winston *Union Republican* as an "ignorant country girl who, having had no advantages, came to the city and fell into the ways of sin."

Robert B. Glenn, the firm's longtime senior member, returned to Winston in 1909 at the end of his term as governor. But he had decided not to rejoin the firm. A popular speaker on the lecture circuit, he traveled the country giving Chautauqua speeches and participating in antisaloon campaigns. "I never expect to practice law any more," Governor Glenn announced to the press in September 1909. "I am making money now with the Rochester Lyceum Bureau and will be with them five months, traveling over the north and south, delivering addresses. Four months of my time will be devoted to the Presbyterian Church, and the other I shall rest."

The firm needed another attorney to fill the vacuum left by Bob Glenn's departure. Clement Manly and William Hendren had their eye on a rising young attorney active in the local courts and in Democratic politics as well. A new year and a new decade were about to begin—a good time to start fresh with a new firm name and a new partner.

Governor Robert B. Glenn joined the governor of New Jersey and a group of that state's Civil War veterans at the dedication of a memorial in New Bern, North Carolina, in 1909.

The North Carolina Division of Archives and History

In 1911, the firm moved to new offices on Liberty Street opposite the courthouse.

North Carolina Collection, University of North Carolina at Chapel Hill Library

B. S. Womble
Attorney-at-Law
Winston-Salem, N. C.

A FIRM CONSOLIDATION *1911 – 1920*

> *"Winston-Salem generally tries to lead the list. We have the largest leaf tobacco market in the State, the largest tobacco manufacturing factory, the finest Court House, the best County Home, the oldest Female Academy, the finest bank building, an imposing Masonic Temple and other things. Winston-Salem is a veritable bee-hive of industry, a place of unlimited possibilities—the city where everybody works."*
>
> J. R. Goslen, editor of
> the Winston *Union Republican* (1911)

"City Solicitor Womble joins the firm of Manly & Hendren," read the notice in the Winston-Salem newspapers during the first week of 1911. "In the future this triple team of leading local lawyers will be styled as Manly, Hendren & Womble." As if to signify the new triumvirate, the firm moved from its old offices on West Fourth Street to new quarters on Liberty Street.

By 1911, over 100 automobiles crowded downtown Winston, "shooting down the street like meteors," according to one observer. Wachovia National Bank had absorbed the Wachovia Loan and Trust Company the year before and was now the largest bank between Atlanta and Washington. R. J. Reynolds Tobacco Company had just moved into a new five-story factory on Chestnut Street. Its Prince Albert smoking tobacco was the best-selling brand in the land. The company would soon build its first factory devoted solely to the manufacture of cigarettes. With the United States Supreme Court's dissolution that year of Buck Duke's American Tobacco Company trust—which Dick Reynolds had made a strategic decision to join 12 years earlier—R. J. Reynolds Tobacco Company was poised to conquer the entire industry.

For all its industrial development, Winston remained

powerfully connected to the rural countryside. Saturday was still "trade day" in Winston. The streets of the business section were crowded from morning until far into the night. During the day, the tobacco warehouses were jammed with wagons from the country bearing leaf destined for the factories. Yet not all developments in the town were so salutary. Saloons selling "near beer" were multiplying and enjoying a brisk Saturday business from farmers, in addition to their regular daily trade from the town's factories. And segregation had come to Winston's residential neighborhoods and streetcars through city ordinance, limiting the freedom of the town's African-Americans.

A few years earlier, in 1907, the Winston press had carried this news item: "Mr. B. S. Womble, of Morganton, N.C., locates in this city for the practice of law and has opened for business in the offices of Mr. David H. Blair, Tise Building." Young Womble had recently arrived in the city after a year of graduate study at the Columbia University School of Law. Ready to hang out his shingle, he started his solo practice on September 7, becoming one of 30 lawyers practicing in Winston.

Bunyan Snipes Womble was born on May 2, 1882, in Chatham County, North Carolina, the son of the Reverend William Fletcher Womble, a Methodist minister, and Olivia Snipes Womble. Educated in the public schools and private academies of the state, he entered Trinity College (now Duke University) in 1900. Lean and lanky at six foot two and 160 pounds, Womble joined the school's fledgling basketball team, which played in the state's first intercollegiate game, a 15-12 loss to Wake Forest. After graduation, he stayed on at the new Trinity College School of Law. He later graduated as one of five members of the school's first class.

"Hands" of tobacco were stacked and ready for auction in this turn-of-the-century view.

THE NORTH CAROLINA DIVISION OF ARCHIVES AND HISTORY

Bunyan Snipes Womble in 1907, the year he arrived in Winston

Courtesy of William F. Womble

B. S. Womble had very few acquaintances in Winston and knew little about the town he came to in 1907. The Winston Bar was reportedly a flamboyant lot, given to florid oratory, Shakespearian theatrics, and a no-holds-barred ethic of legal practice. Some of the first advice he received on establishing himself in the strange town came from none other than R. J. Reynolds. "One day I left my desk and walked across the courthouse square to the O'Hanlon corner, where I joined a group of men standing on the sidewalk," Mr. Womble remembered. "Mr. Reynolds, whom I had already met, saw me and said, 'If I was a young lawyer trying to get a start in Winston I'd let folks know I was here, even if I had to pick a fight with Buxton.' "

Womble declined to engage in fisticuffs with J. C. Buxton, the burly partner of Cyrus Watson in the city's other leading firm, Watson & Buxton. But he did get noticed, quickly making himself known among the leading men of the town. He introduced himself to Clement Manly. With the colonel's help, he succeeded in having the General Assembly enact legislation to establish the office of city solicitor (prosecuting attorney) for Winston. When the city's aldermen met in September 1908 to establish the office, B. S. Womble was selected as the first solicitor of Recorder's Court.

As solicitor, the young attorney soon won his legal spurs, battling the likes of Colonel Buxton, C. B. Watson, and other leading lights of the Winston Bar. From his earliest days in the law, he demonstrated a judicious temperament and a gift for analysis and tight logic. Womble

In 1911, the firm of Manly, Hendren & Womble opened offices on the second floor of this building in the 300 block of North Liberty Street in downtown Winston.

Forsyth County Public Library Photograph Collection

also had a flintlike determination to be the best and a capacity for innovation and hard work. These qualities impressed Colonel Manly, always a keen judge of character and talent. Late in 1910, Manly invited Womble to join the firm.

Like his predecessors, B. S. Womble assumed a role in the community appropriate to a man of his station. He became an active member of the Twin-City Club, was appointed a director of the Board of Trade, helped charter the Winston-Salem Rotary Club in 1915, was named to the Trinity College Board of Trustees the same year, and was elected president of the Trinity Alumni Association the next year. When a Young Men's Democratic Club was organized in Forsyth County in 1912, B. S. Womble was elected its first president.

He even participated in possum hunts, a social occasion enjoyed by young gentlemen (and ladies) of the day. "Young folks drive out into the country in automobiles, and after a hunt of several hours repair to a designated spot, where a tempting supper of possum and sweet potatoes is spread," a Winston correspondent reported in 1907. One 1911 possum-hunting party that bagged seven of the night-prowling animals included the likes of David H. Blair, James A. Gray, Jr., Miss Anna Buxton, and Miss Adelaide Fries, as well as B. S. Womble. R. J. Reynolds was known to enjoy a good possum hunt on a crisp autumn evening in the woods of Forsyth.

As a solo practitioner, B. S. Womble had represented the local office of the Western Union Telegraph Company. He continued to do so with his new firm. "I was kept busy," Womble told a reporter, "by suits against Western Union seeking damages for the mental anguish caused by the company's failure to deliver—or lateness in delivery of—death messages." In one 1912 case argued by Womble, *Lizzie Penn v. Western Union Telegraph Company*, the North Carolina Supreme Court ruled that Penn, a resident of Virginia, was allowed damages for mental suffering for nondelivery of a telegraph, irrespective of whether the message had originated in North Carolina or had simply been received in the state.

An important 1912 case that went all the way to the North Carolina Supreme Court involved two of

B. S. Womble was a member of the first graduating class (1906) of the Trinity College School of Law in Durham, North Carolina. Trinity later became Duke University.

Forsyth County Public Library Photograph Collection

Manly, Hendren & Womble's oldest clients. The firm filed a friendly suit, *City of Winston v. Wachovia Bank and Trust*, in order to test the legality of the city's recent $350,000 bond issue. The question was whether the vote, in which several distinct and unrelated propositions were combined and voted for on a single ballot, was proper and according to law. The court ruled the bond election invalid, holding that when a popular vote is required, the voter should be afforded opportunity to cast his ballot for a single proposition.

The firm's greatest triumph during the decade was a victory shared with the entire community—the uniting of Winston and Salem into one city.

The city had been a work in progress for a long time, to say the least. Robert Gray, an early community leader and the man who bought the first lot in Winston in 1849, had foreseen the day that the two towns a mile apart would be united. In an Independence Day speech in 1876—the same year the firm was founded—Gray proclaimed, "I speak of Winston and Salem as one place. . . . Would that I could speak of them under one name. They are one in identity of interest and future. . . . I hail the coming day [from] which shall rise one united town."

Many business and civic leaders felt the same way. Three years after Gray's speech, the town boards in Salem and Winston appointed a special committee to study consolidating the two towns. The committee recommended that the united halves be named "the City of Salem." A charter was drawn up, approved by both boards, and ratified by the General Assembly. In a public referendum, Salem voters endorsed the charter

In 1913, the community spirit of Salem was joined with the industrial muscle of adjoining Winston to form a new city, Winston-Salem. Within a decade, it would grow into the largest city in North Carolina.

Photograph by G. Allen Aycock

Winston's first town hall, on the corner of Fourth and Main, became the government center for the newly consolidated city in 1913.
FORSYTH COUNTY PUBLIC LIBRARY PHOTOGRAPH COLLECTION

overwhelmingly, but the citizens of Winston, fearing the loss of identity, turned it down almost three to one.

When that vote was taken in 1879, Salem was the larger and more influential of the two towns. It had a long and storied history and had provided the land and much of the leadership for Winston's founding. But the days when it could control the direction of its other half were coming to a close. As it grew and built its industrial muscle, Winston began to overshadow its sister city.

Instead of dictating the name of the new town, Salem found itself fighting to keep its name on the map in the 1890s. Twice during the decade, postal authorities proposed closing the Salem branch office and consolidating it with the office in Winston, to be known as "the Winston branch." Each time, Salem residents dispatched their mayor, Henry E. Fries, to Washington to plead their case. Fries saved the Salem post office in 1891. But by 1899, the best he could come back with was an assurance that the consolidated office in Winston would be known as "the Winston-Salem branch." Many people and businesses—including the newspapers—had been referring to the two towns by that name for some time, but the hyphen took on permanence when it started appearing in postmarks.

Members of the firm had long advocated the joining of the two towns. In an address before the Chamber of Commerce in 1893, Robert B. Glenn had urged civic leaders to revisit the issue. And in 1910, Clement Manly had supported consolidation at a meeting of the Retail Merchants Association.

By 1913, almost everyone considered the two towns one. For many in Salem, the old congregational town had lost its identity and was merely a quiet residential suburb of bustling Winston. It was only natural that the union be legalized.

In December 1912, a group of leading citizens—men such as Clement Manly, Cyrus B. Watson, and James A. Gray, Sr.—prepared a petition calling for

The Salem Boys School, one of the oldest buildings in Salem, was constructed in 1794. Today, it houses the Wachovia Historical Museum.

Wachovia Corporation

a public referendum on consolidation. They chose B. S. Womble to head a special Citizens' Committee on Consolidation, which would be responsible for drafting a bill and lobbying the legislature.

The General Assembly ratified a consolidation act and charter on January 27, 1913. The citizens of each town approved the unification on March 18. On May 6, voters elected Oscar B. Eaton, who had been Winston's mayor for 10 years, as the first mayor of the combined city. Salem, 147 years old, became one of four voting wards of the new city.

"Less than five months after Winston and Salem were joined by a hyphen, an event occurred that ensured the success and growth of the new city and its businesses," wrote Frank V. Tursi in *Winston-Salem: A History*. "Camels arrived. R. J. Reynolds Tobacco Company introduced its Camel cigarettes on October 19, 1913. The brand's immense popularity made Reynolds the leading tobacco company in the world, and the town of Winston-Salem the leading producer of tobacco products."

The emerging conflict in Europe proved a boon to the city's industries. Even before the nation's entry into World War I, Winston-Salem companies were being called on to serve the Allied cause. In 1914, the Chatham Manufacturing Company received a large order for its famous Elkin blankets from the French army. The next year, the J. A. Vance Iron Works sup-

To appeal to American smokers' taste for Turkish tobacco, R. J. Reynolds chose a brand name, Camel, that evoked images of the Middle East. Old Joe, a Barnum & Bailey camel photographed during a 1913 visit by the circus to Winston-Salem, was the model for the dromedary depicted on every pack of Camels.

Forsyth County Public Library Photograph Collection

plied thousands of steel jackets for shrapnel factories. And the J. C. Spach Wagon Works received an immense contract for army escort wagons.

Twin City residents responded with men, materiel, and moral support when Congress declared war on Germany in 1917 and American boys prepared to go "over there." When a patriotic rally to send off the Forsyth Riflemen was organized, it was Clement Manly who was chosen to preside and deliver the opening address to the thousands of citizens gathered at the courthouse square. The attorneys and their wives quickly subscribed to Victory loan drives, supported wartime charities, and worked in public health and welfare activities.

The R. J. Reynolds Tobacco Company filled a government order for 27 carloads of Prince Albert smoking tobacco in 1917. By May of that year, it had shipped 125 more carloads to GIs in France. In addition, the company's cigarette machines worked day and night, turning out 12 billion cigarettes in 1918, double the previous year's total. Bishop Rondthaler called these years "the greatest that the tobacco industry has ever seen."

One by-product of America's involvement in the Great War touched the life of every citizen in every state. This was Congress's passage of the War Revenue Act in 1917, which made the income tax the chief source of federal revenue. On a trip to Washington in 1918, Clement Manly made remarks about the new tax that proved prescient. After a visit with an old friend, Senator Furnifold M. Simmons, chairman of the Senate Finance Committee, Manly told the press, "The income tax act was purposely written to confuse the average person. It can be interpreted in so many ways that no one can escape its provisions." The *Charlotte Observer* noted that if Colonel Manly could not understand the intricacies of the income-tax law, then no one could.

The war years were busy ones for the firm. Manly, Hendren & Womble supported wartime charities such

The poster reached its apotheosis as a propaganda tool—and a high art form—during World War I.

Reproduced from the Bowman Gray Collection of World War I and World War II Posters, Rare Book Collection, University of North Carolina at Chapel Hill Library

Men from Winston-Salem preparing to leave for military service in World War I
Forsyth County Public Library Photograph Collection

as the Red Cross and was among the leaders of the city's Liberty Bond drive, the most successful in the state. W. M. Hendren headed the county's War Advisory Board, which administered some 20,000 oaths over the next two years. Of course, the regular work of the firm continued for clients old and new. Wachovia Bank, Western Union, R. J. Reynolds, and the Southern Railway remained key clients during the decade. But the firm also represented clients such as Dr. A. de T. Valk, a surgeon at the Twin-City Hospital in Winston-Salem. In one of the firm's first major medical malpractice cases, the State Supreme Court upheld the ruling from Wilkes Superior Court, which found no negligence on the doctor's part in diagnosing and treating his patient.

Not all of the firm's clients were men of means and influence. In a 1918 case from Rockingham County, *Slade v. Sherrod*, William M. Hendren represented West Slade, a black man, in a suit against W. J. Sherrod, an owner of the Greensboro Motor Car Company. Slade sought compensation for the loss of his horse and buggy and injury to himself after being struck by Sherrod's car. Mr. Hendren and his co-counsel, the noted attorney P. W. Glidewell, prevailed on appeal, winning damages for Slade in a ruling from the state's highest court.

Mr. Hendren's gesture across the racial divide was a small ray of hope in what proved to be the darkest year for race relations in the history of Winston-Salem. On November 16, 1918, a lynch mob, enraged at the rape and robbery of a white woman and the murder of her husband by an unknown black assailant, gathered at the Municipal Building and attempted to seize a young black man from Durham, Russell High, who had been arrested for carrying a concealed weapon. Despite an appeal by W. M. Hendren and other leading citizens, the mob rampaged down Fourth Street and through Winston's black neighborhoods,

WINSTON-SALEM IN WORLD WAR I

The war effort touched many aspects of everyday life in Winston-Salem, as recounted in this ditty penned by attorney C. A. Reynolds in January 1918:

My Tuesdays are meatless,
My Wednesdays are wheatless,
I'm growing more eatless each day.
My room, it is heatless,
My beds, they are sheetless,
They've been sent to the Y.M.C.A.

The bar-rooms are treatless,
My coffee is sweetless,
Each day I grow poorer and wiser.
My stockings are feetless,
My trousers are seatless,
Oh, Lord, how I hate the Old Kaiser!

looting stores and firing weapons. At least five people were killed in the melee.

The year 1918 also marked the first case argued by W. M. Hendren, a noted constitutional lawyer, before the Supreme Court of the United States. In *Hammer v. Dagenhart*, a case involving the constitutionality of an act of Congress prohibiting the transportation in interstate commerce of goods made with child labor, W. M. Hendren and Clement Manly argued for the appellees. In its decision, the high court affirmed the ruling of the Federal District Court that the law regulating the hours of labor of children in factories within a state exceeded Congress's constitutional authority.

The year 1918 witnessed not only the end of the great European war, but the end of an era for Winston-Salem as well. Within a span of three weeks, the

B. S. Womble (third from left) was part of the delegation of local businessmen who entertained Harvey Firestone, Henry Ford, and Thomas Edison when the famous trio visited North Carolina in 1918.

FORSYTH COUNTY PUBLIC LIBRARY PHOTOGRAPH COLLECTION

A proud R. J. Reynolds with his son Z. Smith Reynolds on the porch of the family's Fifth Street home in Winston-Salem
FORSYTH COUNTY PUBLIC LIBRARY PHOTOGRAPH COLLECTION

city lost both James A. Gray, Sr., president of the Wachovia Bank and Trust Company, and Richard Joshua Reynolds, founder and head of the R. J. Reynolds Tobacco Company. A few days before his death, Mr. Reynolds summoned Colonel Manly, his legal adviser, to visit him at Reynolda, his splendid country home just north of the city. In an affidavit, Manly recalled the scene: "[We] found Mr. R. J. Reynolds in bed, propped up with pillows. He was ill, feeble in body but mind sound and clear, and in the opinion of affiant fully conscious and capable of an understanding of the nature of the transaction hereinafter mentioned. . . . He called [us] to his bedside, and after talking about other matters said that he had asked us to come, as he wanted us to do something for him. He wanted to give two hospital buildings, one for the white people and one for the colored people of Winston-Salem; and that both buildings were to be located on the present hospital grounds of the City of Winston-Salem."

The will otherwise provided that one-third of the estate go to his wife, Katharine Reynolds, and the other two-thirds to the Reynoldses' four children.

"It is possible that I will not return, but I've always expressed the desire to die in harness." These were among the last words Robert B. Glenn spoke to his son as he boarded a train in Winston-Salem to take up his duties as a member of the International Great Waterways Commission in Winnipeg, Manitoba. He never returned, dying "in harness," as he wished, on May 16, 1920. The *Winston-Salem Journal* eulogized him as "a fearless fighter for any cause he was convinced was for the general good." Judge Oliver Allen remembered him as "one of the ablest advocates in the State, an orator and lecturer of national reputation."

An artist's rendition of the sprawling R. J. Reynolds Tobacco Company complex in the third decade of the 20th century

North Carolina Collection, University of North Carolina at Chapel Hill Library

A BUILDING BOOM TOWN *1920 – 1929*

> *"Winston-Salem is forging ahead at a rapid rate. Capitalization of industries went from $34 million to $64 million. Bank deposits increased 60 percent. Some twenty-two new corporations started business with a capital of $3 million. A large reservoir or dam has been built that will reserve a water supply of one million gallons. The population of Winston-Salem is estimated at over 45,000 people. Approximately one hundred homes have been erected in 1919. If you are looking for one of the best little cities in the South, drop in and investigate. The latch-string of Winston-Salem always hangs on the outside."*
>
> *Winston-Salem*
> Union Republican *(1920)*

"Greetings to North Carolina's Largest City!" trumpeted the *Winston-Salem Journal*. On April 14, 1920, citizens of Winston-Salem celebrated the news from the United States Census Bureau that the Twin City's population had reached 48,395, exceeding that of Charlotte by several thousand. Some 5,000 residents turned out for a grand torchlight parade to the courthouse. The town's mounted police led the march, followed by the Salem and Winston bands, hundreds of torchbearers with siren horns, and a line of automobiles that reached for several blocks. After lighting a huge bonfire on the courthouse square, the crowd, described in the paper as "jostling, jesting, and frolicking—but entirely good natured," partied late into the night, drowning out every attempt by public officials to deliver their prepared remarks.

There was indeed much for Winston-Salem to celebrate. The Twin City was one of the top manufacturing cities in the South. Its new plants and ever-increasing production meant more and more workers

The award-winning design of the R. J. Reynolds Tobacco Company Building—the tallest in the Carolinas from its completion in 1929 until 1965—led to a commission to design the Empire State Building for its architects, Shreve, Lamb & Harmon in New York.

North Carolina Collection,
University of North Carolina at Chapel Hill Library

in town. "Investors are swarming into the city like bees," a newspaper columnist wrote in 1920. "They know something good when they see it, and Winston-Salem is on the way up."

The R. J. Reynolds Tobacco Company was the king of the tobacco world, its Camel cigarettes the most popular brand in the world. Two statistics are sufficient to illustrate the might of Reynolds in the 1920s. The company imported so much Turkish tobacco and French cigarette paper for Camels that Winston-Salem—more than 200 miles from the ocean—was ranked by the United States Customs Service as the seventh-largest port of entry in the country. In 1925, Winston-Salem industries (led by Reynolds) accounted for 4.2 percent of the total internal revenue received by the federal government.

Winston-Salem's growing affluence showed itself in a building boom that produced some of the city's grandest homes and commercial buildings. The city's wealthy had begun to leave their Victorian mansions on West Fifth Street for country enclaves on the outskirts of town. R. J. Reynolds had set the tone in 1917, just a year before his death, with Reynolda, his 60-room mansion and 1,000-acre estate. Others soon followed, including Bowman Gray, Sr., the Reynolds executive who began building his Beaux Arts mansion, Graylyn, in 1927. That same year, B. S. Womble built an impressive Neoclassical Revival house on Stratford Road, one of the first fireproof dwellings in the state. Most of the new downtown buildings reached for the sky. The O'Hanlon Building (1915) was the city's first skyscraper. The Robert E. Lee Hotel (1921) and the Nissen Building (1926) were the tallest for a time, only to be surpassed by the 22-story headquarters building of the R. J. Reynolds Tobacco Company. The graceful and elegant Reynolds skyscraper, completed in 1929, brought a fitting end to the frenzied building of the 1920s.

In 1919, city leaders were busy with another constructive effort, establishing the Winston-Salem Foundation, one of the first foundations in the nation whose funds were derived largely from citizens' contributions. Within a few years, two businesses that would become key employers in the city—the North Carolina Baptist Hospital and the Security Life and Trust Company—were established. Both would become clients of the firm.

Nearly 3,000 automobiles could now be found on city streets. Southern Bell counted almost 5,000 telephone customers. A local editor reported that "the city is dotted with soft drink stands and filling stations, and wiener stands are bobbing up like mushrooms. Drinking soft goods and riding in automobiles seems to be the order of the day & a good part of the night." It was the Jazz Age, the era of the speakeasy and bathtub gin, of the flapper and all-night parties. Writing in 1921, the editor of the *Union Republican*

The original North Carolina Baptist Hospital, built in "the wilds of Ardmore" in 1923, was the modest forebear of the sprawling 21st-century medical complex of today.

Forsyth County Public Library Photograph Collection

observed that Winston-Salem's "big city ways" had a dark side: "During the past ten days we have noted six robberies, two hold-ups, the finding of the body of a dead infant, an ex-policeman killing himself, a man deserting his wife and three children, and a young man being given a sound thrashing for being too intimate with another man's wife—all in addition to the usual good-sized docket of liquor cases."

But even as many things in the city of Winston-Salem were changing, one thing remained the same—the Coffee Pot. Though felled by high winds, then knocked over by a rampaging car in 1920, the Coffee Pot was saved by a citizens' appeal from being hauled away to the city junk pile. Erected by Julius and Samuel Mickey in 1858 as an advertisement for their tin shop, the big tin pot at the corner of Main and Belews Creek Streets had become a venerable landmark and the unofficial symbol of Winston-Salem by 1920.

In the first years of the 1920s, there were nearly 100 practicing attorneys in Winston-Salem. Manly, Hendren & Womble was the leading firm in the city and one of the strongest in the state. Twin City lawyers were lobbying hard for federal court to be held in the city and for the establishment of a new judicial district covering Forsyth County. They held their colleague Will Hendren in such high regard that they chose him to lead both efforts. (A new judicial district would take many years, but Winston-Salem did secure a federal court in 1927.)

The Coffee Pot, a venerable landmark in the community since its installation in front of the J. E. Mickey Tinsmith Shop in 1858, became the unofficial symbol of Winston-Salem.

Forsyth County Public Library Photograph Collection

The law was changing, and the lawyers of Manly, Hendren & Womble were changing with it, as they had always done. Modernity and urbanization presented attorneys with a large class of cases utterly unknown to their predecessors: public utilities, municipal corporations, child labor, pensions, and income tax. A lawyer had to become a more diligent student than ever before.

Change had come to the Forsyth County Court, too, in the person of Judge Raymond G. Parker. A glimpse of the local bench and bar in the mid-1920s is provided by Winston-Salem lawyer Roy L. Deal in this memoir of Judge Parker's impact on the court:

> It was as if a thunderbolt had struck among the legal profession in Winston-Salem. According to widespread and time-honored habit, the members of the bar here had been accustomed to trying cases in a more or less haphazard manner. We expected to be able to continue a case at our whim. We were used to taking frequent flings of so-called repartee at opposing counsel. We liked to browbeat the witnesses and say things to the jury which the rules of evidence and strict ethics perhaps forbade. But what an awakening was in store for us and what an education! He immediately changed trials from what had approached endless and chaotic squabbles to swift, clear and fair investigations into the merits of the case. The lawyers ceased bickering with each other and applied themselves much more assiduously to the preparation and trial of their cases, and in observing rules of evidence, rules of court, and rules of courtesy. The results were lasting, and today the Forsyth County bar, perhaps as well as any bar in the State, observes proper methods of conducting jury trials.

The words *prosperity* and *prominence* characterized the work of Manly, Hendren & Womble in the 1920s. The firm—which observed its 50th anniversary in 1926—grew in stature and strength and took on two new associates during the decade: Linville K. Martin in 1920 and Irving E. Carlyle in 1923.

Linville Kerr Martin, a native of Winston, was born on April 30, 1896, to Frank A. Martin and Eva Hendren Martin, a sister of William M. Hendren. After attending public school in the city, he went to Trinity College, where he starred as an All Southern Conference player and captain of the basketball team before graduating in 1917. A second lieutenant in the 258th Aero Squadron of the Army Air Corps in World War I, he returned to Durham after the war and graduated from the Duke School of Law in 1920 before joining Manly, Hendren & Womble later that year.

Irving Edward Carlyle was born in Wake Forest, North Carolina, on September 20, 1896, to Dora Dunn and John Bethune Carlyle, a teacher of the Romance languages at Wake Forest College. He grew up on the college grounds, lettered in basketball and baseball there, and graduated summa cum laude in 1917. After a brief teaching stint at Rocky Mount High School, young Carlyle entered Field Artillery Officers' Training School, from which he received a commission as a second lieutenant in December 1918. Upon release from active duty at the end of the war, he coached basketball and baseball at Wake Forest and taught briefly at Liberty Piedmont Institute in Wallburg, North Carolina. Though Professor Needham Y. Gulley's six-week quiz course at Wake Forest in 1920 was his only formal study of the law, Carlyle passed the North Carolina Bar Examination in 1920. However, on the advice of a favorite professor, Edward Timberlake, Carlyle enrolled at the University of Virginia School of Law. After two years at Virginia, he decided to begin a law practice. In September 1922, he opened a law office in Winston-Salem. Five months later, he became an associate with Manly, Hendren & Womble.

The senior partners remained actively involved in the community during the 1920s.

Clement Manly, a practicing attorney for over 40 years, was one of Winston-Salem's senior statesmen. A trusted adviser to civic leaders and businessmen, Manly was elected vice president of Security Life and Trust when the Greensboro insurance company reorganized upon moving to Winston-Salem in 1924. That same year, Colonel Manly was part of a delegation of

Irving Carlyle (back row, right) with the 1917 Wake Forest College football team, which he coached

MARY IRVING CARLYLE

prominent American attorneys invited to the International Bar Association Conference in London, England.

William M. Hendren served as president of the Twin-City Club in 1920. When the Reynolds family presented the new R. J. Reynolds Auditorium to the city in 1924, it was Hendren who officiated on behalf of the family. A year later, Mr. Hendren's long career of professional service culminated in his election as president of the North Carolina Bar Association. E. S. Parker of Greensboro described the new president as being "as fair a man, as true a friend, and as good a fellow as there is. Some men are born with such an instinct for justice and right, and such a capacity for finding the justice and the right, that we call them natural lawyers. Will Hendren is the kind of lawyer that our profession needs."

B. S. Womble served a term in the North Carolina House of Representatives (1925-27) before his election to two consecutive terms in the State Senate (1927-31), where he chaired the powerful Finance Committee. In the legislature, Womble advocated reforms in voting and child labor. He also supported the teaching of evolution in the public schools and the equalization of public-school funding. Womble quickly became one of the most respected men in the State

The Twin-City Club, a business and professional men's social organization established in Winston in 1884, has long been a popular gathering place for the city's attorneys.

G. ALLEN AYCOCK AND THE TWIN-CITY CLUB

The seven-story Wachovia Bank and Trust Company Building was the tallest in the city when Winston and Salem merged in 1913.

FORSYTH COUNTY PUBLIC LIBRARY PHOTOGRAPH COLLECTION

Senate and was widely mentioned as a future candidate for governor.

With the senior partners so active in professional and civic activities, there was plenty of work for Irving Carlyle and Linville Martin. In March 1923, just after joining the firm, Carlyle was appointed local counsel for the Southern Railway Company, a longstanding client. And in the boom-town atmosphere of Winston-Salem in the 1920s, Linville Martin ran the firm's increasingly busy real-estate practice. Both of the young associates also became quite active in civic and professional organizations, as was the tradition at Manly, Hendren & Womble.

Throughout the 1920s, Manly, Hendren & Womble continued as attorneys for Forsyth County. The firm, which had served for many years as counsel to the city, was replaced by the Board of Aldermen in 1921. Parrish & Deal held the post until 1939, when Irving Carlyle was selected as city attorney.

As attorneys for the Wachovia Bank and Trust Company, the firm continued to represent the bank in any number of cases involving wills and estates, trusts, bankruptcies, municipal bonds, and the like. When at the dawn of the 1920s Wachovia came under attack from a group of 24 Winston-Salem attorneys, the firm found itself in the delicate position of mediating a dispute between its colleagues and a client. The petitioners alleged that lawyers in Wachovia's Trust Department had "encroached upon the distinctive field of the lawyer" by advertising to draft wills on behalf of their clients—a violation of the ethical standards of both the North Carolina Bar Association and the American Bar Association.

In a masterly address at the 1921 meeting of the North Carolina Bar Association, Clement Manly put the controversy to rest. The colonel insisted that neither A. H. Eller nor Gilbert Stevenson, the bank's inhouse counsel, had intentionally violated ethical standards or done anything that was unprofessional. He maintained that while it had always been the clear and consistent policy of the Wachovia Bank and Trust Company to recommend to patrons that they have their

Cyrus Barksdale Watson
1844 – 1916

William Bynum Glenn
1847 – 1892

Robert B. Glenn
1854 – 1920

Clement Manly
1853 – 1928

William Mayhew Hendren
1871 – 1939

Linville K. Martin
1896 – 1954

B. S. Womble
1882 – 1976

Some of the firm's early partners
WOMBLE CARLYLE COLLECTION

Irving E. Carlyle
1896 – 1971

own attorneys draw up their wills, the Board of Directors had nonetheless unanimously adopted an unequivocal policy statement on the matter. "The Wachovia Bank is in hearty sympathy with the Bar of the State in its efforts to prevent improper encroachments upon the distinctive field of the lawyer," said Manly in his closing remarks to the association. "The lawyers connected with the Trust Company are as eager as any of their brethren in the general practice to maintain and support in spirit, as well as conduct, the ancient and honorable ideals of our profession."

In an important case from 1921, the firm opposed Wachovia Bank and Trust, advocating for another longtime client. Mr. Hendren represented the heirs of J. Cicero Tise, a prominent Winston-Salem businessman, in a suit filed by Wachovia, the executor of Tise's estate. Cicero Tise's heirs had challenged the validity of the trust's provisions regarding the development of his summer-resort property in Stokes County, Vade Mecum Springs, as "not only a watering resort, but an institution after the order of a chautauqua." The defendants argued that the purpose of the bequest was invalid, and that the funds in the estate were inadequate. In *Wachovia Bank and Trust Company v. Ogburn* (1921), the North Carolina Supreme Court upheld the validity of Tise's will.

The 400-acre Vade Mecum Springs resort, developed by Cicero Tise in 1890, became one of the first properties administered by the new Winston-Salem Foundation. In 1933, the foundation granted a long-term lease of the property to the Episcopal Diocese of North Carolina for use as a camp and conference center.

The firm was also involved in perhaps the most unusual case in Forsyth Superior Court in the 1920s, one that took 18 years to settle. The case of *Carolina Portland Cement Company v. Washington Mills*, started in May 1903, involved a judgment sought by the plaintiff for the furnishing of cement to Washington Mills for the construction of a stone dam across the New River at Fries, Virginia. The case was decided on behalf of the plaintiff in November 1921, after having been continued 107 times. While Forsyth attorney Lindsay Patterson represented the plaintiff from start to finish, the case for the defendant was first handled by Glenn, Manly & Hendren, next by Manly & Hendren, and finally by Manly, Hendren & Womble.

On October 20, 1927, in the courtroom of the Forsyth County Courthouse, friends and business associates of Clement Manly gathered for the presentation of a portrait of the colonel to the Forsyth County Bar Association, in appreciation for his lifelong service to Winston-Salem and the legal profession. In presenting the portrait, his close friend H. G. Chatham, president of the Chatham Manufacturing Company, said, "In honoring him we have much more honored ourselves. While gloriously one of us, he possesses in such high degree the virtues we desire that he is the ideal of us all. In strength of character and superb ability Clement Manly has few peers, and no superior in North Carolina."

W. W. Fuller, former general counsel of the American Tobacco Company and a lifelong friend of the colonel, said, "No picture of this man's features can be more than a counterfeit of his splendid intellect and sweet character and the nobleness of his soul. They must dwell in the memories of us who know him, and in the faith of those who hear us tell of him."

Clement Manly practiced law until just four days before his death, when illness finally overtook him. As he himself had noted on many occasions, "When the Pale Horse comes to take us away, we are like the Moravians—we are all equal in death."

On November 26, 1928, a little more than a year after the presentation of his portrait to the community, death claimed Clement Manly at the age of 75. Funeral services were held in his native town of New Bern, where W. M. Hendren and B. S. Womble traveled to serve as pallbearers. The next morning, the *Winston-Salem Journal* eulogized him as "the city's great-

Colonel Clement Manly at the time of his election as president of the North Carolina Bar Association in 1905
THE NORTH CAROLINA BAR ASSOCIATION

est lawyer, one of the leaders of his profession in the South, and Winston-Salem's first citizen in many respects."

Upon learning of Colonel Manly's death, Senator Furnifold M. Simmons, his friend of 50 years, memorialized him with these words: "In personality, gracious manners, innate sympathy with his fellows high and low, rich and poor alike, ingratiated him with all classes, and during his life and at the time of his death he was easily one of the most popular and beloved men in North Carolina. Young men loved him, old men trusted him, all respected and esteemed him. His character, his career, his life as a citizen, a lawyer and public man was an inspiration to the young and to the old alike, and his memory will live in the hearts of those who come after him."

These words that Clement Manly wrote for the inscription on the monument to R. J. Reynolds could as easily and as justifiably have been applied to him: "Original in thought; natural in act; justice to all men his guide; energy in boundless measure made up this workman of the world."

Fresh produce and the latest news could be found at the City Market, seen here in the late 1930s.

FORSYTH COUNTY PUBLIC LIBRARY PHOTOGRAPH COLLECTION

Manly, Hendren & Womble

Attorneys-at-Law

THE HABIT OF SUCCESS *1930 – 1939*

"The great development of Winston-Salem has been accomplished largely by local enterprise and local capital. Local initiative has produced the largest cigarette factory in the world. The largest financial institution in the state has been built by men of local birth. Local desire for educational facilities has produced a public school system second to none. But with all this growth there is yet room for greater expansion. Winston-Salem welcomes good citizens, and in welcoming them proposes to make them part of a prosperous and progressive metropolis."

The Industrial Commission of Winston-Salem (1930)

Winston-Salem boasted of its industrial strength at the start of the century's fourth decade. World War I and the 1920s had been bountiful times for Winston-Salem businesses. By 1930, the town produced more cigarettes than any other city in the world, more men's heavy knit underwear than any other place in the country, and more woolen goods and wagons than any other city in the South.

The R. J. Reynolds Tobacco Company—ensconced in its new 22-story office tower, the tallest building in North Carolina—enjoyed another profitable year, its earnings growth some $2 million greater than the previous year. Wachovia Bank and Trust was the largest trust company in the Southeast and the third-largest bank in the South, with branch offices in Asheville, High Point, Raleigh, and Salisbury. And the Chatham Manufacturing Company produced more blankets in 1930 than in any previous year. The time of plenty had, in the words of business historian James Howell Smith, equipped the city with a legacy of "good products and the habit of success." It also made W. M. Hendren and B. S. Womble men of means in the community—if not men of wealth on the scale of the Reynolds and Hanes families.

There were, however, dark clouds on the horizon. The stock-market crash of October 1929 had caused jitters among the city's business elite. Even the high-flying stock of the R. J. Reynolds Tobacco Company—which had been largely immune to the downward momentum of the market—took a dip for a time. But even deep into 1930, the mood among town boosters remained resolutely optimistic. "All this talk about 'hard times' is bunk," wrote the editor of the Winston-Salem *Union Republican*. "On every hand one can see old buildings being razed and new ones erected in their stead. The furniture plants are running on full time and we are told that the big Reynolds plant is running to capacity. There are more automobiles seen on the streets than ever before and people ride all day long and far into the night. We have heard of no one going hungry and certainly the people have enough clothing to wear, even if some of the flappers are rather thinly clad. But it is of their own choosing. No, there are no hard times in this city and will not be if people will go to work and stop talking calamity."

Few banks went under in Winston-Salem during the Depression, but the city almost did. It had to be bailed out by its rich friends. After the stock market crashed in 1929, city revenues dropped precipitously. Strapped property owners knew that the city would take five years to foreclose on their property if they didn't pay their taxes, but that the banks would foreclose on a mortgage almost immediately. So they paid their mortgages and let their taxes ride. The problem for the city was that it had heavy interest payments due on the bonds it had issued for its ambitious street-building program.

Although the aldermen soon began cutting pay and firing some city workers, Winston-Salem had to borrow $500,000 from the R. J. Reynolds Tobacco Company as early as May 1930 to meet city expenses for the rest of the year. By 1933, the city had reduced its budget by more than $1 million and cut its tax rate by five cents. But even these measures were not enough, for in that year, $1.5 million in street bonds came due, and the city had no money to pay them. No bank would lend the city the money, so Mayor George W. Coan, Jr., went hat in hand to the city's most prominent citizens, 15 of whom financed the debt.

Other organizations had problems as well. By the summer of 1930, the Woman's Club of Winston-Salem, a longtime client of Colonel Manly and the firm, was in dire straits. The club was heavily in debt on its building and property on 350 North Marshall Street. Irving Carlyle stepped in to advise the club and help save its good name. With the help of a number of endorsements from prominent local citizens, a loan was secured from the Jefferson Standard Life Insurance Company, and the property was saved.

By 1931, the city's economy proved to be something of a mixed bag. Sales at Reynolds were so robust that the company restored a night shift in one of its plants, adding 200 jobs. Wachovia and the Farmers' National Bank withstood runs by panicked customers late in the year. But the People's National Bank closed its doors in July, joining the Merchants' Bank and Trust Company, which had failed months earlier. Public-works efforts and philanthropic gestures by wealthy citizens helped alleviate the problems of the unemployed, but city leaders were still alarmed by the "sheiks and drugstore cowboys" begging downtown and by the vagrants and rogues who stole gasoline from parked cars. "There has been widespread unemployment," the Reverend Kenneth Pfohl wrote, "and the wheels of industry have moved but a small portion of the time—though there has been improvement in the last months of the year."

Still, Winston-Salem fared better than most communities, cushioned from the worst calamities of the Depression by its tobacco and textile might, its sense of stewardship and philanthropy, and the influx of government funds for public-works programs. Twelve companies—including Hanes Dye and Finishing, Brown and Williamson, and Taylor Brothers—either added new buildings or additions to their plants. Publisher Owen Moon established the city's first radio station, WSJS, in 1930. Eastern Airlines began commercial air service out of the city's Miller Airport in 1935. In 1939, the family of Bowman Gray donated money to the city that helped it secure a Works Progress Administration grant for constructing Bowman Gray Stadium, a project that employed hundreds of local men.

Even so, the city's economy had its share of ups and downs. While many key industries kept their machines running, few factories ran full-time, and jobs remained relatively scarce. Reynolds Tobacco—which employed over half the city's black residents in 1930—was forced to cut its workweek on several occasions, but the company still increased production during the decade without laying off a single regular employee. P. H. Hanes Knitting Company was forced to close its brand-new rayon underwear factory but managed to maintain quality and market share during the Depression. And while New York's International Business Machines Company had enough local business by 1937 to open an office in Winston-Salem, the city's relief rolls that year still contained the names of 10,000 men. The new toy craze in town, the yo-yo, seemed the perfect metaphor for business conditions in the city during the Depression.

With dependable, well-run companies like Wachovia Bank, R. J. Reynolds Tobacco Company, Chatham Manufacturing Company, P. H. Hanes Knitting Company, and Security Life and Trust as clients, Manly, Hendren & Womble weathered the Depression far better than most North Carolina law firms. Colonel Manly's presence was greatly missed, but the firm did not fall apart after his passing, as B. S. Womble had overheard a prominent local lawyer predict a few

The construction of Bowman Gray Stadium in the late 1930s was a boon to men left jobless by the Great Depression.

FORSYTH COUNTY PUBLIC LIBRARY PHOTOGRAPH COLLECTION

years earlier, during Colonel Manly's lifetime. A steady stream of Wachovia cases involving wills, estates, and trusts flowed through the firm's offices on the seventh floor of the Wachovia Building, and both Wachovia and the firm garnered substantial fees for handling the receivership of the Merchants' Bank. Legal work for Reynolds, conversely, often involved personal-injury suits filed by workers and product-liability claims.

The firm also continued to handle a number of railway negligence cases for both the Southern Railway Company and the Southern Public Utilities Company. The utility, which operated the city's electric streetcar system, was purchased in 1936 by another client of the firm, the Duke Power Company, which replaced streetcars with buses.

Manly, Hendren & Womble saw an increase in insurance defense work for a variety of life, fire, and casualty companies, serving local firms such as the Jefferson Standard Life Insurance Company and the Pilot Life Insurance Company and acting as local counsel for national firms such as the Prudential Insurance Company, the Metropolitan Life Insurance Company, the Union Indemnity Company, the Equitable Life Assurance Society (the insurer for Reynolds), and others. The firm remained as local counsel for the Western Union Telegraph Company. By mid-decade, Manly, Hendren & Womble had been selected as local counsel for such national firms as the Standard Oil Company of New Jersey, the American Express Company, Montgomery Ward and Company, and the Duke Power Company.

The most sensational case for the firm in the 1930s involved the mysterious death of Zachary Smith Reynolds in 1932. "Smith" Reynolds, the youngest child of Katharine and R. J. Reynolds, was seven when his father died and barely a teenager when his mother passed away. He and his siblings were brought up by their uncle Will Reynolds and their aunt Kate, a childless couple who suddenly found themselves with an impetuous boy on their hands.

An indifferent student, Smith quit school as a teenager to take up flying, something he became quite good at. He was even more adept at partying. At 18, fickle and immature, he married Anne Cannon, daughter of textile baron Charles Cannon. They divorced within a year, citing irreconcilable differences. "She liked big parties and I like little parties," said Smith Reynolds.

Six days after his divorce in November 1931, he married Libby Holman, a 25-year-old torch singer who had catapulted to fame with the hit song "Moanin' Low" in 1929. Taken with Holman's sensuous good looks after seeing her perform, he immediately asked her to marry him, reportedly telling her that he would kill himself if she refused.

The many parties thrown by the newlyweds at Reynolda became their trademark. The one on July 5, 1932, was typical. Friends from New York and Winston-Salem drank, swam in the pool, and drank some more. By midnight, all the guests had left except Libby's friend Blanche Yurka, an actress, and Albert "Ab" Walker, one of Smith's closest friends.

Ab Walker recounted that he was downstairs at Reynolda about one o'clock the next morning when he heard a muffled shot from the second floor. A drunken Libby soon staggered to the balcony and screamed, "Smith's killed himself!" Walker said he hurried upstairs to find Smith sprawled on a bed with a bullet wound to his right temple. He and Libby rushed Smith to Baptist Hospital, where he died about four hours later.

Smith Reynolds's death was initially ruled a suicide, but a coroner's inquest a few days later decided that Smith had died "at the hands of a party or parties unknown." In August 1932, a grand jury indicted Libby Holman Reynolds for murder and charged Albert Walker as an accomplice.

The shooting, still the most sensational in Winston-Salem's history, attracted reporters from around the country. It had all the elements of a lurid story: a multimillionaire heir, a beautiful singer, mysterious circumstances, and conflicting evidence.

The Reynolds family retained the firm to look into the circumstances surrounding the death of Zachary Smith Reynolds. After several months of investigation, W. M. Hendren and B. S. Womble reported that they had been unable to "discover evidence which in our opinion would justify us in advising the family to join in the prosecution of the indictment."

William N. Reynolds issued a statement to state prosecutors: "If you come to the conclusion that it is right and fair and in the public interest that the cases be dropped, then that action on your part will certainly have no criticism from me or from the other members of Smith's family." The district attorney complied, citing lack of evidence, and no trials were ever held.

Something good did arise from the tragic death of Smith Reynolds. After lengthy litigation over Smith's estate, his siblings used their share, about $7.5 million, to establish the Z. Smith Reynolds Foundation, which has supported many worthwhile causes throughout the South since its founding.

As the 1930s began, William M. Hendren entered his fourth decade as an attorney, all with the firm. He was then serving as a vice president of the Security Life and Trust Company, succeeding Colonel Manly in the position. In 1932, he was elected to the American Bar Association General Council. The previous year, the people of Forsyth County had chosen Hendren to represent them in the North Carolina Senate, following B. S. Womble's two terms in Raleigh. During his first session as a legislator, the *News and Observer* of Raleigh called Hendren "one of the ablest lawyers in the state" but deemed his resolution calling for senators to conduct legislative business on Saturdays "impractical." Hendren's hometown newspaper, the *Union Republican*, weighed in with the opinion that "Senator Hendren will have a hard time reforming these hard-boiled Democratic members who care nothing for the rights of the people, or [for] how much of the taxpayers' money they waste."

The most active phase of B. S. Womble's professional career began in the early 1930s, just as his career in elective politics was drawing to a close. Though prominently mentioned in Democratic circles as a candidate for the state's highest office—the local papers at the time even took to calling him "Governor"—Womble chose another path. "My family was more important," he later told a reporter. In 1932, he was elected president of the Forsyth County Bar Association. In that office, he became a statewide leader in the emerging effort to provide better counsel for indigent defendants. Also that year, he was a founding member of the North Carolina Bar Association Committee on Legal Aid. When the Winston-Salem City School Board needed a chairman in 1933, Womble was drafted for the job; he served with distinction for nine years. He was an active leader in the 1935 campaign for a 20-cent school-tax referendum, which city voters approved. In 1939, he chaired the annual Community Chest campaign for charitable and social-service organizations.

In 1936, B. S. Womble celebrated his 25th year with the firm. As if in commemoration, he received the honor of being unanimously elected as the 41st president of the North Carolina Bar Association. In his nominating address, L. P. McLendon of Greensboro said of Mr. Womble, "For more than twenty-five years this gentleman, this outstanding and successful lawyer, has successfully practiced law in North Carolina, always in thorough keeping with the highest ideals of our profession."

As president of the North Carolina Bar Association, Womble, mindful of the strained relations between attorneys and trust companies such as Wachovia, appointed a Special Committee on Cooperation Between

W. M. HENDREN
B. S. WOMBLE

Associates
L. K. MARTIN
I. E. CARLYLE
W. P. SANDRIDGE

Manly, Hendren & Womble

Attorneys-at-Law

723-734 Wachovia Bank & Trust Company Bldg. Phones 5135-5136

WINSTON-SALEM CITY DIRECTORY (1935)

In the 1930s, lawyers limited their advertising to discreet notices in business and legal publications, such as this listing in a Winston-Salem city directory.

NORTH CAROLINA COLLECTION, UNIVERSITY OF NORTH CAROLINA AT CHAPEL HILL LIBRARY

Lawyers and Corporation Trust Companies, which drafted a resolution authorizing a joint standing committee in conjunction with the North Carolina Bankers Association. Womble also presided at the association's annual summer meeting, which in 1937 was held on board a Bermuda-bound cruise ship, the S.S. *Reliance*.

Mr. Womble and his wife, Edith, had sailed on an earlier cruise, a vacation/study trip to England and France with 11 other American lawyers in the summer of 1931. Upon his return, Womble reported to the local press that both countries had points in their jurisprudence that were well worth studying. He observed that England's stiff penalties for the carrying of concealed weapons had a marked impact on that country's rate of violent crimes, and that France's use of jury trials only in cases of serious felonies resulted in smaller dockets and swifter justice.

William Pendleton Sandridge came with the firm as an associate in May 1930. A native of Roanoke, Virginia, he graduated in 1928 from the University of Virginia School of Law, where he served as editor of the law review. After two years in the legal department of the Chesapeake and Ohio Railroad and successful admission to the North Carolina Bar, he relocated to Winston-Salem, the home of his maternal grandparents.

The junior members assumed increasingly larger responsibilities in the firm, in the profession, and in the community during the 1930s.

Although Linville Martin's real-estate work declined somewhat in the early part of the decade, his practice picked up by 1937, as the city's industries were once again acquiring land, building new plants, and adding to existing factories. Martin, like all the firm's attorneys, was also involved in some trial work. Throughout the decade, "Hip" Martin served as secre-

> *"The best way for a lawyer to advertise himself is to do an outstanding job for a client and get unusually good results, and the client will not only return for more but will tell others about it."*
>
> B. S. Womble

tary-treasurer of the combined Twin-City Club and Forsyth Country Club. In 1939, he was elected president of the Forsyth County Bar Association.

By the 1930s, the local press was describing Irving E. Carlyle as "Winston-Salem's brilliant young attorney," a characterization that reflected his rapid rise in the city's civic and professional ranks. From serving as president of the Junior Bar Association in 1931, young Carlyle went on to the presidency of the Forsyth County Bar Association in 1935. By 1938, he had begun a three-year term on the State Board of Law Examiners. He was elected president of the Winston-Salem YMCA in 1932, chairman of the local branch of the Red Cross in 1933, and a member of the Forsyth County Welfare Board in 1937. His political career also began in these years with a stint as county campaign manager for gubernatorial candidate Cameron Morrison in 1932.

William Pendleton Sandridge also honored the firm's tradition of client service, professionalism, and public service during the decade. Sandridge developed an active trial practice in the state and federal courts, appearing on behalf of such clients as the Southern Railway Company, the Wachovia Bank and Trust Company, and the Metropolitan Life Insurance Company. Elected as the first vice president of the Junior Bar Association in 1933, he was subsequently selected as vice president of the 11th District Bar Association in 1938. He served on the association's Executive Committee in 1939 and 1940.

Winston-Salem newspapers carried this news story in February 1936: "Gordon Gray, who has been practicing law in New York City for the past two years, has returned to Winston-Salem, where he will be associated in the practice of law with the firm of Manly, Hendren and Womble." Gray's father, Bowman Gray, Sr., president of R. J. Reynolds, had died several months earlier, and young Gray returned home to help with his father's estate. Though he practiced with Manly, Hendren & Womble for only two years, Gordon Gray remained a close friend of the firm. He bought the *Winston-Salem Journal*, the *Twin-City Sentinel*, and WSJS radio in 1937. The firm began representation of Piedmont Publishing Company, a relationship that has continued over the years.

One story in particular about Gordon Gray has been passed down in the lore of the firm. It is said that Gray always wore white gloves when he was in

A 1938 photo of the Forsyth Country Club, a favored destination for golf outings and other social gatherings
FORSYTH COUNTY PUBLIC LIBRARY PHOTOGRAPH COLLECTION

Gordon Gray, a 1933 graduate of the Yale University School of Law, joined the firm for a brief period in 1936.
Forsyth County Public Library Photograph Collection

the office because he didn't want to get dirt and dust on his hands. There was no air conditioning in the Wachovia Building at the time, so grime came unbidden through the building's open windows. "Dirt was just rampant," recalled Archie K. Davis, a young bank officer for Wachovia at the time. "In the summertime we'd have to open those huge windows behind us, and the smoke from Reynolds Tobacco would just pour in there. You'd go down there with a lovely linen suit that morning and you'd be as dirty as you could be by that afternoon."

With Gordon Gray's departure in 1939, Linville K. Martin, Irving E. Carlyle, and William Pendleton Sandridge became members of the firm, though the name of Manly, Hendren & Womble was retained.

Mr. Hendren was involved in four high-profile federal cases that decade, three of which were decided by the United States Court of Appeals for the Fourth Circuit and the other by the United States Supreme Court.

The Supreme Court case, *United States v. Chambers et al* (1934), dealt with the constitutional question of what effect the repeal of the 18th Amendment had upon pending prosecutions for violation of the National Prohibition Act. Claude Chambers and Byrum Gibson, the firm's clients, had been indicted for possessing and transporting intoxicating liquors in Rockingham County while the Prohibition amendment had been in force, but the 21st Amendment—which repealed Prohibition—had been ratified before final judgment in the case. The Supreme Court sustained the District Court's dismissal of the indictment. Writing for the court, Chief Justice Charles Evans Hughes ruled that

In 1938, the firm was engaged in a case involving land in western North Carolina originally granted to William Holland Thomas (1805–1893), the famous "White Chief of the Cherokee" and the man most responsible for the creation of the Eastern Band of the Cherokee Nation.
The North Carolina Division of Archives and History

the provisions of the National Prohibition Act "rested upon the grant of authority to the Congress. . . .The people are free to withdraw the authority they have conferred and, when withdrawn, neither the Congress nor the courts can assume the right to continue to exercise it."

The three cases in the Fourth Circuit were all decided within the span of four months in the summer and fall of 1938. W. M. Hendren, nearing his 67th birthday, handled two of the cases himself, but turned to B. S. Womble and Irving Carlyle for assistance on the last.

In one of the cases, *Carolina Aluminum Company v. Federal Power Commission*, Mr. Hendren sought a review of the power commission's finding denying the aluminum company permission to construct a hydroelectric dam on the Yadkin River at Tuckertown, North Carolina, on the grounds that the river was a navigable body of water. Although the petitioners alleged error in the finding, contending that "anyone who has lived along the Yadkin knows that not even small boats can pass over some of the shoals found in the river," Judge John J. Parker denied the petition, noting that the court had authority to review only orders of the Federal Power Commission, not mere findings.

Another case also decided in June 1938 was *United States v. 7,405.3 Acres of Land in Macon, Clay, and Swain Counties, N.C., et al.* The controversy was over the right to a fund paid in a land condemnation proceeding, the question being as to the ownership of 55.9 acres of land in Macon County, claimed on the one hand by the United States as trustee for the Eastern Band of the Cherokee Nation, and on the other by the Nantahala Power and Light Company. The claim of the federal government as trustee was based upon an 1875 grant from the state of North Carolina to William Holland Thomas, the famous "White Chief of the Cherokee." Judge Parker reversed the ruling of the District Court, ruling that title to the land was vested in the United States: "It is beyond the power of the state, either through statutes of limitation or adverse possession, to affect the interest of the United States, and the United States manifestly has an interest in preserving the property of these wards of the government for their use and benefit."

For many years, William M. Hendren had been engaged in a very active practice in the state and federal courts. His partner B. S. Womble observed that, although Mr. Hendren suffered greatly from ill health during the last years of his life, he remained in the practice by force of will until his failing physical strength would permit him to go no farther. Those last federal cases in which Hendren appeared, Womble recalled, were of great importance, requiring long and careful preparation and consuming weeks in trial. From the courtroom, Hendren went to a hospital bed, from which he was unable to recover sufficiently to return to his practice. William Mayhew Hendren died in Winston-Salem on July 19, 1939.

During a visit with William F. Womble in Winston-Salem in 1995, Nell Long, wife of W. M. Hendren's grandson Bill Long, presented the firm with a copy of Mr. Hendren's "Philosophy of Life," the original of which had been discovered by the family among Mr. Hendren's papers some years earlier. Mr. Hendren's credo—a copy of which hangs in each office of Womble Carlyle—begins with these words: "To measure life by the standard of love; to prize wealth as a potential service; reputation as a latent influence; learning for the light it can shed; power for the help it can give; station for the good it can do."

Firm attorneys and staff were actively involved in the war effort, whether in the armed forces or on the home front.

THE BOWMAN GRAY COLLECTION OF WORLD WAR I AND WORLD WAR II POSTERS,
RARE BOOK COLLECTION, UNIVERSITY OF NORTH CAROLINA AT CHAPEL HILL LIBRARY

SERVICE IN A TIME OF WAR *1940 – 1945*

"The heavy fog prevailing on the first day of 1941 is symbolic of the uncertainty which shrouds the future. This is a most crucial year, with the tempo of war increasing every hour and with the threat of a new world order drawing ever nearer—a world order which in its initial states will be anything but friendly to me and my children and to my country. However, I shall face it without fear and shall try to withstand it with all the courage and good will at my command.

"As I face the new year and its increasing responsibilities, I shall strive to apply to all decisions the best independent judgment of which I am capable. It is my resolve to do my own thinking and to do that which I think is best for the greatest number. My home, my family, my friends, my mental and spiritual development, and my growth as a lawyer shall receive a larger share of my effort and thought in the New Year than in 1940 and previous years."

Irving E. Carlyle

By the summer of 1940, nearly all of North Carolina knew that war with Nazi Germany was on the horizon. Like most of the state's citizens, the attorneys in the firm were solidly behind America's opposition to Nazi Germany in the European conflict and would soon take their places in the war effort. "Now, more than ever must the lawyer lead, or the civilization of this Nation and that of England will perish from the face of the earth," said Wilmington lawyer Emmett Bellamy at the annual meeting of the North Carolina Bar Association. "Never before have the activities of the lawyer become so important as now. It is a time for sacrifice."

The entire city of Winston-Salem seemed to be

caught up in preparations for war or war relief by the middle of 1940. Both of the local National Guard companies were called to active duty. Every man in the county between the ages of 21 and 35 had to register for the draft by mid-October. Resident aliens were required to register with the federal government and be fingerprinted. The local branch of the Red Cross increased its membership, raised money for the national fund drive, and began to mobilize for wartime service on the home front. And already by that fall, a posh "Ball for British Relief"—chaired by Linville Martin—had raised enough funds to purchase a new ambulance for the care of civilians wounded in the Nazi bombing raids on England. By year's end, Twin City residents, businesses, and industry were all enlisted in "the arsenal of democracy."

During World War II, Winston-Salem industry prospered as a supplier to the military forces, much as it had done (albeit on a smaller scale) during World War I. Several local furniture plants shifted their production lines to the making of airplane parts. The Briggs Shaffner Company began to forge machine parts for tanks. Across town, the Hanes Dye and Finishing Company made material for gas masks. The P. H. Hanes Knitting Company became so successful in filling huge army contracts for woolen undershirts and heavy underwear that it won three Army-Navy "E" Awards for excellence in defense production. R. J. Reynolds produced billions of cigarettes for Allied servicemen. The company's Foil Division made millions of the aluminum strips dropped by Allied planes to jam enemy radar.

In a number of cases, the departure of old companies made room for new companies, many of them directly related to the war effort. After the Chatham Manufacturing Company left Winston-Salem in 1939 for a new plant in Elkin, the United States government took up the lease on the company's old plant and moved in the National Carbon Company, a manufacturer of submarine batteries. In 1942, the old Planters Tobacco Warehouse became the home of a division of the Allied Aviation Corporation of Baltimore, makers of a new type of amphibious glider constructed of molded plywood. The gliders would later be used in the Allies' invasion of Normandy in 1944.

When Malcolm McLean moved his McLean

Winston-Salem residents tested gas masks in March 1942, in case of poison-gas attacks by enemy infiltrators.

Forsyth County Public Library Photograph Collection

Camel cigarettes were distributed to United States soldiers fighting in the Pacific in 1942.

Forsyth County Public Library Photograph Collection

Winston-Salem, with a population in 1940 of 80,000, was on the way to becoming the leading industrial center of the South.

Lynn Roundtree

Trucking Company from Fayetteville to Winston-Salem in 1943, the city was well on its way to becoming a regional transportation center. A year earlier, the United States Army Air Force's Office of Flying Safety—a 600-man office that investigated all military aircraft accidents—had relocated to Winston-Salem from Washington. Piedmont Aviation Services, the first homegrown airline in the state, was founded in 1940 by Thomas H. Davis, son of a former R. J. Reynolds sales manager, Egbert Davis. Based at the new Smith Reynolds Airport, the fledgling airline company offered airplane sales, maintenance, flying instruction, and charter service. Both McLean Trucking and Piedmont Aviation would soon become significant clients of the firm.

There was work for anyone who wanted it in Winston-Salem during World War II, and plenty of overtime, too, as local plants struggled to keep up with demand. Companies like R. J. Reynolds and P. H. Hanes ran shifts around the clock. Even with women working the night shift in many local plants, labor shortages persisted. Unable to meet demand, Reynolds obtained permission from the Roosevelt administration in 1945 to use German prisoners of war in their factories. Some 250 men from Field Marshal Erwin Rommel's Afrika Korps helped Reynolds make cigarettes for almost a year before being sent back to Germany in 1946.

Those citizens who stayed home in Winston-Salem did their part for the war effort in many ways. City aldermen made vacant lots available for the planting of Victory gardens. Citizens sold war bonds, raised money for war relief, volunteered as air-raid wardens, and provided much-needed social services. And they endured the rationing of "luxury items" such as gasoline, tires, sugar, butter, and cigarettes. Other items not on the rationing list also became scarce, as factories retooled to meet the gargantuan demands of the Allied war effort.

From the outset, the attorneys of Manly, Hendren & Womble were fully engaged in the war effort. B. S. Womble, the firm's senior member, encouraged the same sense of duty, patriotism, and devotion to the community that he always had. His son Bill, whose arrival at the firm had virtually coincided with the start of the war in Europe, was drafted into the United States Army Air Corps in July 1941 and saw action in northern Africa, Corsica, and Italy. His son Calder, who would join the firm in 1949, was a navy pilot in the North Pacific during the war.

In the spring of 1942, Hip Martin was trying to decide whether to run for Congress or go in the army. He chose the latter when, after several months of prod-

Scrap-metal drives such as this one in Winston-Salem in 1941 were a way for everyone to support the Allied war effort.
FORSYTH COUNTY PUBLIC LIBRARY PHOTOGRAPH COLLECTION

The Nissen Building—which housed the entire United States Army Air Force's Office of Flying Safety during World War II—was known around town as "Fort Nissen."

North Carolina Collection,
University of North Carolina at Chapel Hill Library

ding, the Army Air Corps finally accepted him. Martin, who saw action in France, had to lose 40-some pounds to get under the Army Air Corps limit of 200 pounds.

Irving Carlyle, the firm's other World War I veteran, spent the war years helping lead Manly, Hendren & Womble, his community, and the legal profession. In 1942, he was elected by the people of Forsyth County to the State Senate. That same year, he became the first member of the firm to serve as president of the Winston-Salem Chamber of Commerce. Reappointed to the State Board of Law Examiners in 1943, he was selected as president of the North Carolina Bar Association in 1944, just two years after Linville Martin's election.

William P. "Pen" Sandridge, one of the city's leading young attorneys, developed an increasingly busy trial practice during the war years. In 1940, he was elected president of the Winston-Salem Junior Bar Association. He also served on the Budget Committee of the Community Chest campaign, which B. S. Womble chaired that year. In 1944, when Winston-Salem sought one of the new air routes between the Great Lakes and Florida to be awarded by the Civil Aeronautics Board, it was Pen Sandridge who traveled to Washington to represent the city's interests.

During the war years, Irving Carlyle was not just a busy civic leader and politician, but also a masterful trial lawyer with a specialty in municipal law. In July 1939, Manly, Hendren & Womble resumed representing the city of Winston-Salem, a post the firm had held for 14 years beginning in 1908. Throughout World War II and for a number of years afterward, Irving Carlyle did the city's legal work. He regularly attended meetings of the Board of Aldermen; drafted city ordinances, resolutions, and legislative proposals; and represented Winston-Salem in the prosecution and defense of cases brought by or against the city. In this work, he was assisted by William F. Womble until Womble's entry into military service in July 1941 and after his return from service.

Carlyle and W. F. Womble represented the city in a 1940 case, *City of Winston-Salem v. Forsyth County*, an action to recover ad valorem taxes paid under protest and—according to the city—wrongfully and illegally collected. In its decision, the North Carolina Supreme Court affirmed the lower court's decision denying recovery or refund of the taxes. Citing as authority two of the State Supreme Court's own recent rulings in similar cases, and quoting the late judge Willis Brogden, Justice C. J. Stacy's opinion noted that "the divergent views of the law upon the subject were fully set forth in these cases, and it is not deemed necessary to 'beat the same old bush with the same old stick to run out the same old rabbit for another chase.' "

With Bill Womble and Hip Martin in the service

and Irving Carlyle tied up with city business and civic duties, most of the trial work during the war was handled by B. S. Womble and, increasingly, Pen Sandridge. Throughout the war, B. S. Womble was heavily involved on behalf of Reynolds in the federal government's antitrust case against the "Big Three" tobacco companies—American Tobacco, Liggett and Myers, and Reynolds. So involved was the case and so complex the issues that the firm maintained an office in New York City to be close to the other firms' attorneys. In 1944, a jury in Kentucky found the companies guilty of conspiracy in restraint of trade and of monopolizing the tobacco industry, in violation of the Sherman Antitrust Act. A federal Appeals Court upheld the lower court's ruling later that year.

Trust and estate work for Wachovia Bank, personal-injury work on behalf of Duke Power and the Southern Railway, and insurance defense work for companies such as Pilot Life remained mainstays for the firm during the first half of the 1940s, in addition to Irving Carlyle's work on behalf of the city of Winston-Salem. The firm also continued to represent other local government entities, such as the town of Kernersville and Yadkin County.

One case of interest in 1941 was *Washington v. Safe Bus Company*. The defendant, a Winston-Salem business founded in 1926, was one of the largest black-owned transportation companies in the nation. Its motor buses, called "jitneys," provided transportation in the city's black neighborhoods for many years. W. P. Sandridge and the firm represented the bus company in an appeal of the lower court's granting of a petition to examine the company's books and records "for money alleged to be due under the Wage and Hours Law." The high court ruled that the plaintiff, Leonard E. Washington, had not shown sufficient cause to entitle him to such an examination and that, in any case, the Federal Fair Labor Standards Act of 1938 did not apply to local bus carriers.

In 1942, the name of the firm was changed to Womble, Carlyle, Martin & Sandridge, five years after Hip Martin, Irving Carlyle, and Pen Sandridge had

In 1926, Winston-Salem jitney drivers organized the Safe Bus Company, which became the largest black-owned bus company in the United States.

FORSYTH COUNTY PUBLIC LIBRARY PHOTOGRAPH COLLECTION

Black-owned buses, called "jitneys"—slang for "nickel," the price of a fare—were the primary means of transportation in Winston-Salem's black neighborhoods. Irving Carlyle helped jitney drivers obtain their city licenses.

FORSYTH COUNTY PUBLIC LIBRARY PHOTOGRAPH COLLECTION

become members. The former name—Manly, Hendren & Womble—had lasted 31 years; the new name would remain in service for a little over a decade.

In much the same way that business in Winston-Salem was becoming increasingly influenced by large companies based outside the region, so, too, was the practice of law becoming more restricted and losing its vaunted independence. In a speech to the Winston-Salem Bar, noted North Carolina lawyer Kenneth C. Royall—later secretary of the army in the Truman administration—spoke of some of the changes:

> The lawyer's spirit of independence and initiative is being replaced by a spirit of submission to routine tasks. Today important title work comes principally from a title company or an insurance company or a loan company. The preparation of wills and estates was once largely the function of the family lawyer. But now it is the trust company that handles these matters—as well as receiverships and trusteeships. Practically every important tort suit is against either a railroad or an insurance company, whose "home office" bombards the local counsel with directions both as how to compromise and how to conduct the case. All of these companies—title, banking, trust, and insurance—advertise for and solicit business without any legal or ethical restrictions, thus offering competition which the independent lawyer finds it almost impossible to meet.

The members of the firm, ever sensitive to changes in the practice of law, noted that tax law was developing into an important specialty. Discussions about bringing in a lawyer competent in that field had begun even before Mr. Hendren's death in 1939. B. S. Womble, as senior member, made a number of inquiries as to where a young lawyer could get the best training in tax law. In the end, he decided that it was on the staff of the general counsel of the Bureau of Internal Revenue in Washington.

Fortunately for B. S. Womble and the firm, Winston-Salem had a number of connections with the Bureau of Internal Revenue. When Mr. Womble arrived in Winston, he had shared a law office with David H. Blair, who served as commissioner of Internal Revenue from 1921 to 1929. Blair had brought to Washington J. Gilmer Korner, Jr., a well-known Winston-Salem attorney, as a special attorney in the bureau. Womble also knew a Mr. Burroughs, the bureau's assistant general counsel and the man in charge of the Personnel Department.

In the fall of 1939, B. S. Womble traveled to Washington. In the course of his visit, he had an appointment with Mr. Burroughs. In a memoir, Mr. Womble recalled that meeting:

> I told Burroughs that I was going to ask him for some information that he might not see fit to give me but which I would like very much to have. I told him that I would like to have the names of the three young men on his staff who had been

> there from three to five years and whom he considered the top three in that group. He told me that he had never had a request of that kind, but if he had a young man in that group who would have a better opportunity he would not wish to stand in his way. After thinking for a few minutes he gave me the names of three young men, and Leon L. Rice, Jr., was one of the three. After making some investigations of each of the three young men I decided that Rice was the man I wanted and made him an offer to come with our firm as an associate, which he did.

When Leon Rice joined the firm on September 1, 1940, he was only the third lawyer in the state to specialize in taxation. Although young Rice had comparatively little to do in tax law during his first two or three years, the firm insisted that he confine his work solely to that field. He wrote several learned articles on tax-law subjects for leading tax publications and became involved in the tax-law section of the American Bar Association. On the state level, he was a charter member of the North Carolina Bar Association's Committee on Taxation and a frequent speaker at meetings of business and professional groups such as the State Life Underwriters Association.

The firm's first big boost in building a tax practice was Congress's passage of the Revenue Act of 1942. While tax rates under the law skyrocketed to support the unprecedented levels of wartime spending, the 1942 act also allowed tax deductions to employers for contributions made to pension and profit-sharing trusts. This new incentive for employers to supplement Social Security retirement benefits for many of their employees caught on quickly. Leon Rice made an intensive study of the new tax laws affecting retirement plans and was well positioned to serve companies that wanted to install them.

When V-J Day arrived on Wednesday, August 15,

Leon L. Rice, Jr., shortly after joining the firm in 1940

Richard T. Rice

THE RESOURCEFUL B. S. WOMBLE

B. S. Womble's hiring of Leon Rice as a tax specialist is perhaps the most celebrated instance of his remarkable resourcefulness, insight, and knack for innovation. But it was not the first. During his days at Trinity College, he had once run out of money. As the son of a Methodist minister, he paid no tuition, but the cost of his room and board was largely his own responsibility. His lack of funds cost him one night's sleep, he recalled. But by that next morning, young Womble had an idea, as he recounted in a 1960 interview: "I remembered the college bulletin board—a messy affair crusted with notices pasted on and torn off by generations of students. I went to see Dr. Kilgo, the president of the college, and offered to replace the old board with a new one—green cork background in a walnut frame—if he would let me sell advertising to be placed in a border around the board. He agreed. I had the board built, sold the advertising and cleared $175—enough to pay for room and board for an entire year."

The Twin-City Sentinel *trumpeted the end of the war to the residents of Winston-Salem.*

FORSYTH COUNTY PUBLIC LIBRARY PHOTOGRAPH COLLECTION

1945, Winston-Salem celebrated the end of fighting in the Pacific with tumult and shouting. President Truman's announcement of Japan's surrender came over the wires at 7:04 P.M. Within 15 minutes, bedlam broke loose from one end of town to the other. Traffic was blocked to the city limits on nearly every thoroughfare. Confetti streamed from every window on every floor of the Nissen Building. Throngs of people filled the sidewalks along Fourth Street. A reporter for the *Winston-Salem Journal* noticed "a brace of sailors stalking down the street, kissing every girl they met."

Thousands of local citizens had gone to war, including 14 of the city's lawyers. Linville Martin and W. F. Womble would rejoin the firm after the war, and a still younger Womble would soon follow. But 301 men from Forsyth would never return.

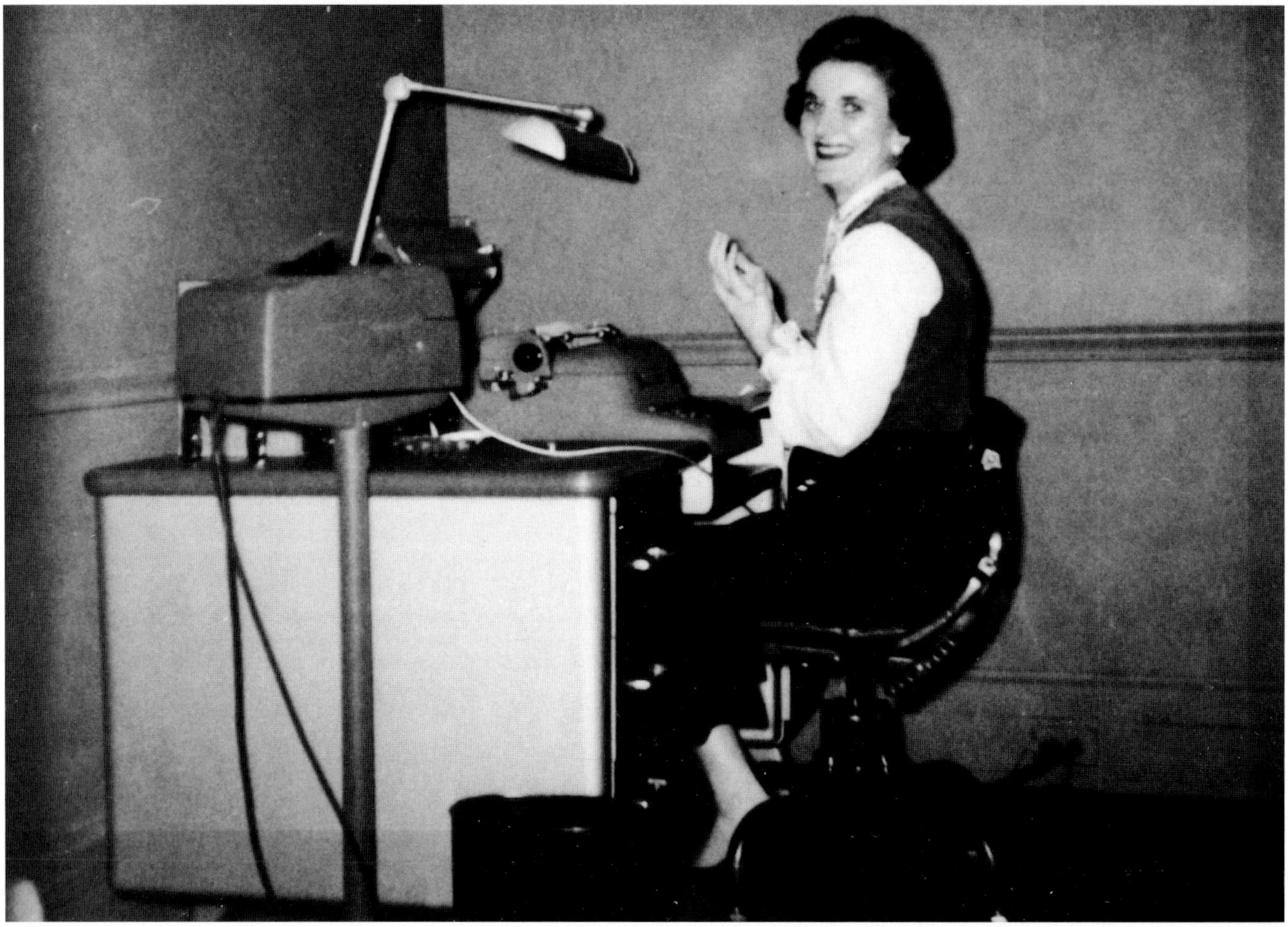

Even in its early days, the firm employed the most up-to-date office equipment.
This 1953 photo shows Pat Wilson, a legal secretary in the firm, using the latest in typewriter technology.
Womble Carlyle Collection

WOMBLE, CARLYLE, MARTIN & SANDRIDGE

ATTORNEYS AND COUNSELLORS AT LAW

WINSTON-SALEM I, N. C.

RETURNING TO RESPONSIBILITIES *1946 – 1954*

> *"Coming out of the war, the practice was not greatly changed for a period. Back in those days, the way a firm practiced law was not a great deal different from the way it had been practiced for a good many years before that. All your dictation was direct dictation—a secretary would take shorthand and then transcribe it. There was no air conditioning in the office. That meant that you were hot in the summer, and you had your windows open. Being left-handed and writing 'upside down and backwards,' as they say, I found that if I was not careful, I would have sweat going across the page as I wrote something. . . . And of course, back in those days, lawyers did not advertise. It would have been improper and unethical to do so. And so, what went out of your office was your only advertisement, other than the advertising you would do by selling yourself."*
>
> William F. Womble

The war years had given the people of Winston-Salem a foretaste of those business and social forces that would soon change the face of their city. Wartime industries had come south and set up shop in the Twin City. Federal agencies had begun to establish offices in Winston-Salem. A number of local women had found new opportunities in the city's defense production plants. And many of the city's African-American soldiers had seen the larger world and gained experience fighting not one but two foes—fascism abroad and racism in their own army.

The GI Bill of Rights—passed in 1944 and authorizing educational benefits for returning veterans—would do more to change the postwar practice of law in the state than any other single event. The veterans who attended law school under the GI Bill came to the bar in great numbers, and they came from circumstances quite different from their prewar predecessors. As historian H. G. Jones noted, "These veterans occupied a special status among a grateful people, and many of them were soon thrust into leadership roles."

But those in uniform came home to a city that was a bit shabby and shopworn. Years of strained budgets during the Depression and the distractions of war had resulted in a community whose infrastructure was frayed around the edges. Most of the city's public services, from the library to the sewage plant, were old and obsolete. Many streets were unpaved and inadequate; road building had not kept pace with the town's growth. Plans for slum clearance and new public housing, a 1941 campaign plank of Mayor Richard J. Reynolds, Jr., had been shelved when Reynolds enlisted in the navy in 1942. Those in uniform were indeed returning to responsibilities in a city that had been marking time.

The postwar boom in Winston-Salem started virtually the minute the war ended. Downtown took a jump to the west. In 1946, Sears Roebuck bought the old West End School site at Fourth and Broad and built a two-block-long department store with rooftop parking. Modern Chevrolet built a new showroom opposite Sears. Many others sought space in the same area.

The Western Electric Company's decision in 1946 to move to Winston-Salem helped change the face of the city. Attracted by the availability of plant facilities, a substantial labor pool, and the welcome extended by the city's industrial leaders, the company moved into the old Chatham Manufacturing plant on Chatham Road, which had been occupied by the National Carbon Company during the war.

When Western Electric began accepting applications on April 29, 1946, an estimated 2,500 people formed a line several blocks long in hopes of helping the company produce military communications equipment. By October 1946, the company had 1,600 people on its Winston-Salem payroll, 90 percent of them hired locally.

What had formerly been a city of homegrown industry suddenly became much less so. Electronics brought high-skill, high-paying jobs to a city known mostly for low-skill, low-paying work in tobacco, textiles, and furniture. For the first time, a major industry was managed by outsiders. Also for the first time,

The Western Electric Company brought newcomers to Winston-Salem and new jobs for city residents when it announced plans to establish a plant in the Twin City in 1946.

North Carolina Collection, University of North Carolina at Chapel Hill Library

a substantial number of employees were outsiders: scientists, white-collar men, people from the Northeast and the Midwest. Western Electric also did something else. It legitimized the unionization of a major local industry.

The population and the local economy diversified. Widespread automobile transportation emerged in the multi-county employment area. And the city's tax base, so long dependent on property levies on stored tobacco, was broadened. Gradually, Western Electric managers joined the established business and industrial leaders in supporting local causes and charities and became a part of the new leadership structure in the city.

The firm played an important role in another of the great events in the postwar history of Winston-Salem: the move of the campus of Wake Forest College from Wake County to Forsyth County.

In 1946, the Reynolds family offered—through the Z. Smith Reynolds Foundation—land and financial support to Wake Forest if the college would agree to move. Irving Carlyle, a member of Wake Forest's Board of Trustees, was appointed to a committee charged with considering the proposal.

The offer posed a wrenching dilemma for many loyal alumni of the college. They could maintain their historic ties to the old campus in Wake County or accept a generous financial proposal likely to ensure future growth. After much soul-searching, Carlyle concluded that the trauma of uprooting his beloved alma mater would in the long run be more than offset by the unique opportunity to move the main campus to the place where the college's school of medicine was already located. In Winston-Salem, the college might have its best—and possibly its only—chance to grow into a great university. His decision made, Mr. Carlyle became a strong advocate of the move and indeed chaired the Winston-Salem campaign for the relocation of the college.

Womble, Carlyle, Martin & Sandridge served as attorneys for the college in this matter. The parties to the agreement asked the North Carolina courts to pass on the validity of the contract under the state's Declaratory Judgment Act. Writing in 1947 for the State Supreme Court in the case of *Z. Smith Reynolds Foundation v. Trustees of Wake Forest College*, Justice Walter P. Stacy affirmed the lower-court ruling declaring the contract valid and enforceable: "Wake Forest College has had a long and honorable career, and whether it nestles in a forest of Wake or stands on a knoll in Forsyth, its mission will remain a quest for truth and a crusade for simple right. We would not deny to this great institution and to those whose faith and good works have made it possible, this vista of a new dawn and this vision of a new hope."

As city attorney, Irving Carlyle—with the assistance of W. F. Womble—played a key role in the city's growth and development decisions immediately after the war.

Recognizing a need for better planning, the city and county cooperated in the establishment of the City-County Planning Board in 1948. Further study indicated the need for an administrative head for the city government. It was Mr. Carlyle who helped convince the aldermen to approve a referendum on adoption of the city-manager form of government. Citizens okayed the proposal by a narrow margin. Winston-Salem's first city manager, C. E. Perkins, began work in May 1948. But a new Board of Aldermen elected in 1951 peremptorily fired Perkins with the support of Mayor Marshall Kurfees, notwithstanding Irving Carlyle's advice that the action was illegal. (The entire saga is recounted in Rixie Hunter's thinly veiled 1966 novel, *The Checkerboard Corridor*.)

In December 1948, on the advice of Mr. Carlyle, the Board of Aldermen adopted a new city zoning ordinance. For the first time in its history, Winston-Salem had a workable zoning ordinance and the

This photo was taken at the time of the last graduation at the old Wake Forest campus, in May 1956.

FORSYTH COUNTY PUBLIC LIBRARY PHOTOGRAPH COLLECTION

In 1951, President Harry S. Truman broke ground for construction of the new Wake Forest campus in Winston-Salem.

REPRINTED WITH PERMISSION OF THE *NEWS AND OBSERVER* OF RALEIGH, NORTH CAROLINA

Attendees at the first meeting of the Winston-Salem City-County Planning Board in March 1948. As city attorney, Irving E. Carlyle was very active in local planning efforts.

Forsyth County Public Library Photograph Collection

determination to enforce it. The 1948 city ordinance, with amendments, was still in use two decades later. County zoning, however, became such a hot political issue that the commissioners let the whole idea die quietly.

In his memoir, *Living, Loving and Lawyering*, Leon Rice recalled the office staff just after the war: "Our offices were on the seventh floor of the Wachovia Bank Building. Two secretaries, Fay Heilig and Kitty Graham, took shorthand and did typing on Royal mechanical typewriters for all the attorneys. Miss Jo Maxwell did the bookkeeping and just about everything else a law office manager of the day and time would do. Nina Marshall, receptionist, completed the non-legal staff."

In light of Winston-Salem's booming economy in the postwar period, the firm gradually needed more lawyers to help handle the load.

In 1948, B. S. Womble's youngest son, Calder, joined the firm. A naval aviator during the war, Calder had finished law school at Duke in 1947 and worked for a year with the North Carolina attorney general's office in Raleigh before returning to Winston-Salem.

Charles Fogle Vance, Jr., a native of Winston-Salem and a descendant of one of the community's old Moravian families, came with the firm in January 1952. A graduate of the University of North Carolina and its law school, Vance had served in the army during the war. In 1949, he opened a law office in his hometown. He then served as assistant solicitor of the Municipal Court from 1951 to 1952. Charlie Vance helped to pick up the slack in the firm's real-estate practice after Hip Martin suffered a stroke in 1951. Like all young associates in the firm in those days, he did some trial work as well.

Leon Rice's work with pension and profit-sharing plans took off after the war. Working with C. A. Bethel of the Trust Department of Wachovia Bank and Trust and Sam L. Booke, actuary for Security Life and Trust Company, Rice played a leading role in drafting trustee retirement plans for a number of regional companies and securing clearance from the IRS.

In 1948, the firm worked on the first public sale

In addition to playing in the Moravian band, Charles F. Vance, Jr., skillfully played the bottles at firm Christmas parties and other events.

Forsyth County Public Library Photograph Collection

OFFICE RULES

When Charles Vance arrived in January 1952, the firm's receptionist, Martha DeHart, penned this ditty and presented it to the new associate:

May I welcome you to the firm, Mr. Vance?
So happy am I that I could dance.
To lengthen your life-span these rules I have written.
Follow them and you will purr like a kitten.

At these rules take no offense.
I'm doing this for your defense.
* For Bunny Womble, you will soon discover,
Is quite a stern man under that sweet cover.

(* He's my favorite but I had to make it rhyme.)

of stock of Piedmont Aviation, just as Piedmont was becoming a feeder airline with a small fleet of DC-3s. Leon Rice collaborated on the stock offering with Al Purrington, Jr., an attorney who regularly represented Carolina Securities Corporation, the underwriter of the issue. (Purrington and his son, Al Purrington III, joined the firm in 1982 when their Raleigh law firm merged with Womble Carlyle Sandridge & Rice to open the Raleigh office.) By 1952, the small but fast-growing Piedmont Airlines had won four new routes from the Civil Aeronautics Board and an unprecedented seven-year renewal of its airworthiness certification.

When it came time to preserve historic Salem from development and to restore the town's roots, James A. Gray, Jr., turned to Leon Rice, naming him to the first Board of Trustees of Old Salem, Inc., when the nonprofit group was founded in 1950. Mr. Rice obtained a favorable ruling from the Internal Revenue Service classifying Old Salem as a public charity, rather than a private foundation. He also was one of the organizers of the Old Salem Restoration Fund Campaign in 1953. He prepared a booklet for donors on the tax advantages of charitable gifts to the organization.

Leon Rice was also involved in the organization of the Mary Reynolds Babcock Foundation in 1953. The firm had represented Mrs. Babcock for a number of years, beginning with a series of cases pertaining to the disposition of the estate of her father, R. J. Reynolds. Mr. Rice helped draft the corporation's charter and bylaws, confirmed the tax-exempt status of the foundation, and served as secretary-treasurer of the new nonprofit. Begun with $12 million worth of R. J. Reynolds Tobacco Company stock, the foundation has become one of the largest and most respected charitable organizations in the state.

In the immediate postwar period, the firm continued to build on its traditional strengths in business and corporate law. The R. J. Reynolds Tobacco Company and Southern Railway remained major clients, and the firm's association with Wachovia Bank and Security Life and Trust increased with the interest shown by many companies in setting up pension and profit-sharing plans under the revised federal tax laws. Advice and counsel for local companies such as McLean Trucking and Pilot Freight also increased, as businesses tried to respond to pent-up consumer demand. Insurance defense work for companies such as Metropolitan Life and the Equitable Life Assurance Society continued apace; the firm also did occasional work for national companies such as the Royal Indemnity Company and Lumbermen's Mutual Casualty Company.

The firm's representation of the R. J. Reynolds Tobacco Company included a variety of labor-law matters. For many years, William P. Sandridge assisted the company in talks with workers, in wage negotiations (black workers at RJR's Winston-Salem plants had organized a local chapter of the Tobacco Workers Union in 1943), and in disputes before the National Labor Relations Board. Soon after the company successfully broke a month-long strike by African-American workers in May 1947, the leadership of the national union

A Piedmont Aviation DC-3, the workhorse of the company's airplane fleet after the war

FORSYTH COUNTY PUBLIC LIBRARY PHOTOGRAPH COLLECTION

Winston-Salem became a trucking center after the war.
McLean Trucking, a client of the firm, was an industry leader.

THE NORTH CAROLINA DIVISION OF ARCHIVES AND HISTORY

mounted a year-long effort to organize white workers in Reynolds's cigarette-making and packing departments. Union agents were sent to Winston-Salem to direct the organizing campaign. They met with small groups of workers in their homes, published a newspaper for workers, set up a club room with refreshments for white workers, and sponsored Saturday-night square dances at the union hall of Local 22. Famed folk singer Woody Guthrie traveled to the city in December 1947 to perform at a square dance and union benefit concert. While visiting Winston-Salem, he wrote a song about the city called "Against th' Law."

Legal work for textile companies such as Spray Cotton Mills had long been part of the firm's business and remained so during the postwar period. In 1951, William P. Sandridge served as counsel for the Arista Mills Company—an old client and Winston-Salem's oldest business—in a case that went to the United States Court of Appeals for the Fourth Circuit. Writing for the court in the case of *Textile Workers Union of America, CIO v. Arista Mills Company*, Judge John J. Parker sustained the judgment of the lower court in favor of Arista, declaring that the company had not been guilty of breaching a collective bargaining agreement with the union. The union's contention that striking workers should have been treated as laid-off employees under the contract was without merit, said Parker, because "the striking workers ceased to be employees upon the termination of the strike."

"My becoming active in good works outside the firm was consistent with firm tradition, and the firm encouraged it," wrote Leon Rice. Within a few years of joining the firm, he was elected president of the Family and Child Service Agency (a role he served from 1945 to 1947) and chairman of the Winston-Salem chapter of the American Red Cross (a position he held from 1946 to 1948). In 1952, Rice served as president of the Forsyth County Committee on Public Solicitation. He was named president of the Community Council in 1953.

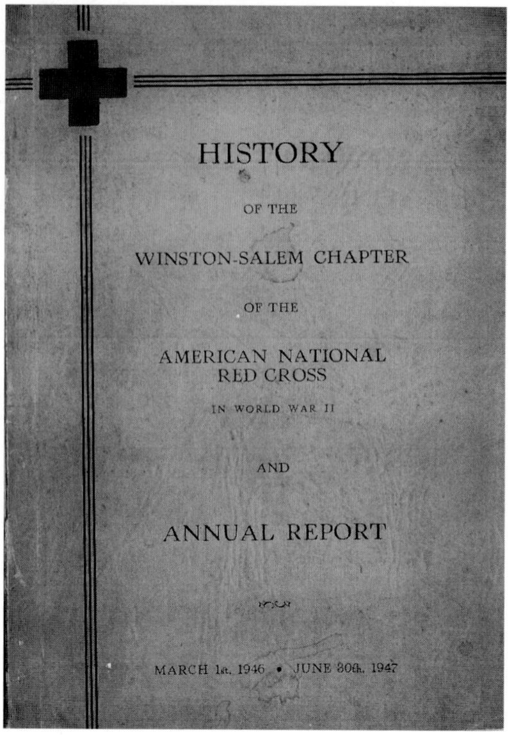

Pen Sandridge and Leon Rice were campaign chairmen for the Winston-Salem Red Cross at the end of World War II.

North Carolina Collection, University of North Carolina at Chapel Hill Library

B. S. Womble led the 1948 Citizens' Committee effort for a 15-cent increase in the Winston-Salem supplementary school tax, headed a 1952 fund-raising campaign in northwest North Carolina for the state's Methodist colleges, and presided over the Patrons' Group for the Arts Council Follies the same year.

Irving Carlyle served in the State Senate again during the 1945-46 term; he served concurrently on the State Advisory Budget Commission. In the State Senate, he chaired the powerful Finance Committee, served on the Rules Committee, and irritated many of his fellow Baptists by supporting a liquor referendum bill in 1945. When his long service on the State Board of Law Examiners ended in 1949, he was ap-

This June 1947 photo shows attorneys B. S. Womble and Norman Stockton opening the cornerstone box of West End Methodist Church. From its earliest years, the firm has encouraged attorneys and staff to be involved in local religious organizations.

FORSYTH COUNTY PUBLIC LIBRARY PHOTOGRAPH COLLECTION

pointed to the North Carolina Board of Public Welfare, a post he would hold for 15 years. Known as "Mr. Democrat" in Forsyth County and throughout the state, he was not afraid to take a courageous or unpopular stand. He supported Frank Porter Graham in the 1949 primary campaign for the United States Senate, though most of the state's leading Democrats backed the other candidate, attorney Willis Smith. As a delegate-at-large to the 1952 Democratic National Convention, he was one of the first to back the candidacy of Adlai Stevenson, whom he supported again in 1956.

William F. Womble chaired the Community Chest campaign for 1949. In 1953, he was elected to the first of three consecutive terms in the North Carolina House of Representatives.

Following in the footsteps of Leon Rice, Calder Womble chaired the local Red Cross fund-raising campaign in 1951 and was elected president of the Forsyth County chapter of the Red Cross in 1953.

During the postwar years, Pen Sandridge served on the boards of the Winston-Salem Chamber of Commerce and the Forsyth Citizens Planning Council. He was president of the United Fund drive in 1952.

The firm lost one of its senior members on October 3, 1954, when Linville Kerr Martin died. The native and lifelong resident of Winston-Salem had held numerous elective offices in bar organizations, alumni associations, veterans' organizations, and the Methodist Church. Mr. Martin continued to come to his office in his later years. Just a few months before his

William F. Womble (center) chaired Winston-Salem's Community Chest drive in 1949, part of the Womble family's tradition of leadership in charitable fund-raising.

FORSYTH COUNTY PUBLIC LIBRARY PHOTOGRAPH COLLECTION

Gordon Gray (right) with Mr. and Mrs. Linville K. Martin in October 1949. During his nearly three decades as an attorney, "Hip" Martin helped establish the firm's real-estate practice.

FORSYTH COUNTY PUBLIC LIBRARY PHOTOGRAPH COLLECTION

death, he was elected president of the Forsyth County chapter of the Duke University Alumni Association.

When Senator Clyde R. Hoey died in office in 1954, there were strong indications that Governor William B. Umstead would appoint Irving E. Carlyle to fill the vacancy. Umstead's intentions appeared to be confirmed when he asked Carlyle to be the keynote speaker at the State Democratic Convention.

On May 17, 1954, just four days before the convention, the United States Supreme Court handed down its decision in *Brown v. Board of Education of Topeka, Kansas*, ruling that compulsory racial segregation in the public schools was unconstitutional. There was immediate sharp reaction against the court's decision in the state and throughout the South. Irving Carlyle, one of the state's leading Democrats, was disturbed that no political leader came forward to declare that the court and its decision must be respected.

Toward the end of his remarks at the convention, Carlyle quietly added these words: "The Supreme Court of the United States has spoken. As good citizens we have no choice but to obey the law as laid down by the Court. To do otherwise would cost us our respect for law and order, and if we lose that in these critical times, we will have lost that quality which is the source of our strength as a State and as a nation."

Those 68 words proved to be a bombshell. Prominent Democrats across the state asked, "What happened to Irving?" Some murmured that he had lost his mind. But Irving Carlyle was just being what he had always been—straightforward, courageous, and unconcerned with personal consequences.

Nothing more was heard about his appointment, which went to Judge Samuel J. Ervin, Jr. Mr. Carlyle never expressed any regrets. When asked about his decision, he would break into a wry grin and say, "It was the most influential speech I ever made."

"THE GIRLS" OR "OLD BUN WOMBLE HAD A FIRM"

Old Bun Womble had a firm, E-I-E-I-O.
And in that firm he had some girls, E-I-E-I-O.
With a peck peck here and a dictate there,
Here a record, there a file, everywhere a letter letter,
Old Bun Womble had a firm, E-I-E-I-O.

In a little room about twelve feet tall,
With absolutely nothing on either wall,
With a yellowish floor—a sickly tan,
And altogether bare as your hand;
A lavatory here, a transcriber yonder,
How they do any work is hard to ponder.
This little room, two by four,
Houses three girls—lately four.
From nine to one and from two to five,
Here they work in this little dive.
It's a buzz buzz here and a call call there—
Enough to make a good girl swear!
These little girls, they do our work,
Always faithful—never a shirk.
If it isn't a brief or a verbose letter,
It's a summons to court for some poor debtor;
Or more likely still, an answer is due;
And whoever does it is in a stew.

Chorus

Now, Kitty, she works for Irving and Pen;
And these two fellows are really he-men
When it comes to loading down a girl
With every kind of thing in the world.
Irving draws ordinances and does things for the city;
But he's good about records. What a pity.
When it comes to a Dictaphone, Pen is a flop,
When he could put it on records as easy as not.

Chorus

Lynn is the gal of Leon and Bill;
Whenever she's working, she works with a will.
Bill, he draws answers and contracts and such
And then, like his daddy, redrafts them right much.
Now, Leon is the tax and pension plan man,
And does other things whenever he can.
But the thing Lynn hates most and would give it the ax
Is a claim for a refund on an income tax.

Chorus

Civic boosters depicted Winston-Salem as
a dynamic business center with distinct social and cultural amenities.
NORTH CAROLINA COLLECTION, UNIVERSITY OF NORTH CAROLINA AT CHAPEL HILL LIBRARY

EXPANDING OPPORTUNITIES *1954 – 1965*

"In the early 1950s, Charlie Vance had come with us, initially to work in real estate because Hip Martin had had a stroke and was unable to continue the practice. Then, as Charlie got into some other things, Wade Gallant came with us and was also in real estate for a short time. Then Wade found that he was better suited for banking and other areas of practice. So, about that time, Les Browder came with us, and he became the longtime partner in our firm who has headed up the real-estate practice. Also about that time, Grady Barnhill came with us, straight out of Wake Forest Law School. He got into litigation right off the bat and hit the ground running and has been a very important member of our firm, in the area of litigation particularly."

William F. Womble

In the latter half of the 1950s, Winston-Salem enjoyed a stable, healthy economy that was largely immune to the recessions and unemployment problems that plagued some other parts of the country. During the decade, the city's payroll nearly tripled and its employment total almost doubled. The "Big Four"—R. J. Reynolds Tobacco Company, P. H. Hanes Knitting Company, Hanes Hosiery, and Wachovia Bank and Trust Company—had enjoyed strong growth since the end of the war. The city's major trucking companies—McLean, Pilot, and Hennis—kept pace with Winston-Salem's key industries. And newcomers such as Western Electric, Bassick-Sack, and Duplan continued to bring new products, new people, and new ideas to the Twin City.

In the 1950s and 1960s, Reynolds was one of the

bluest of the blue-chip companies. The tobacco giant introduced its first brands of filtered cigarettes—Winston in 1954 and Salem in 1956. By 1958, the popularity of the new brands and the company's old standbys—Camel cigarettes and Prince Albert pipe tobacco—made Reynolds the largest tobacco company in the nation once again, a ranking it had lost to American Tobacco back in 1941. When the company's new Whitaker Park facility opened in 1961, it was the largest cigarette factory in the world.

Despite the continued strength and financial health of the city's Big Four companies, Winston-Salem's industrial base was by the 1960s shifting toward national companies whose ownership and corporate headquarters were elsewhere. The Chamber of Commerce recognized the trend and began lobbying executives of many of the country's leading industries to open new facilities in Winston-Salem. As the city and its suburbs grew in these baby-boom years, the shopping center—that unique artifact of the automobile age—made its appearance. Thruway Shopping Center opened in 1955, Northside in 1958, Parkway Plaza in 1960, Reynolda Manor in 1963, and Sherwood Plaza in 1964. Womble Carlyle attorneys and staff patronized these postwar shopping meccas; the firm's real-estate practice also had a hand in developing a number of them.

Camel and Prince Albert, two of the best-selling brands of the R. J. Reynolds Tobacco Company, helped carry the name of Winston-Salem to the far corners of the world.

North Carolina Collection, University of North Carolina at Chapel Hill Library

A NEW WIND BLOWS IN DIXIE

A major change during the 1950s was the arrival of air conditioning, which some historians have called the "turning point in 20th-century Southern history." All of the office windows on the east, south, and west sides of the Wachovia Building were blocked, and air conditioners were installed. No longer did attorneys need to have a handkerchief handy to keep perspiration from dripping on legal documents. Gone were the days when they had to take a book off the shelf, blow across the top of it, and shake it a few times to rid it of the omnipresent dirt and dust carried in through open windows.

It was a simpler time, a more informal time. The firm didn't have a real budget, there was no personnel manual, and few attorneys kept time records. Pen Sandridge recalled that they would do work for the Southern Railway all year, then sit down in December and say, "Now, let's see, what did we do for the railroad this year, and how much should we bill them?"

Barbara Sims (center) served as legal secretary with the firm for 45 years.

WOMBLE CARLYLE COLLECTION

From seven lawyers in 1954, the firm grew to 10 lawyers and four staff members by the end of the decade. One of the largest practices in the state, it had offices on the seventh floor of the Wachovia Building. B. S. Womble, Irving Carlyle, Pen Sandridge, and Leon Rice were the senior partners. "They were leaders, and they would convince you to follow," Calder Womble remembered. "They had good reason for wanting the firm to go in a certain direction, or to do certain things. Back then, you had six or eight or 10 people who saw each other every day and usually had lunch together. You didn't need to have a firm meeting to know what somebody was thinking or talking about or wanted to do. At that time, you just did it." Calder W. Womble was named a partner in 1954 and Charles F. Vance, Jr., in 1957.

Barbara Sims, who had come with the firm in 1953, was legal secretary for both Mr. Sandridge and Mr. Carlyle, the senior members who were most active in trial practice. "They were absolute gentlemen, and they loved the law, just loved the law," Barbara Sims remembered. "Mr. Carlyle and Mr. Sandridge were completely opposite in their political views. But they got along so well together, and they would sometimes try cases together. Mr. Carlyle would often describe their contrasting courtroom styles by saying, 'Yeah, Pen tells 'em the facts, and I make 'em cry.' "

During this period, William F. Womble functioned as the managing partner, responsible for hiring both lawyers and staff. For a long time, Mr. Womble was able to tell a young lawyer coming with the firm that no one had left its employ for many years, and that anyone who had come with the firm had made partner. "I was able to say to the people who came with us as lawyers that to come with our firm is a little bit like being born and dying. You don't pay anything to get into the firm. When you go out, you do not have an equity interest that goes with you. The firm was just the firm, and whatever the firm has stays in the firm, except that all of the income is divided among the partners each year."

Gradual expansion was the watchword in those years. Legal work for Wachovia Bank and Trust Company, R. J. Reynolds Tobacco, and the Southern Railway Company were the bread and butter of Womble Carlyle during the decade, in addition to Irving Carlyle's substantial work as Winston-Salem city attorney. The relationship with Wachovia—which celebrated its 75th anniversary in 1954—not only provided a steady stream of business and referrals but also gave the firm a certain institutional solidity and a stamp of respectability in the business community. Also during this period, Western Electric became a client of the firm. At the same time, the firm continued its substantial representation of individual clients concerning a wide variety of personal and business concerns.

Insurance defense work for Security Life and Trust Company, the Equitable Life Assurance Society, and the Metropolitan Life Insurance Company made up a significant part of the firm's business. Textile-mill clients included Burlington Mills Corporation and Spray Cotton Mills. Two local transportation companies, McLean Trucking and Pilot Freight, were clients. It was also during this period that the firm began to represent the Transcontinental Gas Pipe Line Corporation. Municipal clients from outside the city included the town of Kernersville and the town of Morganton. Pen Sandridge remained a valuable counsel to a number of prominent companies and a trusted litigator. In the field of taxation, Leon Rice represented companies such as R. J. Reynolds and Carolina Biological Supply Company in matters before the state and federal courts. Mr. Rice also served as general counsel for Thomasville Furniture Industries and assisted in that company's first public stock offering. Charles Vance was involved in all manner of litigation work, including antitrust and labor cases.

Wade M. Gallant, Jr., a graduate of Wake Forest College and its School of Law, joined Womble, Carlyle, Sandridge & Rice on August 20, 1955. A Raleigh native, he had been a Latin scholar and concert pianist at Wake, from which he graduated at the top of his class. He did some real-estate work for about a year and a little trial work before becoming a specialist in banking and corporate law, securities in particular. The firm made him a partner in 1963.

A year after Gallant joined, on June 1, 1956, the firm brought in Leslie Browder to take over the real-estate practice. A Winston-Salem native, a Duke undergraduate, and a Wake Forest School of Law graduate, Browder had been a sole practitioner in the Twin City for two years before coming with the firm. He had come to know Charlie Vance and Wade Gallant in the course of his work. Les Browder recalled the thing that impressed him most: "This firm has a wonderful internal philosophy. I am not speaking about work ethic and all of that, because there are a lot of other firms that have the same philosophy. The firm has, over the years, developed the concept that you save your competition for your adversaries and you do not compete internally with your colleagues. You simply do not compete internally. It just won't work. It may work for a

Wade M. Gallant, Jr., one of the first securities lawyers in North Carolina, joined the firm in 1955.

WOMBLE CARLYLE COLLECTION

Leslie M. Browder became a real estate lawyer with the firm in 1956, after the death of Hip Martin.

WOMBLE CARLYLE COLLECTION

while, but it will not work long-term. Every dollar that you make and that every other lawyer in the firm makes, you are going to get a part of it. . . . The more that the bottom line increases, the more you get. It is just that simple."

H. Grady Barnhill, Jr., who clerked with Womble Carlyle in the summer of 1957, joined the firm as an associate in September 1958 after graduating from the Wake Forest School of Law at the top of his class. He became very involved in litigation from the start, working with I. E. Carlyle and W. F. Womble on cases involving the city, doing insurance defense work, and handling personal-injury cases for clients of the firm. Grady Barnhill was admitted as a partner on January 1, 1963, along with Les Browder and Wade Gallant.

Allan R. Gitter, a graduate of R. J. Reynolds High School, Washington and Lee University, and the University of Michigan School of Law, came with Womble Carlyle in 1962. Gitter, who covered Board of Aldermen meetings for a local radio station while waiting to take the state bar exam, had been approached by W. F. Womble about doing some legal research for the firm in conjunction with its role as city attorney. On becoming an associate, Gitter immediately moved into litigation, training under Irving Carlyle and Grady Barnhill.

William Pendleton Sandridge, Jr., joined the firm in September 1961. A graduate of the University of North Carolina and the University of Virginia School of Law, Sandridge had served a two-year tour of duty in the United States Navy before coming with the firm as an associate.

Excellence in quality of work and client service was expected of all new associates. Les Browder recalled his first conversation with B. S. Womble after being hired:

> Mr. B. S. Womble was an imposing figure. He could intimidate you by just giving you a look. He didn't have to say a word, but he set a standard of perfection which everybody understood. And he articulated it very carefully when I first came to the firm. It was only said once. He said, "Les, we're glad to have you, wonderful for you to be here. You know, we've invested 60 years developing the reputation of this firm, and everything that you send out from this office will add or detract from that reputation. So it's up to you to be sure that nothing goes out that detracts, and should you do something that does that, we will bring it to your attention. And if you are not able to correct it, you will be asked to leave." That's all that was ever said. And he meant it, too. He wasn't going to coddle anybody.

While Winston-Salem had a reputation for being something of a closed society composed of a few leading families, the firm was noted for helping integrate new associates into the community. Just as B. S. Womble had "talked up" Leon Rice to just about everybody in the Twin City, the Wombles and the Carlyles and the Sandridges made new lawyers such as Wade Gallant and Les Browder feel at home, entertaining them and introducing them around the city.

The remarkable Wombles continued to amaze with their dedication and commitment to service. In one month, June 1960, B. S. Womble became chairman of the Board of Trustees of Duke University; William F. Womble assumed the presidency of the Winston-Salem Chamber of Commerce; and Calder Womble was elected to lead the 1960 fund-raising campaign for Forsyth County's United Fund. With Calder's election, they became the only three men from the same family in the city's history to head the Community Chest/United Fund campaigns. As B. S. Womble often reminded his sons, "Everything that is good about your life came out of this community, and you owe it back."

B. S. Womble was 78 years old when he accepted the chairmanship at Duke. The university was in crisis over the firing of President Hollis Edens and the issue

Brothers Bill and Calder Womble with their father, B. S. Womble, in the firm's library in 1962

William F. Womble

of whether to enroll African-American students. Mr. Womble calmed the waters during his term as head of the trustees, shepherding the board through to the successful selection of a new president, Dr. Douglas M. Knight. And after initially opposing integration of the student body, he changed his position upon hearing presentations made by student leaders and visiting with students across the campus. Thereafter, he encouraged the trustees to welcome African-American students to the university. After three years as chairman, Mr. Womble stepped down in 1963.

The next year, both Womble sons were on hand for a dinner party at the Old Town Club marking B. S. Womble's 53rd year with the firm. Partners, associates, and staff members attended the occasion, hosted by Leon Rice. Miss Jo Maxwell, who had worked for Mr. Womble from 1908 until her retirement in 1956, was in attendance as a special guest of the firm. In his remarks to the assembled guests, Mr. Womble proudly spoke of the firm's commitment to education, noting that every partner in the firm was either presently serving as a trustee of a college or had served in that capacity.

The firm's attorneys served the community in myriad ways. W. P. Sandridge served on the board of the Winston-Salem Foundation in 1955 and with the Winston-Salem Hospital Commission in 1959. Leon Rice began a long association with the Mary Reynolds Babcock Foundation in 1954 and led a 1955 committee of the North Carolina Eye Bank that helped advise

THE SPIRITUAL DIMENSION OF SERVICE

Let me mention that during tonight's proceedings you will hear of our firm's involvement in the business and professional affairs of Winston-Salem and in other cities where we have offices. Our firm has also had a prominent role in the religious life in the communities we serve.

Colonel Clement Manly came to Winston-Salem from New Bern, North Carolina. He was one of the first Roman Catholics in this city. In the 1920s he was a moving force in building the St. Leo's Catholic Church.

B. S. Womble was born in Chatham County, North Carolina, the son of a Methodist minister. He and his sons Bill and Calder have been active in the Centenary United Methodist Church and in other Methodist organizations, such as Duke University, where Mr. B. S. was a Trustee, and Arbor Acres, the Triad United Methodist Home.

Pen Sandridge was an active Presbyterian, as have been Rod Ligon and our Chairman, John Garrou. They served as Elders of the First Presbyterian Church here, and John sings in the choir.

Irving Carlyle and Leon Rice were leaders in the Baptist faith. Both had close ties to Wake Forest, and Leon was a founder of the Knollwood Baptist Church.

Charles Vance, a Moravian descendant, was prominent as a Trustee of the Home Moravian Church and also of the Southern Province of the Moravian Church. Charlie did about all there is to do in the Moravian Church. He taught Sunday School, sang in the choir and played the alto horn in the Moravian band.

Ken Michael and Gusti Frankel have been active in the Winston-Salem Jewish community. They are members of the Board of Governors of Temple Emanuel. Ken has devoted hundreds of hours as the Chairman of the Long Range Planning Committee and Chairman of the Design Committee, leading to the construction of a new sanctuary.

Our Washington office, through John Hagner's leadership, helped organize a home for the frail elderly, the St. Mark Presbyterian House, of Rockville, Maryland. For fourteen years, John and his colleagues have provided all of the legal services, pro bono, for this home.

Twenty years ago Terry Parker, in Atlanta, founded the National Christian Charitable Foundation. This is a donor advised fund that has assets of $350 million. Last year it distributed $80 million to 3,600 charities, mainly churches and religious organizations. Terry has established over one hundred religious nonprofit organizations over the years. He recently met in Washington with President Bush and members of his administration on the President's faith-based initiatives program.

Thus not only in the past, but very much in the present, members of the firm have demonstrated personal religious conviction and have contributed to the religious life of their communities. We trust that this part of our heritage will continue.

Remarks by
Linwood L. Davis
at the Newcomen Award Ceremony, April 2001

lawyers on ways to increase public awareness of the Eye Bank's needs. Calder Womble was elected president of the Forsyth County Junior Bar Association in 1958 and was an active board member and fund-raiser for the Winston-Salem Arts Council in the late 1950s. Charles Vance served as a member of the Home Moravian Church Board of Elders and the Salem College and Academy Board of Trustees. Wade Gallant's interest in public mental-health services began in these years. He began working with the city's Associated Family and Child Service Agency in the 1950s and served as its president from 1962 to 1965.

During the decade, the firm built on its record of distinguished service to city government. Irving Carlyle—who turned down William Umstead's request to manage his gubernatorial campaign in 1952—scaled back his political activities. In an April 1955 letter to Governor Luther Hodges, he admitted being somewhat out of the loop politically: "With Bill Womble being in the Legislature and with his father being on an extended trip to Europe, I have been so busy here in the office this winter and spring that I have not been able to keep very closely informed on what is taking place in the General Assembly."

Mr. Carlyle continued as attorney for the city and related entities such as the School Board, the City-County Planning Board, and the Zoning Board of Adjustment. In governmental matters, he was ably assisted by W. F. Womble and H. Grady Barnhill, Jr. Mr. Carlyle was a key adviser to the city on the issue of consolidation of the city and county schools, a measure approved by the voters in 1963. He also represented State Senator Max Thomas in his effort to have the courts authorize an election for lieutenant governor in 1962 to fill the unexpired term of H. Cloyd Philpott, who had died in August 1961.

Irving E. Carlyle (right) and Frank A. Daniels were sworn in as members of the North Carolina Board of Public Welfare in 1953. Mr. Carlyle served on the board for 15 years.

Reprinted with permission of the *News and Observer* of Raleigh, North Carolina

Throughout the Eisenhower years, Leon Rice was busy building the region's premier corporate tax practice. Mr. Rice worked closely with Maddrey Cooke of Booke & Company, the state's first pension firm, helping draft pension plans and advising companies on the tax consequences of their plans. Rice also became active in the Taxation Section of the American Bar Association and served as chairman of the section's Committee on Pension and Profit-Sharing Plans. In his memoir, Mr. Rice wrote, "My activities in the ABA Section of Taxation materially influenced my standing as a tax lawyer and resulted in considerable business referrals from fellow section members across the country."

In 1957, his book *Basic Pension and Profit-Sharing Plans* was published by the American Law Institute of the American Bar Association. Coauthored with Edward M. Schlaudt of New York, the book was designed as a practical, easy-to-read handbook to help lawyers, business executives, and corporate directors understand the fundamental aspects of employee benefit plans.

The way in which Bill Womble fulfilled the office of president of the Winston-Salem Chamber of Commerce in 1960 tells much about the man. He described his two major goals for the organization in writing: "First, we must increase and diversify our industrial growth. Second, we must—by deeds, words, publicity and the like—work towards creating a *deserved* public image of the Chamber as being for the development of the *total* community. I fear that too many people think of the Chamber as the guardian of limited vested interests." He wanted to avoid even the appearance of being self-serving, of excluding legitimate voices and simply maintaining the status quo.

As a representative in the North Carolina General Assembly, he showed the courage of his convictions. When the 1957 State House of Representatives was considering a bill requiring the National Association for the Advancement of Colored People and other organizations active in the integration struggle to open their records to public scrutiny, Bill Womble was one of the few in the lower house to rise in opposition: "I say to you that if you or I or any other citizen should want to organize or belong to a dues-paying group that either supports or opposes the separation of the races in the use of public facilities we should be permitted to do so with freedom and dignity, as we might on any other proposition of public concern without being singled out for treatment and burdens which this bill would impose. . . . I humbly beseech you to hark to the heritage that is ours as North Carolinians and Christians, and let reason overrule prejudice, and out of our sense of wisdom and justice to all people to vote against this bill."

W. F. Womble was held in high regard throughout his years in the legislature. In 1955, he was one of the authors of a bill creating the first statewide Board of Higher Education; he was appointed one of the members of the inaugural board later that year. In 1958, Womble was one of 15 prominent state attorneys appointed to the Court Study Committee, chaired by Judge J. Spencer Bell; the committee proposed a sweeping reform of the court system in North Carolina. In 1963, Bill Womble chaired Winston-Salem's "Experiment in Self-Reliance," a partner in the North Carolina Fund, the state's innovative attempt to eliminate the causes of poverty and illiteracy in local communities.

In 1961, William P. Sandridge, Sr., won a huge victory in the California courts in a case that drew considerable public attention. The suit, *Piedmont Publishing Company v. Rogers*, centered around the first television station in Winston-Salem, WSJS-TV. It pitted Gordon Gray, a friend and former associate of the firm, against silent-screen star Mary Pickford and her husband, actor Buddy Rogers.

Piedmont Publishing Company and Pickford had decided to collaborate in applying for a license for the new station in 1953, forming a joint venture under the name of Triangle Broadcasting Corporation. Piedmont paid for two-thirds of the stock in the new company, while Pickford purchased the remaining third. An agreement signed by the two parties gave Piedmont an option to purchase Pickford's stock within six years at a price to be determined by Triangle Broadcasting's independent accounting firm. If Piedmont did not exercise its option within the allotted time, Pickford was to have an option to purchase half of Piedmont's interest in Triangle.

When Gordon Gray attempted to exercise his purchase option, Pickford and Rogers demurred, claiming that Triangle's accountants had undervalued the price of the company's stock and misrepresented the station's earnings. Piedmont Publishing sued Mary Pickford and Buddy Rogers in Los Angeles County Superior Court in 1958.

After two trials in California lasting a total of 20

Movie star Mary Pickford and her husband, actor Buddy Rogers, in 1961
William P. Sandridge won a case on behalf of Piedmont Publishing Company against Pickford in the California courts. The case involved a North Carolina television station license.
COURTESY OF CORBIS CORPORATION

weeks, a two-judge panel of the California Court of Appeals ruled in Gordon Gray's favor, stating that Piedmont had intended to pay Miss Pickford a fair price for her participation in securing the television license and in making the station a successful venture.

W. L. Maynard, comptroller for both Piedmont Publishing and Triangle Broadcasting, characterized Pen Sandridge's handling of the case as "absolutely magnificent." Mr. Sandridge had twice bested the finest legal talents in California on their home turf. The defendants' attorneys had come to realize that Sandridge was anything but the guileless, naive country lawyer they may have thought. By the end of the trial, they had developed a tremendous respect for him. Coincidentally, while in California, Pen Sandridge received news of his induction as a fellow of the American College of Trial Lawyers, one of the highest honors accorded in the legal profession.

Irving Carlyle remained in the spotlight not only as one of the state's leading Democrats but also as a fearless public citizen. When Governor Luther Hodges supported several bills in 1956 designed to prevent forced integration of the public schools, Mr. Carlyle was one of only a handful of prominent Democrats in the state—black or white—to come out against the legislation. "I have read the several bills," he commented. "Running through much of the proposed legislation is the term 'child of another race.' This seems to indicate that the laws are based upon racial differences or the purposes of preserving racial segregation in the schools by public funds furnished by the state. It still seems to me that this procedure is of doubtful legality and will probably be held invalid by the Supreme Court of the United States. . . . This is a long backward step that ought never to be taken by North Carolina."

He had long been a staunch supporter of equal rights for all men regardless of race, creed, or color. In the mid-1920s, he had helped African-Americans in Winston-Salem gain city licenses to operate jitney buses in black neighborhoods. He was active in the North Carolina Conference of Christians and Jews for many years. And in the 1960 presidential election, he spoke up for the candidacy of John F. Kennedy, a Roman Catholic, even writing a letter to the editor of the *Biblical Recorder* reminding the state's Baptists that "the United States is a nation founded upon religious freedom."

Mr. Carlyle was the yellowest yellow-dog Democrat of his time in the state of North Carolina. He truly believed—to the bemusement of some of his partners—that there was no such thing as a good Republican, because, as he would say, "if you really were a right-thinking person, you would not be a Republican!" In one of his standard speech texts, "Why I Am a Democrat," Mr. Carlyle stated, "The Democratic Party has always promoted the public interest in terms of the greatest good for the greatest number. It puts human rights above property rights. It works constantly for the good of all the people rather than for the benefit of the privileged few."

As the year 1965 closed, the firm was preparing for a move to the new Wachovia Building. Since 1920, when the firm was known by the name of Manly, Hendren & Womble, the attorneys and staff had done business in the Wachovia Building on the corner of Third and Main; Colonel Manly's fireplace was on the seventh floor. Now, the firm was packing and readying for new offices in the tallest building in the Carolinas. "We felt that we were really expanding and taking on a financial challenge," William F. Womble remembered. "Our rental rates were increasing from about $2.25 a square foot to about $4.25 a square foot. We were leasing nearly half a floor, which meant that we were nearly doubling our space, occupying 7,000 or 8,000 square feet in that new building. It all seems modest today, but it was a big challenge at the time."

WE WORK HARD

"It should go without saying that hard work is a must for every attorney in the firm. We often prevail over opposing counsel because we have worked hard, dug deep and are better prepared. We get the facts, research the law in depth, *think* things through, exercise judgment based on ability and experience, confer among ourselves, and so on. This takes time, and a lot of it. Abraham Lincoln, when asked how long a man's legs should be, replied 'Long enough to reach the ground.' That is the way I view the responsibility of an attorney in this firm, with respect to the time he or she should devote to law practice."

Leon Rice, *Living, Loving and Lawyering*

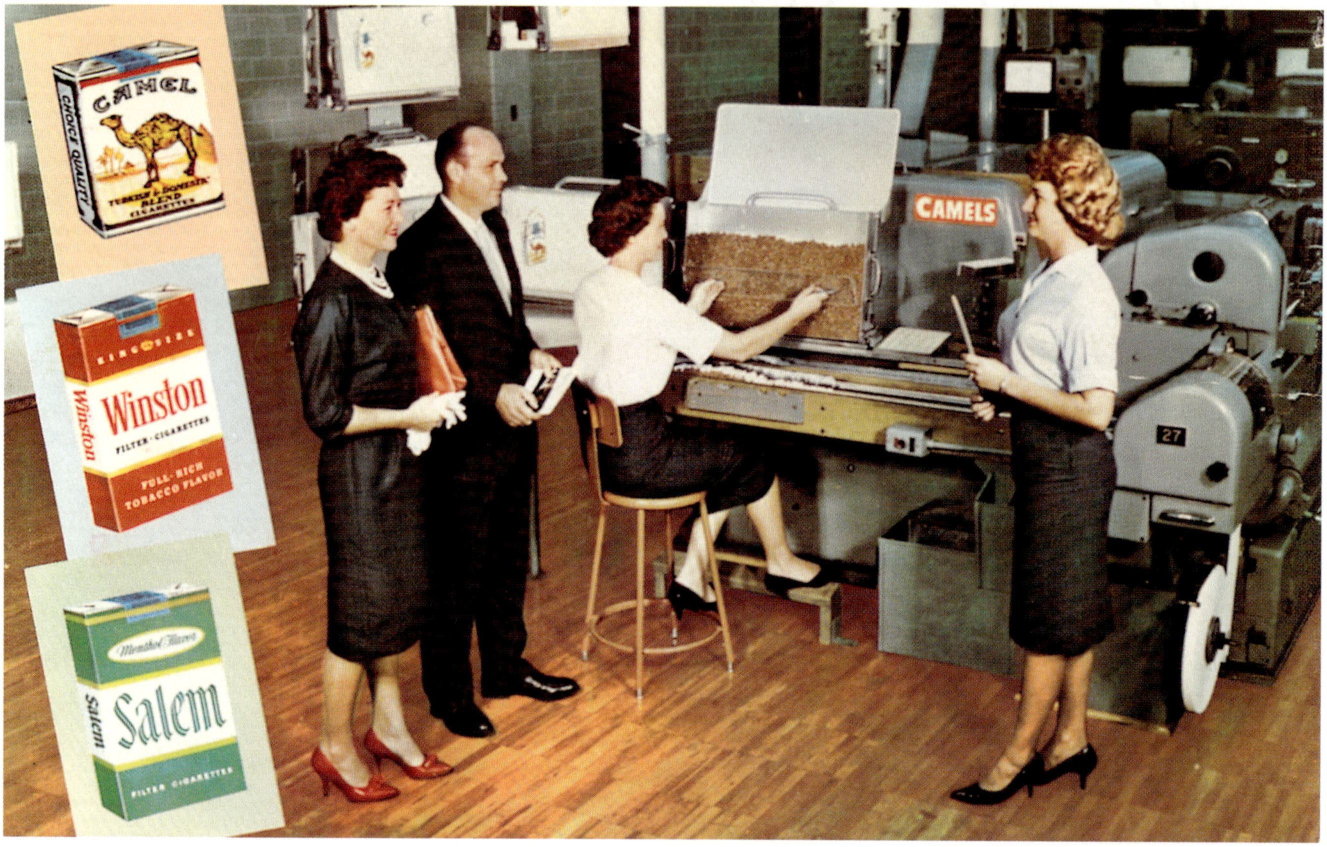

Visitors enjoying a personalized tour of the R. J. Reynolds Tobacco Companyin the 1960s

LYNN ROUNDTREE

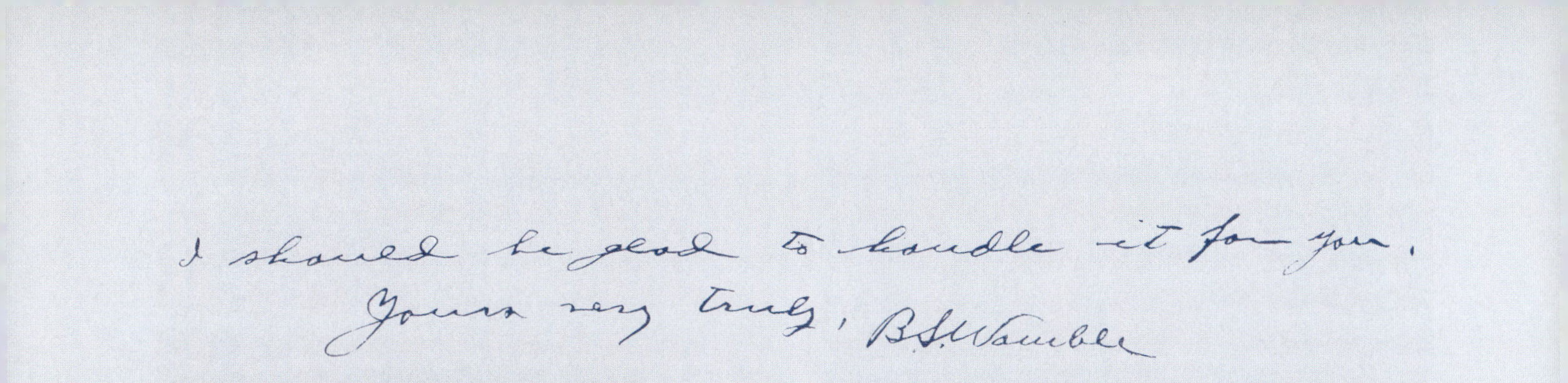

BEGINNINGS AND ENDINGS *1966 – 1976*

> *"By the mid-1960s, we were preparing to move out of the Wachovia Building on Third Street, where the firm had been since 1920, and into the new Wachovia Building on the east side of the courthouse square on Main Street. At that time, we probably had 12 to 14 lawyers. By the time my father died in May 1976, the firm had 36 or 37 lawyers, over 10 times the size when he joined it in January 1911."*
>
> William F. Womble

The growth of Winston-Salem business and industry from the mid-1960s followed the now familiar "home and away" pattern. Since World War II, the expansion of both Winston-Salem's homegrown companies and its national corporations had brought prosperity to the city and new clients to the firm.

One future client, the Joseph Schlitz Brewing Company, began contacts with the Chamber of Commerce in April 1965 that resulted in the completion in May 1970 of a $45 million brewery capable of producing 4.4 million barrels of beer per year. Like Western Electric's arrival two decades earlier, it marked the largest investment in county history to the time. It also served to attract satellite companies, in this case newcomers such as the Continental Can Company and the Owens-Illinois Glass Company. Industry-hunting expeditions—like the one Chamber of Commerce president Bill Womble had led back in 1960—attracted 27 new companies by 1969, including electronics maker AMP and the Gravely Tractor Company.

Meanwhile, a few of the city's homegrown giants continued to grow into companies of national and even international stature.

A major development was the merger in 1965 of

A view of bustling Fourth Street in Winston-Salem in 1970

FORSYTH COUNTY PUBLIC LIBRARY PHOTOGRAPH COLLECTION

the Hanes Hosiery Mills Company with the P. H. Hanes Knitting Company to form the Hanes Corporation, a uniting of family enterprises begun separately at the turn of the century by brothers John Wesley Hanes and Pleasant Henderson Hanes. With former Hanes Hosiery president Gordon Hanes at the helm as CEO, the combined company brought out new product lines and expanded its operations internationally. The company's L'eggs brand of one-size stockings, introduced in 1970, broke records for hosiery sales in drugstores and supermarkets. By 1974, it was the leading brand of hosiery sold in the United States.

The R. J. Reynolds Tobacco Company, one of the firm's largest clients, continued its growth. By 1966, the company's Winston brand had become the best-selling cigarette in the nation. Its Camel and Salem brands also continued to enjoy strong sales. The company began to plow more of its profits into research. Researchers based at the company's Bowman Gray Development Center, which opened in Winston-Salem in 1968, patented several new methods for processing cigarette tobacco more efficiently. Manufacturing operations and licensing agreements were expanded abroad. But there were also signs of big changes to come in the company's business. In 1967, the company had formed a new parent company, R. J. Reynolds Industries, Inc. That same year, a new subsidiary was created, RJR Foods, which acquired several well-known food companies, such as Hawaiian Punch and Chun King.

The Wachovia Bank and Trust Company's stature and strength were reflected in its new 26-story skyscraper, the largest office building in the Carolinas upon its completion in February 1966. The bank's total resources had passed the $1 billion mark for the first time late in 1964. By the end of 1965, the bank was the 37th largest in the country and the largest in the Southeast. Its International Division, founded in 1961, was growing rapidly in response to the state's booming export trade.

The year 1966 was an auspicious one for the firm. Attorneys and staff were, of course, excited about the move into spacious new offices in the Wachovia Building. But they were also proud of an honor conferred upon one of their own. Following the tradition set by Clement Manly, William M. Hendren, B. S. Womble, Linville K. Martin, and Irving Carlyle, William F. Womble was serving as president of the North Carolina Bar Association.

The question of whether to admit qualified African-Americans to membership in the association came to a head on Bill Womble's watch. (Womble had already helped lead efforts to desegregate the Forsyth County Bar Association in 1963.) After a series of rejections of black applicants to the bar association, the faculty of the Duke University School of Law voted in December 1965 to discontinue support of bar association activities. In a statement to the press shortly thereafter, William F. Womble responded to the faculty at his alma mater: "I agree with the proposition that applications for membership in the North Carolina Bar Association should be considered and voted on without regard to race. On the other hand, I regret that the Duke Law Faculty has seen fit to withdraw its support of our Continuing Legal Education program. . . . I hope that we shall be able to work things out so that the cordial relationship heretofore existing between the North Carolina Bar Association and the Duke Law School may be resumed."

In June 1966, W. F. Womble helped lead the association's effort to remove the whites-only clause from its constitution. Finally, in April 1967, two

Henry E. Frye (second from right) being sworn in as a justice of the North Carolina Supreme Court in 1983 Sixteen years earlier, William F. Womble had helped lead efforts to secure his admission to the North Carolina Bar Association. Frye was one of the first two African-Americans admitted to the North Carolina Bar.

COURTESY OF THE *WINSTON-SALEM CHRONICLE*

African-Americans, Julius L. Chambers and Henry E. Frye, became members of the North Carolina Bar Association, making it the first bar association in the South to admit blacks to membership.

In the mid-1960s, Womble Carlyle continued to be the firm of choice for many of the largest corporations in the area, including longstanding clients such as Wachovia Bank, R. J. Reynolds Tobacco Company, Duke Power, Piedmont Aviation, and Cannon Mills. Major insurance clients included Aetna Life and Casualty and Security Life and Trust Company (later Integon Corporation). An observer described Womble Carlyle as "an excellent general practice firm with a strong corporate full-service environment and strengths in tax, corporate and business advice, and business and commercial litigation." The firm was about to begin a growth spurt in all these practice areas. A fresh generation of lawyers with a variety of backgrounds and experiences would soon arrive to help usher the firm into a new era.

Calder Womble and Wade Gallant handled most of the banking and finance work for the firm, in addition to corporate securities. By the 1960s, Wade Gallant had become the principal attorney for Wachovia Bank and one of the finest securities lawyers in the state. He also served as a director of the Brenner Companies, Inc., of Winston-Salem and of Thomas Built Buses, Inc., of High Point.

On the real estate side, the firm's practice continued to evolve under Leslie Browder's direction. What had begun as a relatively small residential and commercial practice grew with the economy of North Carolina and the western Piedmont. Les Browder's section became sophisticated in commercial and industrial real estate transactions and worked closely with the firm's Corporate Section on mergers and acquisitions when real estate was involved. Commercial site acquisition for financial institutions, textile firms, furniture manufacturers, and other local companies was a major part of the work of the Real-Estate Section. "In real estate practice you take pride in your monuments," Les Browder wrote. "We put together the whole block where the old Wachovia building went, demolished it, and built the Wachovia building on it [in 1965]. I did a lot of the title work on the old Nissen building. And the Belews Lake facility of Duke Power—I bought every square foot of that."

Browder also served as general counsel to Wake Forest University at the same time that his partner, Irving Carlyle, was a trusted adviser and member of the university's Board of Trustees. In this role, Browder was responsible for acquiring property for the university, its Bowman Gray School of Medicine, and North Carolina Baptist Hospital. Beginning in the mid-1960s, Les Browder also became general counsel for Piedmont Federal Savings and Loan, a local institution.

In these years, Pen Sandridge enjoyed a reputation as one of the finest lawyers in the state. He was recognized as an expert in antitrust law, a trusted corporate adviser to companies such as Cannon Mills, and a gentlemanly colleague beloved by the attorneys and staff in his own firm. John Garrou, a young associate at the time, recalled a case in which he and Charles Vance defended the Vulcan Materials Company, a longstanding client of Mr. Sandridge and the firm. The plaintiffs had filed a suit against Vulcan contending that explosions at a Vulcan quarry operation had caused cracks in the plaster of their house. Garrou suggested that the firm set off a small, controlled blast near the house and retain a seismologist to certify the seismograph readings. He recounted Mr. Sandridge's response:

> He said, "Well, you could do that. Or you could do what I did one time when I had a case like this. I went out in front of the house and set up two soft-drink bottles. One was set upright, and the other was put on its top, with the mouth

touching the mouth of the other bottle. I put those soft-drink bottles down there, and then we went and set off a blast, just like the blast that the plaintiff was complaining about. The soft-drink bottle didn't fall over. The jury understood."

Mr. Sandridge said, "I did something else. We went into the courthouse, and I looked around, and I noticed that there were cracks in the plaster of the courtroom. I went back into the Jury Room, and I noticed that there were cracks in the plaster there as well. So when I argued to the jury, I said, 'You know, cracks appear in plaster in houses and dwellings and buildings, and I'll bet when you go back in that Jury Room, if you'll look around, you'll find cracks.' " And he said that the bailiff told him that the first thing those jurors did was start looking around. And he heard them saying, "There's one" and "Look, there's another." He won that case, needless to say.

By 1965, Leon Rice was regarded as one of the finest tax and pension attorneys in the country. The firm's tax practice had almost more work than it could handle. Murray Greason, Jr., recalled the nature and scope of Mr. Rice's practice in those years: "Leon did everything that was tax related, including employee benefits and pension plans, which were driven largely by taxes. He did the estate planning and the estate administration, because death taxes drive a lot of that planning process. He did tax controversy work, contesting with the Internal Revenue Service or the North Carolina Department of Revenue about whether people owed more tax or not. And he did mergers and acquisitions."

Greason, hired by the firm in August 1965, wanted to be in litigation and was willing to learn how to be a courtroom lawyer "by carrying the bag for Irving Carlyle and Grady Barnhill," as he later put it. But before his first day at Womble Carlyle, Leon Rice, Bill Womble, and Grady Barnhill approached him about helping Leon Rice in the Corporate and Tax Section "for a few months to a year" to help relieve Mr. Rice's heavy workload. (Rice was busy advising on public stock offerings to businesses such as Lowe's Companies and Thomasville Furniture Industries.) Though Murray Greason did at first try a few cases with Irving Carlyle and Allan Gitter, he soon settled into a corporate and tax apprenticeship under Leon Rice, who said that Greason "took to tax law like a duck to water."

While Charles F. Vance was primarily involved in

This photo shows Murray C. Greason, Jr., a Wake Forest School of Law student, and his wife, Joan, hanging a picture in their student apartment in 1961. Mr. Greason joined the firm four years later.
Forsyth County Public Library Photograph Collection

labor law, he was, like W. F. Womble, something of a generalist, doing both litigation and transactional work, spending a good deal of time on wills and trusts and other work for Wachovia Bank, the Moravian Church, and Salem College and Academy. In litigation, Mr. Vance represented such clients as Piedmont Publishing Company, Vulcan Materials Company, and the Transcontinental Gas Pipe Line Corporation.

By 1967, the firm had 14 attorneys and was the largest in the state. It was a modern operation on the cusp of the computer age, yet an institution still with something of an old-fashioned feel. Murray Greason remembered the informal nature of the firm at the time:

> Miss Annie Drake was the only staffer we had who was not a full-time secretary, except for Frances Austin, who answered the telephone and sat on the front desk. Miss Annie kept the books. I remember when Price Waterhouse was engaged as our first accounting firm. They were amazed because she used single-entry bookkeeping, and they could not straighten it out, couldn't figure out where she started from. And I remember she had one of these calculating machines that was a couple of feet long and eight to 10 inches wide, with a big crank handle on one side. She would punch numbers into the keyboard, and then she would pull the crank, and it would calculate. She knew what she was doing, and she was good and accurate, but just not in step with PW's modern methods.

One of the watershed events in the firm's history was its handling of the Piedmont Aviation, Inc., litigation between 1968 and 1971. On July 19, 1967, a Piedmont Aviation 727 jet airliner was involved in a midair collision with a Cessna 310 over Hendersonville, North Carolina. All five crew members and 74 passengers on the jet were killed, as were the three occupants of the Cessna.

Piedmont's insurance carrier, Aviation Underwriters, approached H. Grady Barnhill, Jr., about handling the case. Pen Sandridge thought it would be good for the firm to break into a line of work that had previously been dominated by a handful of national defense firms that worked with the aviation insurers.

The case ultimately involved 150 actions, over 130 eyewitnesses, and some 20,000 pages of depositions. Linwood Davis, who was hired by the firm in 1967, assisted throughout. Eddie C. Mitchell, an associate at the time, contributed near the end. And Jimmy Barnhill helped with the settlement discussions. But by and

CARLYLE'S CUSPIDOR

Several stories survive in firm lore about Irving Carlyle and his cuspidor. Mr. Carlyle liked to chew tobacco. When he was going somewhere, he carried a paper cup with him for use as a makeshift spittoon. One time, his secretary, Barbara Sims, went to a baseball game with Irving Carlyle and his wife, Mary Belo. Mrs. Carlyle insisted that Sims sit beside Mr. Carlyle. At first, she wondered why. But when she looked down and saw her tobacco-spattered ankles, she understood.

Mr. Carlyle kept a cuspidor in his office for many years in the old Wachovia Building, but at some point, Robert Hanes, president of Wachovia Bank, decided to ban all cuspidors from the building. Right after the firm moved into the new Wachovia Building in 1966, Mr. Carlyle brought his back. From all the way down the hall, visitors to the firm's 24th-floor offices could clearly see the cuspidor at Mr. Carlyle's right side in his corner office, if the door was open. Soon after the move, Mr. B. S. Womble appeared at Mr. Carlyle's door and in his deep, resonant voice said, "Irving, do you think you could put it over on the other side of the desk?" To which Mr. Carlyle immediately replied, "I'm sorry, Mr. Womble, but I just don't spit left-handed."

The crash of a Piedmont Airlines jet near Hendersonville, North Carolina, on July 19, 1967, led to the firm's involvement in major aviation litigation. Eighty-two people lost their lives in the crash.
AP/WIDE WORLD PHOTOS

large, the success of the case was due to the indefatigable efforts of Grady Barnhill, with sage advice from Pen Sandridge.

Linwood Davis recalled the case: "Starting out, there was always the question out there of whether we could stay on the field with the big boys. But it wasn't too long before the big guys recognized Grady Barnhill as their equal or better. He ran circles around most of them—really, all of them. They developed an enormous respect for Grady and, as a result, for our firm."

This multiparty, multistate litigation brought Womble Carlyle to the forefront among North Carolina law firms involved with aircraft insurance carriers. For the first time in American aviation history, all cases arising out of a major air crash were settled simultaneously. As a result of the Piedmont case, the firm became North Carolina counsel for the major national aircraft insurance carriers and began to handle an increasing volume of aircraft and product-liability litigation. More importantly, the case put Womble Carlyle in the "major league" of litigation with the large New York and Washington law firms, a strength that the firm would build upon in the years to come.

In Grady Barnhill's absence, Allan Gitter picked up most of his cases, quickly learning how to effectively manage a very large volume of insurance defense cases. In those years, he came into his own as a first-rate litigator and began a long tradition of training the firm's new associates in litigation as they came along.

The period from the mid-1960s to the mid-1970s saw a mushrooming of litigation for the firm. Besides the Piedmont case, the firm began to represent—at the urging of Allan Gitter—the statewide caseload of the North Carolina League of Municipalities and, later, the North Carolina County Commissioners Association.

The growth in litigation and in corporate practice required a steadily increasing stream of new associates. The firm's class of 1965 included an associate for the Corporate Section, E. Lawrence Davis. A graduate of Princeton University and the Duke University School of Law, Davis came with the firm after two years of active duty as a captain in the United States Army. Davis had grown up in Winston-Salem, the town to which his grandfather Egbert Davis, a top salesman for R. J. Reynolds Tobacco Company, had come from Yadkin County. As a young associate, Davis helped represent municipalities such as the town of Kernersville and corporate clients such as Piedmont Aviation. Lawrence Davis served two terms in the North Carolina House of Representatives before being elected to the first of two consecutive terms in the State Senate in 1974. Through his work in Raleigh, he became involved in state governmental relations matters for clients such as Vulcan Materials and the Goodyear Tire and Rubber Company.

David A. Irvin, a graduate of Davidson College and the University of North Carolina School of Law, joined the firm in September 1966. Like most junior associates, he did some defense work under Allan Gitter and Grady Barnhill for several years. He then moved to the Labor Section with Pen Sandridge, Sr., and Charles Vance, where he represented clients such as the Chatham Manufacturing Company and Cannon Mills before the National Labor Relations Board. Into the 1970s, Irvin helped defend longtime clients such as R. J. Reynolds, Wachovia, and Integon in class-action suits brought under Title VII of the Civil Rights Act of 1964.

Lawrence Davis's brother, Linwood L. Davis, also a graduate of Princeton University and the Duke University School of Law, came with Womble Carlyle in September 1967. While interested in corporate and tax practice, he also wanted to gain some litigation experience, and so was introduced to Grady Barnhill, who, as Linwood Davis put it, "made me the lead briefcase carrier on the Piedmont case for three years." After the Piedmont case was settled, Linwood Davis returned to the business side, where he apprenticed under Leon Rice and Murray Greason.

William A. Davis II, a native of High Point and a graduate of the University of North Carolina and the Duke University School of Law, came with the firm in July 1968. He apprenticed under Leon Rice, doing mostly tax and estate planning and "controversy work," contending with the Internal Revenue Service and the North Carolina Department of Revenue. The core of the Tax Section's clients in those years included textile firms such as Chatham Manufacturing, furniture companies such as Broyhill Industries, and financial institutions such as Wachovia Bank.

Kenneth A. Moser, a graduate of Wake Forest and its School of Law, joined Womble Carlyle in September 1968 to help pick up some of the workload caused by the Piedmont litigation. Like most young corporate associates, he worked on projects for every partner in the firm. Due to the firm's needs at the time, he ended up doing trust and estate work and a wide variety of litigation for the next six years.

John L. W. Garrou, a graduate of Princeton University and the University of North Carolina School of Law, came with the firm in September 1967. During the late 1960s and early 1970s, he assisted W. F. Womble in a number of school desegregation cases in the federal courts on behalf of the Winston-Salem/Forsyth County Board of Education. But after a few years, he moved into the firm's Corporate and Tax Section.

Jimmy H. Barnhill, who had clerked with Womble Carlyle in the summer of 1962, was hired in October 1968 to help shoulder the backlog in the Litigation Section caused by his brother Grady's involvement in the Piedmont Aviation case. "For three or four years,

Allan Gitter, Dave Irvin, and I were working just to keep our heads above water, trying Allan's backlog of cases and then Grady's work on top of that," Jimmy Barnhill recalled. "Just as soon as we got through with court one week, we started on the next week's cases."

Zeb E. Barnhardt, Jr., came with the firm in 1969, also as an associate in litigation. He worked with William F. Womble on city matters, among other things.

The year 1974 saw the downfall of a fellow student of Leon Rice's at the Duke University School of Law—Richard M. Nixon, who resigned as president of the United States on August 9. In 1936, young Rice, a senior, had approached Nixon, class of 1937, about running for president of the Duke Bar Association. Nixon agreed. Rice went on to manage his campaign, and Nixon won his first election. Years later at a Duke alumni banquet, Nixon, then vice president, told the audience that "Pinky" Rice had been his first campaign manager. "For a long time, I was proud of that," Rice noted. "But when Watergate came, I never was so disappointed in anybody as I was in him. He sold out to politics, as I see it."

Another important development for the firm was the signing of its first Partnership Agreement. Drafted in 1968 by Leon L. Rice, Jr., the document—which became effective on January 1, 1969—was the first formal written document on the sharing of income in the firm's history, such matters before that time having been based on tradition, mutual understanding, and trust. The new agreement related largely to the management of the firm, the sharing of net income, and the retirement of partners. The Partnership Agreement also created a Partnership Management Committee to manage the firm and the practice. The committee was composed of the five partners senior in service with the firm who were under the age of 65.

Within the firm, Leon Rice was known as "the Master of the Red Pen" for his insistence on proper English usage and excellence in all communications that went out under the firm's signature. Two generations of Womble Carlyle attorneys have vivid memories of how Mr. Rice would "bleed on the page" of any document presented to him. One of his understudies, Linwood Davis, recalled the Rice method: "You had to have it right. You had to have the facts right. You had to have the law right. You had to have the analysis right. You had to have the conclusions right. And you had to express it correctly, succinctly, and in a well-organized fashion. It was wonderful training. And once you were 'Leonized,' it became part of your approach to things—to meet the client's needs with the most professional product, and the product that conveys the message in the most meaningful way."

Mr. Rice had suggested that the firm should drop the commas from its name. In 1983, the partners agreed. About that time, the members also decided to adopt Womble Carlyle Sandridge & Rice as the "brand name" of the firm, rather than having to periodically reconsider changing the name with the comings and goings of partners.

As the 1970s began, Womble Carlyle continued to hire associates at a rapid pace. But in 1971, the firm made the decision to bring in a lateral attorney. Roddey M. Ligon, Jr., one of the state's top experts in governmental law, came with the firm after stints as attorney for Forsyth County and Forsyth Memorial Hospital and 13 years as a professor of law and government at the Institute of Government of the University of North Carolina. At the university, he had specialized in medicolegal matters and problems of county government, public welfare, public health, and domestic relations. Ligon had gotten to know W. F. Womble while doing the county's legal business, and it was Womble who extended an invitation to join the firm. "Irving Carlyle and Bill Womble had done an excellent job representing the city of Winston-Salem and other governmental entities,"

Mr. Ligon remarked in an interview. "So when I came along, I just stood on their shoulders."

When William F. Womble's son, William F. Womble, Jr., joined the firm in January of the same year, it marked the third generation of the family at Womble Carlyle. Like his father, uncle, and grandfather before him, he had studied at Duke University, earning his J.D. in 1967. However, his entry into the practice was delayed by the Vietnam War, in which he served as a lieutenant in the United States Navy from 1967 to 1971. He started trying cases with Allan Gitter right away and by 1974 was defending clients regularly before juries throughout northwest North Carolina. During one week, he successfully defended three cases in jury trials back to back. He worked with Grady Barnhill in aviation litigation, principally for Cessna Aircraft, then took on a broad range of product liability defense work.

Donald F. Donadio, a Wake Forest graduate, joined the firm in 1972 after nearly five years in the army's Judge Advocate General Corps in West Germany. He did a little bit of everything at first—real estate work, litigation for the city, some corporate work—before settling into a corporate finance apprenticeship under Calder Womble and Wade Gallant.

W. Andrew Copenhaver also came with the firm in 1972, out of the University of North Carolina School of Law. He began in business litigation under Charlie Vance and Pen Sandridge and soon moved into handling employment discrimination cases and class-action suits, working closely with Dave Irvin.

Dennis W. McNames, a graduate of the University of North Carolina and the Wake Forest University School of Law, came with the firm in 1973 to work with Les Browder in real estate matters.

Elizabeth L. Quick and Robert Quick were the first married couple hired by Womble Carlyle. They came as part of the 1974 class of associates out of the University of North Carolina School of Law. Elizabeth Quick began work in estate planning and administration, a relatively new specialty for the firm at the time. She worked with attorneys such as W. F. Womble, Charles Vance, Pen Sandridge, and especially her chief mentor, Leon Rice. In an interview, Betty Quick recalled another aspect of the "Rice method":

> Leon Rice had a great talent with words—wordsmithing was an art with him. But he also taught good habits, which is also a mark of a great teacher. I can remember one time that I wrote a memo or a letter or something and cited a section of the Internal Revenue Code, and I thought that I knew what I was talking about. Well, after Mr. Rice read it, he led me into his office and said, "Did you go back and look at that particular section of the code?" And I acknowledged that I had not. He opened the volume with that section in it and said, "Always, always, when you cite a section of the Internal Revenue Code or any authority, don't rely on your memory. Go back and look at it and read it again." That's a wonderful piece of advice that I have passed on to many young lawyers.

There was concern among some of the partners as to whether women could handle the workload and how clients would react to "real smart young ladies,"

> *"He imbued me with the traditions of this firm of high quality work, exemplary ethics, common sense, sound judgment, fair dealings, preciseness in the use of the King's English, community (including church and charity) service, bar association involvement, and so on."*
>
> Leon L. Rice, Jr., on B. S. Womble

as one attorney called them. And there was some apprehension about how women would fit in, both among the "old boys club" of attorneys and the predominantly female staff. But those concerns and fears quickly faded. "Lawyers are lawyers, and in this firm, they respect each other for that. She soon was treated just like anybody else," Pat Kight, a longtime staff member, remembered of Betty Quick.

Also in 1974, William C. Raper, a University of North Carolina undergraduate and Vanderbilt University School of Law graduate, came with the firm. Bill Raper had clerked for Judge J. Braxton Craven, Jr., on the United States Court of Appeals for the Fourth Circuit and had worked for Sam Ervin, Jr., on the United States Senate Subcommittee on Constitutional Rights. Upon joining Womble Carlyle, he started trial work under Allan Gitter—"a trial a week, sometimes two," he recalled—and then with Grady Barnhill.

Keith W. Vaughan and W. G. Champion Mitchell came with the firm at the same time in August 1975. Vaughan, a Wake Forest undergraduate and University of Georgia School of Law alumnus, began almost immediately doing trial work with Allan Gitter, Grady Barnhill, Bill Raper, Jimmy Barnhill, and Pen Sandridge. Champ Mitchell, a Raleigh native and North Carolina graduate, joined the Corporate Section.

Womble Carlyle Sandridge & Rice was involved in a number of important and memorable cases in the decade following the move to the new Wachovia Building in 1966.

In *Swann v. Charlotte-Mecklenburg School Board* (1971), the landmark United States Supreme Court case that authorized busing as a means of achieving racial balance in the public schools, William F. Womble filed an amicus brief on behalf of the firm's client, the Winston-Salem/Forsyth County Board of Education.

In 1968, Mr. Sandridge and W. F. Womble prepared a brief for the United States Supreme Court on behalf of the Carolina Container Corporation. In *United States v. Container Corporation of America* (1969), the high court ruled that the corrugated container industry had engaged in a pattern of price fixing, thus violating the provisions of the Sherman Antitrust Act.

The firm was also involved in the famous Winston-Salem National Guard Armory case. On September 27, 1969, an explosion in the supply room of the armory killed three men and severely burned four others. Civil suits were brought against the city alleging that the injuries and deaths resulted from the city's negligent operation of a sanitary landfill on property belonging to the armory. In an important ruling on the scope of governmental immunity, the North Carolina Supreme Court ruled in 1972 in *Koontz v. City of Winston-Salem* that the city was "exercising powers voluntarily assumed for its own corporate benefit . . . and receiving revenues over and beyond incidental income," thus excluding it from protection under the legislature's grant of governmental immunity.

Irving Edward Carlyle died at his desk in his home on Saturday, June 5, 1971. Though officially semiretired after several years of heart problems, he had in recent months stepped forward to co-chair the newly formed North Carolina Committee to End the War in Indochina. Ever interested in education, he was also putting the final touches on an address he was to deliver the next week before the legislature's Joint Commission on Higher Education, which was considering a proposal to break up the state's university system. In a draft of his speech, Mr. Carlyle wrote, "To dismantle and deconsolidate the Consolidated University would be a terrible mistake."

Thousands packed Wait Chapel at Wake Forest University for the funeral services of Irving Carlyle, class of 1917, just hours after the members of the class of 1971 had received their diplomas on the lawn outside. The *Winston-Salem Journal* eulogized him with these words:

He was the happiest warrior of them all. Show him a shining cause that was friendless, show him a victim of injustice who stood alone, and Irving Carlyle girded himself for the battle.

He fought best, perhaps, for causes that were hopeless, and almost as much for the fun of battle as for the winning. And when it was over, he bore no grudges.

His beliefs were simple and unshakeable. North Carolina is the fairest state under heaven. Tar Heels are the noblest breed of men (though sometimes a bit ornery). The University at Chapel Hill is the proudest jewel in the state's diadem. Anglo-Saxon law and the United States Constitution are the most soaring creations of the human mind and spirit. And the Democratic Party is the first and last best hope for all Americans.

He loved the law. It was his career but it was also his passion. He was not one of those latter-day law-and-order men who say, "This law is for me and that law is for thee." The law must be the same for everyone—rich man, poor man, beggar man, thief . . . and black man, too. For that equal-justice-to-all kind of law he was prepared to sacrifice anything. . . .

Perhaps, then, of all the Tar Heels born and bred he was the most deserving to stand beside Tennyson's perfect knight, for certainly his code was the same: "Live pure, speak true, right wrong, follow the King—Else, wherefore born?"

"Perhaps, then, of all the Tar Heels born and bred he was the most deserving to stand beside Tennyson's perfect knight, for certainly his code was the same: 'Live pure, speak true, right wrong, follow the King—Else, wherefore born?' " These words were spoken during a tribute to Irving Carlyle in 1971.

FORSYTH COUNTY PUBLIC LIBRARY PHOTOGRAPH COLLECTION

In the American bicentennial year, the firm was witness to several endings just as the third century of the nation's independence was beginning.

On June 1, 1976, Roddey M. Ligon, Jr., argued a motion before Judge Hiram H. Ward in the federal courtroom in the United States Post Office Building in Winston-Salem. It would be the last matter ever heard in that beautiful and historic courtroom before the move of the District Court to the city's new Federal Building.

Just two weeks earlier, on May 17, 1976, the firm's senior member, Bunyan Snipes Womble, had died at the age of 94 in his 70th year as an attorney at law. In the 65 years since he joined the firm, it had grown from three lawyers to 36. Even into his 90s, he had continued to come downtown to the firm's offices occasionally and to attend meetings of the Rotary Club.

In a resolution of appreciation, his fellow Rotarians marked his passing with these words:

> We record with deep sorrow the death of B. S. Womble on May 17, 1976, at the ripe age of ninety-four years. Our friend and brother Rotarian was among those who founded Rotary, the first service club in Winston-Salem, in October 1915. He was the last survivor of our charter members and the oldest member of this club. . . .
>
> It is interesting to recall that he commenced practice as a solo practitioner with his office on the east side of the Court House Square and, as time passed, moved to the north side, the west side and the south side, and back again to the east side in the new Wachovia Building. For many years and at the time of his death he was one of the most distinguished lawyers in our state and the senior partner in one of the oldest law firms in the state. Those who knew him professionally, either as associates in the practice of law, fellow lawyers or clients, knew him as an exceptionally able lawyer, loyal and tenacious in the protection of the interests of those he served. Mr. Womble embraced in full measure the legal principle that, "No privilege exists that is not inseparably bound to duty."
>
> Throughout his life he remained resolutely committed to his principles. He had high character, firm convictions, and absolute integrity, all combined with a quiet and unassuming manner. In short, he was a Christian gentleman.

"No privilege exists that is not inseparably bound to duty."

B. S. Womble

Winston-Salem celebrated the American bicentennial on July 4, 1976, with picnics, games, and concert music.
FORSYTH COUNTY PUBLIC LIBRARY PHOTOGRAPH COLLECTION

WOMBLE, CARLYLE, SANDRIDGE & RICE

ATTORNEYS AND COUNSELORS AT LAW

WINSTON-SALEM, NORTH CAROLINA

PLANNING FOR THE FUTURE *1976 – 1982*

> *"When I was hired in 1979, we had 50 lawyers—all in Winston-Salem, all on two floors of the old Wachovia Building. Wachovia was gracious enough to let us eat lunch in their cafeteria each day. And that was the best communication tool that the firm has ever had, and I miss it to this day. They had round dining tables that would seat 10 people, and you would have a mix of lawyers seated together. You would hear what's going on here and what's going on there, so you had a really good feel of everything that was happening in the firm. And it kept everybody kind of pulling together on the same team."*
>
> Hassel L. Parker

The growth rate of Womble Carlyle accelerated in the 1970s. Law-school enrollments burgeoned throughout the decade. This increase in law-school students and admissions to the bar made available a large crop of would-be attorneys just as the firm's corporate and litigation workloads were rapidly increasing for a host of local, regional, and national clients. From just two associates in 1965—W. Pendleton Sandridge, Jr., and Allan R. Gitter—the firm counted 13 by early 1976.

In the 1970s, specialization increased in the legal profession, and Womble Carlyle was not immune from the trend. Attorneys in the Corporate and Tax Section were now focusing their practices in estate planning, securities, and mergers and acquisitions, rather than serving as the jack-of-all-trades generalists of old. The firm's litigators were concentrating, too, in areas such as aviation, antitrust, and employment discrimination. By the early 1980s, Leon Rice joked with his successors in the Corporate and Tax Section that "it now takes

20 lawyers to do what I did *alone* up to about 20 years ago."

Just as the Civil Rights Act of 1964 had affected the firm's governmental clients during the previous decade, subsequent civil-rights laws such as Title IX and the Age Discrimination in Employment Act brought new business to the firm in the 1970s. Also, the passage by Congress in 1974 of ERISA—the Employee Retirement Income Security Act—changed the firm's pension practice dramatically. The crafting of corporate pension plans had once been something of a cottage industry for the trio of the firm, Wachovia Bank and Trust Company, and Booke and Company. Now, such work was codified in a single, standardized set of rules governing all benefit plans nationwide.

William A. Davis recalled the day when a copy of the newly enacted ERISA law arrived at the firm's offices: "Leon Rice took one look at those 300-odd pages of statute, and he looked at me and said, 'You know, I'm not going to do this.' Now, I'm not the smartest person in the world, but I knew that I was supposed to say, 'Well, I'll do it.' So I became an employee-benefits lawyer for a while and did almost all my practice there." Joining Bill Davis in employee benefits in January 1974 was Michael D. Gunter, a graduate of Wake Forest and the University of North Carolina School of Law. Mike came with the firm after completing an M.B.A. at the Wharton School of Finance at the University of Pennsylvania.

By 1976, Womble Carlyle had 21 partners and 13 associates. It remained the largest law firm in North Carolina, and one with an enviable list of clients. The firm continued as general counsel for Wachovia Bank and Trust, Chatham Manufacturing Company, the city of Winston-Salem, Hanes Dye and Finishing Company, Thomasville Furniture Industries, and Piedmont Publishing Company. In recent years, it had also become general counsel for companies such as Wachovia Realty Investments, Wachovia Mortgage Company, Thomas Built Buses, Brenner Industries, and Brad Ragan, Inc. New clients added in the last decade included Associated Aviation Underwriters, Fairchild-Hiller Corporation, Piedmont Natural Gas Company, the Joseph Schlitz Brewing Company, and the Ford Motor Company.

By the summer of 1976, William P. Sandridge, Leon L. Rice, Jr., and William F. Womble were the firm's senior partners, B. S. Womble having died in May of that year. William F. Womble, who had been the managing partner since his father ceased his active practice, had stepped aside in 1974 so that Leon Rice could head the Partnership Management Committee. Mr. Rice completed his term as PMC chair in December 1977, when W. F. Womble resumed the chair. Rice continued to attend meetings at the committee's request. Also serving on the PMC at that time were Calder W. Womble, Charles F. Vance, Jr., Wade M. Gallant, and H. Grady Barnhill, Jr.

William F. Womble remained a highly valued business counselor in the community and continued to try cases, including several antitrust suits in the late 1970s. Calder Womble maintained his close relationship with Wachovia Bank (as did Ken Moser and Bill Davis) and assisted Piedmont Aviation with financing and lease arrangements for the company's fleet of aircraft. Don Donadio, who was developing a practice as one of the state's first bond attorneys, remembered the key roles that Bill and Calder Womble played in his career:

> I think that Bill Womble was an important mentor, in his care and attention to detail, in his very careful drafting, in just the little things that he'd tell you about—things that you'd think were generalities at the time, but as you'd look back on them, you would see that they were very worthwhile things that he was saying.
>
> The other person who probably had the strongest influence on the way that I prefer to practice

law is Calder Womble. At the time that I joined the firm, Calder was the nearest thing to a businessman lawyer that we had. Calder understood business, and he also had just a superb understanding of human nature. He would always approach negotiations with an understanding of what motivated people to reach a certain result. And probably the thing that he impressed me with the most was just the understanding that you should never expect the other side to act in a way that is contrary to its own interests. Now, that is so obvious, but it is so often missed when you go into negotiations. All of my mentors in the firm were never anything other than very genuine, honest people. They had a tremendous sense of who they were, and were just terrific people to pattern your life after.

Leon Rice, who turned 65 in 1977, maintained his busy tax practice, barely slowing down at all. One partner recalled that he regularly recorded 1,600 or 1,700 billable hours a year even in the late 1970s. Still, he always made time for others and was unfailingly courteous. Pat Kight, who worked for him on occasion, remembered that every day, without fail, he would say, "Thank you for your good work today."

Pen Sandridge continued to advise business clients and worked on some significant antitrust and employment discrimination cases. "He may have been the most personable of all the senior partners, and was just a lot of fun to work with," Murray Greason remembered.

Bill Raper, a midlevel litigation associate at the time, recalled Sandridge's gentlemanly ways and matchless skill at sizing up a problem and finding a solution:

Pen's door was always open. Sometimes, I would get overwhelmed about how to handle a case. And I'd go in there and say, "Mr. Sandridge, you got a minute?" He never said no. I don't care what he was doing, he would say, "Sure, Bill. Come sit down." So I'd sit down and say, "Okay, here's the situation." And I'd talk for 20 minutes. And he'd just listen and listen and listen. And after I'd finished, he'd look at me, smile, and say, "Well, that's an interesting situation. Have you thought about maybe doing this?" And I'd sit there and say to myself, "Oh, that just about solves everything." He had an incredible ability to sit back, listen to a complicated situation, and distill it down to a workable plan. He was a true gentleman and superb at what he did.

Charles Vance handled a variety of litigation matters, including employment discrimination, antitrust, labor, and First Amendment cases. He served as a mentor for young associates such as Andy Copenhaver. Bill Raper, who had been recruited by Mr. Vance, said, "He was a true gentleman, smart as a whip. Soft-spoken in person but tough in the courtroom. Just a wonderful fellow."

The period from the mid-1970s to the early 1980s saw a boom in Womble Carlyle's litigation practice. Grady Barnhill, who headed the firm's Litigation Section, handled several high-profile medical and legal malpractice cases, as well as a number of wrongful death and personal-injury cases.

An important case for Grady Barnhill and the firm involved the defense of Eastern Air Lines, Inc., in an appeal of damages awarded to the victims of a crash of an Eastern Air Lines jet near Charlotte, North Carolina, on September 11, 1974. The crash resulted in the deaths of 69 passengers and two crew members and serious injuries to nine passengers and two crew members. Bill Raper argued the case of *Arnold v. Eastern Air Lines*. Grady Barnhill was on the brief. Senator Sam Ervin also was "of counsel" on the appellate briefs, at the request of Bill Raper.

Cavelle Lund, longtime secretary for Grady

Leon L. Rice, Jr., served as managing partner of the firm from 1974 to 1977.
WOMBLE CARLYLE COLLECTION

William Pendleton Sandridge, 1904–1982
WOMBLE CARLYLE COLLECTION

Barnhill, remembered a trial from the 1970s in which her boss demonstrated his trademark courtroom style:

> One morning, he called me from the courthouse—he was trying a case, and it was in the second day, I think—and he said, "Cavelle, my wife is going to come by and hand you a paper bag. You bring that bag down to me at the courthouse as fast as you can go. Run, 'cause they're getting ready to start court." And I said okay. So I go down to the front of the building, and Mrs. Barnhill comes by and hands me the bag, and I ran down to the courthouse. When I got into the courtroom, the jury had just come in. They were sitting, watching everything that was going on, but proceedings hadn't started yet.
>
> Grady was sitting at the counsel's table in a brown suit, and I handed him the bag. He took out a brown sock. Then he leaned over and took off his shoe and put his foot up on the table, took off his green sock, and put on the brown sock. Then he looked over at the jury and just grinned, and they just ate it up.
>
> He really could play to the juries, and they all loved him because he had a funny sense of humor and was just brilliant.

The inimitable H. Grady Barnhill, Jr., dean of the firm's litigators

Photograph by G. Allen Aycock

Thirty-four lawyers strong at the beginning of the nation's bicentennial year, Womble Carlyle continued to hire attorneys to meet the needs of a growing and increasingly sophisticated practice. New associates were added at a rapid rate as the firm began to consider and accept applicants with a greater variety of backgrounds and educational experiences. Seventeen associates were added between 1976 and 1981, including Leon Rice's son, Richard T. Rice, in 1977; Garza Baldwin III, Michael E. Ray, and George A. Ragland in 1978; S. Fraley Bost, Anthony H. Brett, and Keith A. Clinard in 1979; and Hada V. Haulsee and Stephen A. Yeagy in 1981.

The increase in large corporate litigation also required additional experienced attorneys. In 1978, the firm hired a seasoned trial attorney from a Greensboro law firm, Daniel W. Donahue, who was involved in substantial product-liability cases for clients such as the Ford Motor Company. Such was the volume of product-liability cases that the firm established the position of special investigator.

In 1980, the firm represented the estate of Edwin Duncan, Sr., founder of Northwestern Bank, in a dispute over the trust under the will of David Crockett Duncan, father of Edwin Duncan. By the terms of the will, Edwin Duncan received the net income of the trust during his lifetime. Upon his death, the trust was to be continued for the benefit of Edwin's children and grandchildren, and was ultimately to be distributed to descendants farther down the line. The Internal Revenue Service contended that the trust violated "the Rule Against Perpetuities." If correct, this meant that the trust assets belonged outright to Edwin from the time of inception of the trust and remained his property until his death. Several hundred thousand dollars of real-estate taxes and possibly gift taxes were riding on this issue, the determination of which was a matter of state law.

Although the Wilkes County Superior Court upheld the validity of the trust, finding that the Rule Against Perpetuities had not been violated, the firm still needed a decision from the state's highest court in order for the decision to be binding for federal income-tax purposes. Leon Rice petitioned the North Carolina Supreme Court for certiorari, and the writ was granted by the court.

It was decided that retired senator Sam J. Ervin, Jr., a former North Carolina Supreme Court justice, should be brought in as co-counsel on the case. Pen Sandridge also contributed many hours. The night before oral arguments were to be heard, Senator Ervin joined Leon Rice and Elizabeth Quick for dinner to discuss their different arguments. It was decided that the senator would lead off, with Quick to follow.

Betty Quick recalled the way Senator Ervin began oral argument before the justices: "I remember so well that one of the first things the senator said was, 'Now, you know that I tend to talk too long. I want to make sure that you cut me off, that I don't go on too long, because I want to make sure that you hear from this pretty little lady.' Of course, all eyes in the courtroom turned to me, and I must have blushed 50 shades of red. But needless to say, the court did not cut him off. They gave him all the time he needed, and they gave me the time that I needed as well."

"Senator Sam was superb," Leon Rice wrote, "and he predicted after the argument that we would win." The senator surmised that the courts did not like the Rule Against Perpetuities and would go to great ends to keep it from being used to frustrate the intent of the creator of a trust. He was right. In *Joyner v. Duncan*, the North Carolina Supreme Court upheld the David Crockett Duncan trust in its entirety.

Sometime later, a University of North Carolina law professor commented that, while the law wasn't necessarily on the side of the firm in this case, *Joyner v. Duncan* was an example of "good lawyering at its best."

Betty Quick played a part in one of two "firsts" registered by Womble Carlyle around the turn of the century's ninth decade. In 1981, Elizabeth L. Quick

Former United States senator Samuel J. Ervin, Jr., worked as co-counsel with the firm on several high-profile cases after leaving Congress.

THE NORTH CAROLINA BAR FOUNDATION

became one of the first female partners in a major North Carolina law firm. Two years earlier, in 1979, the firm had hired the first African-American lawyer to join it or any other large North Carolina firm, Anthony H. "Tony" Brett. Tony began working under Roddey M. Ligon, Jr., on hospital-law and municipal-law matters and assisted W. G. Champion Mitchell on antitrust cases.

In his memoir, *Living, Loving and Lawyering*, Leon Rice noted the rapid changes in office staffing, technology, and procedures: "In the 1970s paralegals were brought in as part of the effort to relieve the workload and keep down client charges. Computers helped speed record-keeping and word processing, grinding out the expanding and never-ending words, words, words, that characterize the law practice of today. Photocopiers produced reams upon reams of paper, a far cry from the old system of carbon copies and Thermofax. To the regret of many of our older heads, running a law office became big business and conducting a law practice a complex and multi-faceted endeavor."

Anita Brannan, who came with the firm in 1972 as assistant office manager, assumed the role of office manager in 1976. She was responsible for human resources and facilities. Working with the Partnership Management Committee, she helped draft the firm's first budget in the 1970s, began the first time and billing systems, produced the first office manual, and helped select and implement the first computer system.

Womble Carlyle hired its first paralegals in 1975. One of them, Marie Rodden, remembered that initially the firm "didn't really know what a paralegal could do, what their training was. But Allan Gitter started giving me a little work, and it just kind of developed from there." There was a period of adjustment for both parties. The paralegals had quite a bit to learn about the way the firm did things, and the legal secretaries had to gain confidence in the paralegals' skills. Many of the legal secretaries had grown accustomed to doing just the kind of work now being assigned to the paralegals.

"As we began to get more and more paralegals, we realized that they were really helping lighten the secretaries' load, because the secretaries didn't have to stop what they were doing and go over to the courthouse for something," Claudia Lyda observed. "Or when we would have closings, the paralegals were responsible for getting all the signed documents together and seeing that everyone got copies of the proper documents."

Beth Keiger, hired as a legal secretary in 1977, remembered how the firm was like a small, close-knit family: "We worked hard and generally did what was needed to get the job done. Everybody pitched in. Back then, we knew what each other was doing, so it was easier to help. We used to be up and down the halls a lot more, talking about what we were doing. I miss the sound of the electric typewriters typing away, be-

Womble Carlyle's staff has long been recognized as the foundation for the firm's success. Pictured in this photo from the early 1980s are Mary Emmons, Sandra Macemore, Peggy Boyer, Pat Kight, Joyce Cobb, Claudia Lyda, and Betty Stephenson. They represent 165 years of service with the firm, as of 2001.

THE WINSTON-SALEM TRANSIT AUTHORITY

cause it was like energy—*Ta-ta-ta, ta-ta-ta-ta-ta-ta. DING.* You really felt the flow of the office, the pulse of the place."

Womble Carlyle Sandridge & Rice made a strategic decision to invest in technology in a substantial way starting in the mid-1970s. While the firm had traditionally acquired the latest innovations in office technology—which in the mid-1970s consisted of the MTST automatic typewriter and the "Mag Card" word processor—it decided by 1976 to install the Comptek Barrister 300 System, a minicomputer running a proprietary legal word-processing and accounting software package. The firm established a centralized Word Processing Center and gradually installed more Barrister terminals around the office. It continued to expand and update the Barrister system until the mid-1980s, when the personal computer brought affordably priced computing power to every desktop.

At a partners' retreat in Roaring Gap, North Carolina, in June 1979, the firm took a long, hard look at itself and its prospects. While Winston-Salem was in the most industrialized part of North Carolina, it was neither the largest city in the state nor the fastest growing. For some time, the firm had looked to out-of-town referrals for a significant share of its business. Some of the firm's largest clients were becoming interested in statewide representation, a kind of one-stop shopping for legal services. William F. Womble recalled the times: "In the 1970s, you could see a trend of big firms from other parts of the country spreading and becoming regional or even national firms in their reach, with a tendency to swallow up smaller firms in the effort to become even bigger. And it became apparent that we either needed to grow our own firm or be absorbed by another firm, because if we didn't do one or the other, we would lose out. We preferred to grow our own firm."

Management consultants from Price Waterhouse advised the firm to carefully consider expansion into other markets. The consultants brought in for the partners' retreat made another recommendation—namely, that the firm hire a professional administrator. Other large law firms around the country were beginning to move in that direction.

A Firm Study Committee, chaired by Roddey M. Ligon, Jr., began the firm's first efforts at long-range planning. A Growth Study Committee, chaired by Calder Womble, began to examine the possibilities of expanding into other markets. The partners also decided that the firm had reached such a size that it needed to be run more professionally. No longer did a partner have the time to handle administrative matters and practice law at the same time. Like other large law firms, Womble Carlyle realized that it needed a capable professional manager to handle the day-to-day running of the firm's administrative matters.

The partners appointed a Law Office Administrator Committee, chaired by Pen Sandridge, Jr., to develop a job description and conduct a search for a firm administrator. One candidate, Colonel Hassel L. Parker, an army intelligence officer with extensive command and staff experience in human resources, budget and finance, and computer systems, quickly rose to the top of the list. Mr. Parker recalled how his job specifications coincided with those of Womble Carlyle:

> I had decided to retire from the army, and so I started looking around to find something that would let me build on the skills that I had developed in the military. Law firms had just started to grow to a size large enough to need some professional management, and I thought that this would be an interesting and exciting second career. I happened to have sent a letter to Womble Carlyle telling them of my interests at the very time that they had decided to add someone.
>
> Once I started interviewing, and the more I talked with people who had been in law firms, the

Loyal staff members salute Colonel Hass Parker on the occasion of a special birthday in the late 1980s. Shown left to right are Don Adamick, Pat Kight, Anita Brannan, Jean Anglin, and Terry Wiley.

WOMBLE CARLYLE COLLECTION

more I realized the cultural differences. I interviewed with a pretty sizable firm in Birmingham, and one of the senior partners asked me, "What value could you bring to our firm?" I said, "Well, I think I know quite a bit about technology and computers, and it seems to me that we need to increase efficiencies in law firms." And he said, "We really don't need computers in law firms." In other interviews, the only thing that the interviewer wanted to talk about was the size of the partners' offices and the politics of keeping everybody satisfied. So then when I talked to a firm that was really focused on client service, teamwork, and adding value, and treating people with respect and dignity, the choice became very, very clear.

From the beginning, the firm was receptive to Parker's suggestions and followed through on its decision to delegate administrative authority to a nonlawyer. Some staff members initially had concerns about bringing in an outside administrator. The anomalous position of the administrator—a member of the staff but also of the management team—took time to resolve. But each side was patient with the other, and differences were worked through. Murray Greason, who as managing partner worked with Mr. Parker on a daily basis for nine years, observed, "Hiring Hass Parker was one of the smartest things we ever did. Not just hiring him, but making a conscious decision that he was going to be a heavyweight executive, not an order-taker and an inventory manager. We gave him the responsibility, and he took it and ran with it. It got a lot of the operational stuff off the desks of lawyers, where it would languish. It simply wouldn't get done because we would always respond to the client rather than internal matters."

A firm retreat at the Tanglewood Manor House near Winston-Salem in May 1980 focused largely on issues related to growth. The Firm Study Committee reported that a survey of the partners—conducted by Lesley Powell, a young paralegal at the time—indicated that a substantial volume of client matters could be better handled by offices in Raleigh and Charlotte. The committee recommended that the firm focus on one city—Raleigh—at the outset. After deliberations, the partners established a special committee to investigate the feasibility of opening an office in Raleigh and to make recommendations on the best way to accomplish this.

The partners' retreat the next year focused on the possible advantages of forming a professional corporation. The partners also authorized discussions with Purrington & Purrington, a small Raleigh firm noted for its real-estate and trust work, about a possible merger. By the end of 1981, the prospects for such a merger were looking favorable. Pen Sandridge, Sr., who had been encouraged to attend the retreat by other senior partners, reminded the group that "while we are growing, let's not forget that really the basis of our growth is client relationships, and we mustn't sacrifice that."

On April 2, 1982, the firm lost one of its legends with the passing of William Pendleton Sandridge, who died at the age of 77 after a year's battle with cancer. On hearing of his death, R. C. Vaughn, Jr., president of the Forsyth County Bar Association, said, "He was acknowledged as a fine lawyer, a leader and a gentleman. When you dealt with him you could rely on his knowledge of the law and his integrity. He was the epitome of the best that the bar has to offer."

W. L. Maynard, who had worked with Mr. Sandridge while secretary-treasurer of Piedmont Publishing Company, recalled Pen Sandridge's performance in the Mary Pickford case in California in the early 1960s: "Pen told them that he was just an untrained country lawyer who didn't know much about big-city ways. And then he proceeded to strip them of their britches."

Members of Womble Carlyle's Management Committee at a May 1982 meeting: Charles Vance, Jr., Lawrence Davis, Wade Gallant, Calder W. Womble, Grady Barnhill, William F. Womble, Don Donadio, Les Browder, and Murray Greason

THE *WINSTON-SALEM JOURNAL*

BRANCHING OUT *1982 – 1987*

> *"I think that there were several pivotal points for the firm in the 1980s. The firm's decision to expand geographically outside of Winston-Salem, and the opening of an office in Raleigh in 1982. The firm's willingness to invest in technology to a greater degree than other law firms. The opportunity to open an office in Charlotte in 1984. And the decision to become involved in the smoking and health litigation in 1985. At each of these moments, the firm showed great foresight."*
>
> Hassel L. Parker

Womble Carlyle Sandridge & Rice had 35 partners and 19 associates at the outset of 1982. As the year began, Calder W. Womble assumed the chairmanship of the Partnership Management Committee from William F. Womble, who had reached the mandatory retirement age of 65 the previous year. After four years of leading the firm, Bill Womble assumed the role of consulting partner under the Partnership Agreement.

The firm stood ready to move in new directions. Prospects for the successful opening of a practice in Raleigh looked promising. There were compelling reasons for establishing a beachhead in the Capital City: access to banking and corporate clients in eastern North Carolina; opportunities for advocacy efforts before the state legislature and other governmental bodies; and the chance to build a bond and public finance practice. But the expansion would also require substantial investments of capital, partners' time, and staff resources—and perhaps even a reduction in partners' incomes for a couple of years. But the choice was relatively easy for a firm that had always looked to the future.

On February 20, 1982, the partners unanimously approved a motion to open a Womble Carlyle

Charles Vance and Calder Womble shared a story en route to a North Carolina Bar Foundation meeting.
WOMBLE CARLYLE COLLECTION

Al Purrington, Jr., who joined the firm in 1982 when it opened its Raleigh office, was honored at a North Carolina Bar Foundation Justice Fund ceremony.
WOMBLE CARLYLE COLLECTION

Sandridge & Rice office in Raleigh. In conjunction with the opening of the Raleigh office, Al Purrington III would come aboard as a partner, while his father, Al Purrington, Jr., would have an "of counsel" role in the firm. When the Raleigh office opened its doors for business on June 1, 1982, Womble Carlyle became the first major firm in the state to have an office in another city.

Don Donadio, already a frequent visitor to Raleigh doing public-finance work, and Lawrence Davis, who had served in the state legislature, made the decision to relocate to the Capital City. The partners decided that the Raleigh office would focus on corporate law, public finance, securities, commercial real estate, and government relations. Calder Womble scouted locations in Raleigh and handled negotiations, while Director of Administration Hass Parker rented the office space, hired the support staff, and tied in the computers and telephones; anyone in the firm could be reached by dialing a four-digit extension.

"We got here to Raleigh in the middle of a recession," Don Donadio recalled, "and Lawrence and I

When Womble Carlyle opened its Raleigh office on June 1, 1982, the firm became the first in North Carolina to operate an office in another city.

Photograph by Michael Back

The prosperity of Winston-Salem and the R. J. Reynolds Tobacco Company have been closely intertwined.
CORBIS CORPORATIOIN

thought that we'd have to be going back to Winston two or three days a week for a while to have enough work to do. That didn't turn out to be the case."

Deborah J. Hylton, the first associate hired in the Raleigh office in the summer of 1982, liked the opportunities afforded by the new office: "In my interview, it seemed that Womble was offering the best of both worlds—a sophisticated practice with the biggest firm in the state, and yet in a small, brand-new office where you know everybody and quickly make a difference. . . . But I often tell the story of how revolutionary it was for the firm to conceive of a lawyer right out of law school not training in the Winston-Salem office. I had to go to Winston-Salem for two months to be 'Wombleized.' And of course, the great advantage of that was that the other 65 lawyers in the firm were on two floors of the Wachovia Building, so by the end of those two months, I knew everybody in the firm and had worked for half of them."

Three associates were added within a year. Over the next couple of years, it became clear that clients wanted a full range of legal services from the Raleigh office. In 1985, Elizabeth Riley and William Moore were hired for the Litigation Section. The following year, the firm added C. Eugene Boyce and Carole S. Gailor as lateral partners in insurance defense and family law, respectively.

In 1985, the firm assisted in the representation of Wachovia Bank in its acquisition of the First Atlanta Corporation and the forming of a new banking holding company, First Wachovia Corporation. Because of the firm's close relationship with Wachovia Bank, the partners began looking at expansion into the Atlanta market, with the intent of better serving Wachovia and leveraging that relationship into work with other clients of the bank.

As specialization increased in the legal profession, Murray Greason, John Garrou, and Bill Davis became responsible for much of the mergers and acquisitions work of the firm, having delegated other areas to fine younger lawyers—retirement planning to Michael Gunter and estate planning to Elizabeth Quick, for example. In the mid-1980s, the economy was strong, corporate work was plentiful, and mergers and acquisitions work was at a high point.

The firm's Litigation Section enjoyed robust growth. Led by section head Grady Barnhill, the firm's litigators built on their traditional strengths in labor and employment discrimination, insurance, negligence, antitrust, and product liability and expanded their representation in areas such as health care and environmental law.

Allan Gitter continued to lead the firm's insurance defense efforts and its representation of the North Carolina League of Municipalities. The work of Roddey M. Ligon, Jr., on behalf of the city of Winston-Salem grew. Along with Anthony H. Brett, he increased the firm's reputation in the field of hospital law. Charlie Vance and Dave Irvin tried a number of employment discrimination cases for the firm, and Mr. Vance worked with young attorneys such as W. Andrew Copenhaver on several antitrust and First Amendment lawsuits. William F. Womble, Jr., and a team of young lawyers advanced the firm's reputation on a number of high-profile product liability cases.

Thanks to a growing economy and a healthy demand for its litigation and corporate services, Womble Carlyle added an unprecedented 34 attorneys in the 1980s.

Perhaps the single biggest event in the recent history of Womble Carlyle Sandridge & Rice was the opportunity to represent the R. J. Reynolds Tobacco Company in smoking and health litigation. In 1984, the company approached Womble Carlyle to serve as in-house counsel/adviser in litigation and to provide guidance and direction to a national law firm, which would coordinate the defense for RJR Nabisco. (The company had purchased Nabisco Brands in June 1985.)

The firm had already been working for several years on smaller RJR initiatives, such as an initial document-coding project and a multistate effort to win regulatory approval for a cleaner-burning cigarette, which Reynolds later introduced under the brand name Premier. Managing Partner Calder Womble recalled the full and frank discussions among the partners about accepting this major assignment from Reynolds: "It was an amazing time. We spent weeks trying to decide whether to take on the project. It was a big opportunity, and clearly we would have to expand rapidly, but it was something that could end completely within a very short time. We talked and talked about it but finally decided that if we could handle the logistics without overwhelming the firm, we would receive more national contact than we could possibly gain anywhere else."

The R. J. Reynolds Tobacco Company, which had been sued on the smoking and health issue since the 1950s, had warehouses full of documents pertaining to the matter. Millions of documents needed to be coded and archived. Womble Carlyle attorneys convinced the company that lawyers had to be involved in reviewing documents and making decisions as to attorney-client privilege, and that the firm could manage the entire project.

Suddenly, the firm's personnel needs expanded greatly. Paralegals were needed to review enormous quantities of documents. Highly competent attorneys were needed to evaluate documents and supervise the paralegal staff. Partners with very strong practices were being diverted to an area that could disappear nearly as quickly as it had appeared. Almost overnight, Womble Carlyle went from a firm of 60 partners and associates to one with 40 contract lawyers and 200 contract paralegals scattered across several buildings in downtown Winston-Salem.

Hass Parker recalled an early conference with the client in Manhattan: "I remember going to New York in the summer of 1984 and sitting in a meeting with the in-house lawyer from the client and the counsel from another law firm. They were talking about the size of the project to review these documents, and the lawyer from the New York firm said, 'Well, there's no big problem. I have one paralegal, and my secretary can help, and we can start the document review.' Our Womble lawyer said, 'Well, we need at least 40 paralegals working by the first of September.' It was then about the 10th of August. And he turned around and said, 'We have no problem doing that, do we Parker?' Well, of course, there was only one answer to that question."

Champ Mitchell, Grady Barnhill, Keith Vaughan, Andy Copenhaver, and Dan Donahue were the partners who led the smoking and health work on behalf of Reynolds, with help from associates such as Mark Holton, Cy Johnson, and Mark Poovey. Copenhaver, who had done some trade-practices work on behalf of Reynolds, recalled being approached by Grady Barnhill about working on smoking and health: "I told Grady that I really wasn't interested. Well, the next thing I knew, I was down in Calder's office with Grady, hearing how the firm really needed me being involved. It was decided that I would spend 50 percent of my time on smoking and health. Well, within six months, that was 100 percent."

While the work on smoking and health litigation made extraordinary demands on Womble Carlyle, it exposed the firm to a number of other prominent law firms, gave it additional experience in handling major litigation, brought national exposure, and proved that the firm's work was indeed equal to that of any in the country. Bill Raper remembered how the firm accepted the challenge of the smoking and health project and rose to the occasion: "We knuckled down, hired incredible numbers of lawyers and paralegals at one time, and produced for our client. And then we were smart enough, as a firm, to capitalize on that experience. We had document retrieval technology. We developed lawyers with niche expertise in areas such as document management. Not many other firms around had that, and we saw it as a real opportunity to take that in other directions."

Through its work for Reynolds on smoking and health litigation, Womble Carlyle got a head start on other firms in employing technology to solve problems for clients. With the advice of Price Waterhouse, the firm developed state-of-the-art computer technology for storing and retrieving massive quantities of documents. As the firm decided to invest in technology in a significant way, it looked to Hass Parker to provide leadership.

With the support of the Partnership Management Committee, Hass Parker invested substantial funds in technology. In 1984, the firm purchased an updated version of the Barrister system. Computers in each of the offices were connected by the latest in telecommunications links, and laser printers were installed in each office. The smoking and health project required massive computing power for litigation support. The advent of the personal computer in 1984 led to a pilot project the next year in which personal computers were placed in the offices of new associates. By early 1987, the firm had authorized substantial expenditures for upgrades of computer equipment in Raleigh and a new system for the Winston-Salem offices capable of providing every secretary with a computer terminal.

Opportunities in Charlotte prompted the opening of an office in that city just two years after the Raleigh office opened. In the fall of 1984, J. Carlton Fleming, a well-respected attorney in the Charlotte firm of Fleming, Robinson & Bradshaw, agreed to come

On October 1, 1984, Womble Carlyle opened an office in Charlotte, the business and financial center of the Carolinas.

CHARLOTTE REGIONAL PARTNERSHIP

with Womble Carlyle to open an office in Charlotte.

David Johnston moved from Winston-Salem to Charlotte to join Carlton Fleming. Two young associates, Lesley Powell and David Conaway, came to Charlotte immediately. They were soon followed by Garza Baldwin and Cy Johnson. Within a few years, the Charlotte office counted companies such as Interstate Securities Corporation, J. A. Jones Construction Company, and Food Lion, Inc., as clients.

With the opening of the Charlotte office on October 1, 1984, Womble Carlyle became the first firm in North Carolina with offices in the three largest population centers and financial centers of the state.

In 1982, when Womble Carlyle opened its Raleigh office, the firm had 59 lawyers. By 1984, when the Charlotte office opened, the firm counted 72 lawyers. By the end of 1985, Womble Carlyle had just over 100 lawyers in its three offices. The rapid increase in attorney hiring earned it the distinction of being one of the 10 fastest-growing law firms in the nation.

Womble Carlyle's explosive growth at mid-decade led the partners to reexamine how the firm administered and governed itself. It had become clear that additional staff was needed to manage the firm's increasingly sophisticated and complex systems and to maintain and improve the quality of service to clients. By 1985, a personnel manager, an accounting manager, and a services supervisor were added to provide more effective support for attorneys in client matters. A year later, office administrators were added for the Charlotte and Raleigh offices. The new hires gave Director of Administration Hass Parker more time to focus on long-range planning, firm growth, and other issues of major importance.

In 1986, Womble Carlyle engaged Price Waterhouse to assist the Firm Study Committee and Special Task Force in studying the issues involved in the smoking and health representation. The consultants' central recommendation was that the management structure of the firm should be changed to provide more centralized planning and direction and a more balanced representation. To this end, the partners approved the establishment of a three-member Executive Committee with the authority to conduct the day-to-day business of the firm and do long-range planning. It also agreed to further organize the firm along section lines and to appoint section heads. And it reorganized the Partnership Management Committee into a smaller, broader-based committee. Price Waterhouse submitted a long-term planning document to guide the firm's continuing deliberations on how best to continue making strategic investments.

In the interest of serving its corporate clients, Womble Carlyle had itself quickly grown into a big business. The increasing numbers of attorneys and staff and the growing investment in technology necessitated the hiring of office managers, a personnel manager, and technology trainers. But even with all of the growth and modernization, senior attorneys and staff ensured that the firm's most venerable traditions and values survived. If an associate treated a staff member in a disrespectful manner, that attorney was soon called into the office of one of the senior partners and counseled on proper behavior and decorum.

On October 1, 1986, Leon Leftwich Rice, Jr., became a retired consulting partner, having been with the firm for 46 years and one month. In his memoir, *Living, Loving and Lawyering*, he looked back with great satisfaction at the practice he had helped build:

> The tax practice that B. S. Womble brought me to Winston-Salem to establish has had right much to do with the growth of the firm. Clients were brought in for tax services that would not

have otherwise come. Clients we serviced in tax matters remained for services in other matters, usually corporate in nature. Our fees in tax and tax related matters are perhaps better than average because of the amounts involved, responsibility assumed, results obtained and ability to pay. This growth of business and income called for additional attorneys to do the work. One of my great satisfactions has been to have a part in the development of the group of tax and corporate law specialists who have come with our firm over the years. . . . It makes me feel very humble in a way, and very rewarded in how good Winston-Salem and the firm have been to me.

Mr. Rice, who told a reporter in October that he was "looking to the future, toward the year 2000," died unexpectedly in Winston-Salem on April 25, 1987, scarcely six months after beginning what he called his "second fifty years of the practice of law." He had graduated from the Duke School of Law in 1936 and had practiced law with his father in Anderson, South Carolina, briefly before joining the Office of the Internal Revenue in Washington, where he was when B. S. Womble brought him to Winston-Salem in 1940. His protege, Murray Greason, said of Rice, "I owe a great deal of whatever success I've had to the fact that Leon Rice introduced me to the great clients that he had, turned me loose with those clients, let me inherit those clients, and just generally was a true friend."

THE RULES OF RICE

"We act for the firm. The client is that of the firm, not of the individual attorney serving the client. The firm has a heritage of clients, standards and a reputation set by those who have gone before. It is up to us to build on the foundation established by predecessors and to the best of our abilities, enhance the quality of service to clients, keeping in tune with the times."

Leon Rice, *Living, Loving and Lawyering*

Womble Carlyle's interest in downtown redevelopment was reflected in the move of the firm's offices to One Triad Park in 1987.

PHOTOGRAPH BY G. ALLEN AYCOCK

INVESTING IN THE FUTURE *1987 – 1996*

"With over 140 lawyers on board in Winston-Salem, Raleigh, and Charlotte by 1987, the close-knit family that the firm once was has necessarily been divided into sections covering the several areas of practice in which the firm engages. However, through various means, we try—and I believe succeed remarkably well—in keeping the lines of communication open within the firm, working together as a team and conducting the high-quality practice for which the firm is known. We continue to be the largest law firm between Richmond and Atlanta and don't deny the allegation that we are also the best."

Leon L. Rice, Jr.

By the fall of 1987, Womble Carlyle Sandridge & Rice employed some 170 lawyers, up from 40 at the start of the decade and 117 just two years earlier. The firm's new offices in Raleigh and Charlotte each now counted more than 10 attorneys on staff.

On Easter weekend of 1987, the firm began moving its nearly 250 employees to One Triad Park, the 19-story glass office tower on Second Street that anchored a $100 million development project. Calder W. Womble had led Winston-Salem Civic Ventures, the blue-ribbon citizens' review panel that spearheaded redevelopment of the downtown. The move into the new quarters, located just a couple of blocks from the firm's former offices in the Wachovia Building, was completed over the Fourth of July weekend.

The last months of Calder Womble's term were busy ones. Not only were there the tumult and excitement of the move to One Triad Park, but the move of RJR Nabisco's corporate headquarters from Winston-Salem to Atlanta in the fall of 1987 led the firm to accelerate its work toward establishing a major presence in Atlanta, in all likelihood through a merger with

"We always respected each other and worked with each other rather than against one another. We believe in integrity and in working together for the good of the firm."

Calder Womble

a full-service Atlanta firm. The firm was of course eager to maintain and enhance its relationships with two of its oldest clients, RJR Nabisco and First Wachovia Corporation, but it also saw an Atlanta office as a way of increasing its presence regionally, nationally, and internationally.

Womble Carlyle was aggressively courted by a number of Atlanta firms in the late 1980s and held merger talks with several of them. But as Murray Greason said, "we just didn't find the right marriage partner." The firm did open a small office in Atlanta in September 1993 after Wachovia relocated its corporate banking, corporate finance, and international banking operations to Atlanta. The Atlanta office was staffed by two Womble Carlyle partners, James E. Lilly and Christopher E. Leon.

Having reached the age of 65 in 1987, Calder Womble prepared to turn over the reins of the Executive Committee. The man whom Murray Greason called "the world's youngest 65-year-old" assumed the role of consulting partner but also volunteered to assist in several ongoing firm management matters. With his corporate background and his knowledge of business, Calder Womble had possessed the skills needed to lead the firm at a time of tremendous growth. "I liked a number of the administrative areas because I enjoy working with people and finances," Womble told an interviewer. "But the fun part of practicing law is working with a variety of people, and having the feeling that you're playing a part in helping them achieve their goals. It's still a lot of fun."

Murray Greason accepted the role of managing partner. On January 1, 1988, at the age of 51, he became the youngest person to head the Partnership Management Committee. One of his first activities as head of the partnership—other than commending and thanking Calder Womble for his "substantial contribution to the progress of the firm"—was to appoint the firm's first section heads: Bill Davis as head of the Business Section; Bill Raper and Bill Womble, Jr., as coheads of General Litigation; Rod Ligon as head of the Trade, Employment, and Governmental Regulations Section; and Don Donadio as head of the Financial Representation and Real Estate Section. The establishment of sections was yet another example of the need to further systematize the firm's practice and distribute management responsibilities in light of growth. The firm was subsequently reorganized into "practice groups" in 1992.

With the support of Grady Barnhill (head of the firm's Litigation Section), the Partnership Management Committee, and the senior partners, Greason always took care to instill the firm's core values in the minds of young associates and to remind them of the firm's traditions. Greason and Barnhill, each in his own way, epitomized the spirit of Womble Carlyle for their generation, building on the traditions they had learned firsthand from their own mentors, Leon Rice and Irving Carlyle, who in turn had learned them from B. S. Womble.

It was not always easy. Leading a group of independent, highly intelligent attorneys is "like trying to get butterflies to fly in formation," as Greason liked to say. In most large firms, there is a natural rivalry between the Corporate and Litigation Sections. For Womble Carlyle, that creative tension has generally manifested itself in good-natured bantering between the two sides. "We work on things that people want to happen," Greason would playfully point out to Barnhill, "rather than tragedies that need to be unwound." Barnhill, not to be outdone, would point out that corporate types "aren't real lawyers because they don't go in a courtroom."

Yet in this era of rapid growth and change, a sense of trust and mutual respect among the attorneys and staff remained the bedrock of the firm. The partners took care to listen to each other, talked through whatever issues emerged, and then proceeded to move the firm forward. Just as B. S. Womble had imbued Leon Rice with the firm's tradition of high ethical standards, quality work, sound judgment, and fair dealing, so Murray Greason's generation worked to carry forward the Womble Carlyle heritage of trust, mutual respect, and shared responsibility.

As the year 1988 neared a close, the firm lost one of its senior partners when Wade M. Gallant, Jr., succumbed to cancer on December 9. A recognized expert in banking and corporate law, Gallant had served for a number of years as principal attorney for Wachovia Bank and Trust Company and as director of a number of corporations, including Brenner Companies, Inc., in Winston-Salem and Thomas Built Buses, Inc., in High Point. William F. Womble, Gallant's partner for 25 years, memorialized him with these words: "Wade Gallant was an excellent lawyer; a lifelong, avid student of the law; an ardent advocate; an innovative thinker, capable of handling difficult, complicated matters in a manner that attracted and gained the respect of clients; a man totally loyal to clients and his firm; a valued partner who made important contributions to the firm's substantial growth and development during his years with us."

Litigation had changed a great deal in the span of just two decades. "Mediation, the growth in sheer number of attorneys, the emergence of some superb female trial lawyers, and the growth and development of in-house counsel are the chief differences I see," said Jimmy H. Barnhill. "Back when I started in the late 1960s, the chief counsel for companies like Wachovia and RJR were very capable, but they didn't have any staff. Outside counsel would run the case and send them the bill. But by the late 1980s, the corporate in-house counsel were extremely capable attorneys who had come up through the private-practice route. They knew just about as much as you did about trying a case. Whereas the in-house counsel in early days generally did not have any trial experience, and they just deferred to you."

Other litigation—especially antitrust and product liability cases—was booming as well in the late 1980s, so much so that the firm had a difficult time employing enough attorneys to handle the workload.

Bill Womble, Jr., represented clients in product liability litigation mostly in North Carolina. He recognized that the growth of the firm and the product liability defense practice called for a client base beyond the state's borders. He recalled that in 1987, Charlie Vance told him of an attorney Mr. Vance knew in Chicago who was seeking national counsel for one of the leading manufacturers of components for propane systems, RegO Company. That company, like most of those in propane-related industries, was embroiled in separate product liability cases in nearly every state. Bill welcomed the opportunity and successfully interviewed on behalf of the firm with counsel for the Chicago owners of the business. By September 1987, Bill and Dan Donahue learned the propane industry and formed a small team of litigators. They successfully defended RegO thereafter nationally and in the Virgin Islands.

The firm's work for RJR Nabisco accelerated in

late 1987 and early 1988 from its already brisk pace, as ancillary projects were added to the main smoking and health project. New associates and paralegals were hired, and the firm even put out a call for additional weekend secretarial help. In a January 1988 report to the Executive Committee, a partner involved in Reynolds matters weighed the benefits and the costs of the projects: "The firm's involvement in these matters for Reynolds provides a great opportunity to expand our base. It will [also] provide an opportunity for young associates to learn regulatory and administrative law, and introduce them to premium law firms throughout the United States. On the other hand the demands of the work are extremely high, creating stress, a heavy travel schedule, a loss of opportunity to participate in community activities, and a drain on family relationships."

Within six months, the tobacco industry would suffer its first loss in court over the smoking and health issue. On June 13, 1988, a jury in federal District Court in New Jersey hearing the case of *Cipollone v. Liggett Group, Inc.*, awarded $400,000 in damages to the Cipollone family, finding the tobacco companies guilty of using misleading advertising and contributing to the death of Rose Cipollone, a cigarette smoker. Over 300 lawsuits had been filed against the industry since 1954, yet none prior to *Cipollone* had succeeded in exposing so many confidential industry research documents on the health effects of smoking. The United States Court of Appeals for the Third Circuit later threw out the damage award in *Cipollone* and ordered a new trial.

Meanwhile, other tobacco lawsuits were working their way through the courts, some of them over the issue of whether the federal warning labels on cigarette packages protected the tobacco companies from liability. In 1992, the United States Supreme Court ruled that in some cases involving conspiracy, the package labels did not completely shield the tobacco industry from liability.

For a time after the high court's decision, neither side wanted to try smoking and health cases without knowing what the law ultimately would be. Most plaintiffs' attorneys could not afford to prosecute such expensive litigation if the jury awards were to be small. On the other hand, the court had exposed the cigarette companies to potential liability in the deaths of smokers and opened the door for disclosure of more confidential industry documents. "It knocked the props out from under us in certain respects," said Murray Greason.

Ross Johnson, chief executive officer of RJR Nabisco, announced in October 1988 that he was heading a management team that intended to take the company private through a leveraged buyout. Other investors joined in the bidding, which culminated in the acceptance by the RJR Nabisco Board of Directors of a bid of $109 a share by Kohlberg Kravis Roberts and Company, a New York investment firm. The deal, worth $25.4 billion, was a boon for stockholders but a bust for the tobacco company, which quickly lost sales and market share to its competitors.

At the same time, the nation's economy was entering a recession. Company mergers and acquisitions work decreased, as did product liability litigation. The firm's leadership worked hard to cut costs, reallocate resources to more efficiently deliver services, and use the best talents of the firm on any particular matter from any of the firm's offices. It also made sure that the firm's young partners would be guaranteed the same income as in the previous year, regardless of net income for 1990. The firm brought a number of attorneys into partnership—including a number who had made significant contributions to the smoking and health litigation—despite the economic downturn and the surplus of legal talent in the firm.

In 1990, Bill Sullivan, who had been a partner in a major Washington, D.C., law firm, joined Womble Carlyle for the specific purpose of rebuilding its bankruptcy practice. Over the next several years, this task was accomplished with the able help of lateral partner Kay Donahue, a veteran bankruptcy attorney from Greensboro, who joined the firm in 1991.

An important event was the development in 1991 of a long-range strategic plan for the firm. The Partnership Management Committee established a Long Range Planning Committee and brought in consultants from Ernst & Young to assist in developing the plan. Womble Carlyle's strategic plan committed it to becoming a strong regional firm capable of providing a wide range of legal services throughout the Southeast. To that end, the firm continued to entertain overtures for possible mergers with firms in the region, particularly in Atlanta but also in Washington, D.C.

During the recession of 1991, the firm reexamined its costs and assets. The Long Range Planning Committee recommended reorganizing the firm into nine practice groups and eight sub-practice groups. The committee also studied new practice areas such as intellectual property. And the Executive Committee authorized a study of whether the firm should leverage its technical and management expertise into a consulting service. Also, after studying the pros and cons of remaining a partnership, the partners voted to become a professional limited liability company (PLLC), effective April 1, 1994.

Even as the firm was cutting costs to make up for a temporary decline in business, it remained committed to the growth and development of the Charlotte office. In recent years, the Partnership Management Committee had been emphasizing the need for a strong litigation team in Charlotte to add to its initial strengths in corporate, bankruptcy, and real estate. Murray Greason approached Bill Raper about moving to Charlotte and heading the litigation practice there. Raper agreed. He was joined by partner Jim Cooley, an experienced litigator who had come with the firm in 1984. Together, they persuaded three other litigators—G. Michael Barnhill, Timothy G. Barber, and Debbie W. Harden—to help build a business litigation group in the Queen City. It was a strategic decision by the partners to expand the firm in the booming Charlotte area, the state's commercial and financial center.

In the 1990s, Womble Carlyle also renewed efforts to build the firm's governmental, administrative, and regulatory practices, both in Raleigh and in Washington. Ashley O. Thrift, a former top aide to Senator Ernest Hollings of South Carolina, came with the firm in May 1992 to assist clients with legislative, regulatory, and international trade issues. Alexander "Sandy" Sands, a former state senator from Rockingham County, was hired in 1995 to head the governmental relations practice in Raleigh.

The Raleigh office continued to grow at a measured pace. Just as in Charlotte, the firm realized that a full range of legal services should be offered in Raleigh. Thus, litigation attorneys began to be added to an office whose initial strengths had been in corporate law, public finance, securities, and commercial real estate.

C. Eugene Boyce, who had come to the Raleigh office in 1986 to handle insurance defense and general business litigation, soon became involved in several plaintiffs' cases on a contingent-fee basis. In 1989, he took a case on behalf of a friend, retired Superior Court judge James H. Pou Bailey, and other retirees whose pensions had been taxed by the state of North Carolina. Beginning in 1991, Gene Boyce filed a series of class-action suits on behalf of retirees, including state retirees (the *Bailey* case), federal retirees (the *Patton* case), and disabled retirees (the *Emory* case).

The firm and Boyce also represented North Carolina taxpayers in the *Smith/Shaver* class action, a 1995 challenge to the constitutionality of North Carolina's intangibles tax. In February 1996, the United States Supreme Court ruled that the state of North Carolina had unconstitutionally favored in-state companies in the way that it collected its levy on the value of stocks and bonds held by taxpayers. Bill Raper and Keith Vaughan argued the case before the high court.

It would be another two years before the class-action suits began to pay off for the plaintiffs. In 1998, the co-counsel for the class, Boyce (who had left the firm in 1996) and Keith Vaughan (representing the firm), reached a settlement in the pension cases valued at $799 million. A year later, the North Carolina General Assembly agreed to a $440 million class-action settlement in the intangibles tax case.

Needing more expertise in managing both the finances of the firm and its sophisticated computerized litigation support system, the Executive Committee authorized Hass Parker to search for an individual with a background in accounting and database management. The firm was fortunate to find someone with that unusual combination of skills: Terry M. Wiley. Not long after Wiley's arrival in March 1988, the firm began a move away from the Barrister system, in part because of its limited capabilities in litigation support. Based on recommendations made by computer consultant Don Holland, the Firm Management Committee authorized a gradual phase-in of a personal computer local area network and the immediate purchase of new timekeeping and billing software in 1989.

In the early 1990s, the firm reaffirmed its decision to invest substantially in technology. With strong support from Hass Parker and Terry Wiley, the Firm Management Committee saw technology as a means of adding value to client services and supporting the continued geographic expansion of the firm. "I was a little too old to become agile with the computer myself," Murray Greason observed. "But when the suggestion came forward that we invest in technology in a big way, at least I had enough sense to say, 'Go to it, boys. Spend the money. I'll just get out of the way.' "

The first step in the mid-1990s was to establish a wide area network linking all offices by telephone, fax, and e-mail, permitting lawyers to allocate resources as needed from any location, as well as to establish direct, secure connections with clients and their legal departments. In May 1995, Womble Carlyle became the first law firm in North Carolina with an Internet website (www.wcsr.com). Soon after that, it further linked its offices with videoconferencing capability.

A major boost to the development and marketing of the firm's technical expertise came with the hiring of Marvin Chavis as director of technology and training in 1993. Chavis, an attorney and vice president at CMS/DATA —developer of the financial management system used by Womble Carlyle—quickly generated excitement throughout the firm about using technology to improve service to clients. His exuberance for technology solutions was infectious, often spreading to the firm's clients. Unlike some other firms where the "techies" were consigned to the back office, Chavis made sure that his troops were in the field assisting the firm's attorneys. "We're out there helping the clients right along with the lawyers," Chavis told *AmLaw Tech* magazine.

In the early 1990s, Womble Carlyle continued to reach out to the communities it served. In 1991, the Winston-Salem office initiated a pilot pro bono program to assist the Forsyth County District Attorney's Office in the prosecution of child sexual-abuse cases. In a press release, Grady Barnhill noted, "We are pleased to be joining the district attorney to help the children of our community. We are committed not only to the sponsorship of the training program, but to donating a substantial amount of lawyer time to the program." Attorneys Kurt Stakeman, S. Fraley Bost, Jeffrey L. Furr, and Richard T. Rice spearheaded the effort on behalf of the firm.

In 1993, Womble Carlyle became one of the first

Murray Greason, Managing Partner from 1988-1996

Photograph by G. Allen Aycock

The Director of Financial Systems Terry M. Wiley, now Executive Director, demonstrating Womble Carlyle's state-of-the-art videoconferencing equipment in 1996

Courtesy of Marshall Marvelli

Marvin Chavis, Director of Technology from 1993-2000, as photographed by AmLaw Tech *for a cover story on the firm's technology program.*

PHOTOGRAPH BY JOHN EMERSON

businesses in Winston-Salem to build a house for Habitat for Humanity. The idea came from a lunchtime conversation among Kay Donahue, Pen Sandridge, and Les Browder about a Habitat house built by the Guilford County Bar Association, according to Ken Carroll, a partner in the Winston-Salem office at that time. Carroll headed up the project. "From that, they got the feeling that maybe a firm of our size could take on a project like that," he said. "It just sort of steamrolled from there. We've had a tremendous response from our lawyers and staff. A hands-on opportunity to do something in the community is what makes this project so attractive and interesting and exciting for us." Pat Kight coordinated volunteers to work on Saturdays, and Al Sorrell lined up food and refreshments for workers at the job site. In the year 2000, the Charlotte office would help in the building of a Habitat house in the Queen City.

Within the span of three days in May 1996, in the final months of Murray Greason's term as managing partner, the firm made two key strategic decisions. On May 13, after months of deliberations and negotiations, the members voted to merge with the Parker Johnson Cook & Dunlevie firm in Atlanta. Then, on May 16, the Firm Management Committee gave partners Deborah Hylton and Ken Carroll permission to investigate the steps needed to open a new office near Research Triangle Park, a fast-growing center of high-tech, biotechnology, and start-up companies in the Raleigh-Durham area. After coordinating a business plan with the Firm Management Committee and the Raleigh office, the firm's Research Triangle Park office opened early the next year.

Murray Greason, who had served as managing partner since 1987, relished a return to the practice of law and to having more time to devote to family and leisure. As early as 1992, he indicated to the partners that he would be "perfectly satisfied to return to the practice of law full time, if this is the pleasure of the partnership." In any event, he did not plan to serve as chairman of the Firm Management Committee beyond September 30, 1996. The firm acceded to his wishes to find a successor by 1996, when he would turn 60.

At his last Firm Management Committee meeting as managing partner, Murray Greason was honored with this resolution by his successor, John Garrou: "Murray has presided at well over one hundred of these partner meetings, and this is the last. He has helped us through some of the toughest decisions in the long history of this great firm. In doing so he has epitomized strong leadership, unquestioned integrity, respect for individuals, and respect—even reverence—for this institution. Everything that Murray has done has exemplified the knowledge that we are not simply a collection of lawyers held together by convenience or economic self-interest, but a true firm, an institution, a living, dynamic organism which is dependent on all of us, but which exists beyond our collective selves."

John L. W. Garrou, chairman of the Firm Management Committee since 1996, is leading Womble Carlyle into the 21st century.

PHOTOGRAPH BY G. ALLEN AYCOCK

EMBRACING CHANGE *1996–*

> *"If you look at our firm in comparison to other law firms, we are very open—almost eager—to embrace change. As an institution, we don't have any fear of it. We're proud of our history and where we've come from, but we understand the value of change. Why is that? I think that, over time, the firm has developed a confidence in its leadership and a willingness to defer to firm leadership on issues that, in other firms, the partners insist on deciding for themselves."*
>
> John L. W. Garrou

John Garrou, the vice chairman of the Firm Management Committee, became the managing member (partner) of Womble Carlyle Sandridge & Rice, PLLC, on September 24, 1996. In his opening statement as head of the committee, he envisioned a bright future for the firm: "We are poised to enter a great new era. The opportunities are boundless. We have a number of advantages over other firms in this new marketplace, the most important and meaningful of these being our sense of unity and pride in our membership in this firm, and our relationships with one another."

Womble Carlyle Sandridge & Rice's merger with the 20-year-old full-service Atlanta firm of Parker, Johnson, Cook & Dunlevie on June 1, 1996, marked a major turning point. Never before had the firm incorporated more than a two-lawyer practice or established a full-fledged office outside of North Carolina. But the move to Atlanta had long been pondered, and the combination had been carefully considered by both firms. Steven S. Dunlevie, former managing partner of Parker Johnson, noted that it had quickly become clear that the two firms were cut from the same cloth: "It was a good fit because we're alike both in the way we service clients and in the way in which we treat our attorneys and staff. We do not feel as if we have been acquired. Womble Carlyle is really like a big Parker Johnson."

Womble Carlyle expanded its presence in the Atlanta market in 1996 through a merger with the respected firm of Parker, Johnson, Cook & Dunlevie. Pictured here, left to right, are Steven S. Dunlevie, Robert F. Cook, G. Donald Johnson, and Terrill A. Parker.

PHOTOGRAPH BY JOHN DISNEY

Parker Johnson partners R. Russell Berry and Steven Dunlevie worked closely with Murray Greason and the Firm Management Committee to smooth the transition, and the Womble partners already in Atlanta—James E. Lilly and Christopher E. Leon—helped pass on the firm's culture, history, and traditions. Staff from the Winston-Salem office, particularly Hassel L. Parker and Donald H. Adamick, made numerous trips to Atlanta to tie in the new office with the systems in the firm's other offices.

The Atlanta firm was highly respected in the region, with particular strengths in business litigation as well as corporate, regulatory, securities, banking, and real-estate law. Parker Johnson's 25 lawyers represented a number of impressive corporate clients in the region, including Hayes Microcomputer Products, Inc., Transit Group, Premier Bancshares, Inc., and Reliance Trust Company.

"Our clients' business needs are expanding regionally, nationally, and even globally," said Murray Greason in a press release announcing the merger. "Our clients recognize that Atlanta is truly an international center of commerce, and that a strong presence in Atlanta is essential for our firm to continue to serve our clients."

By 1996, the firm—with some 265 lawyers in Atlanta, Charlotte, Raleigh, Research Triangle Park, and Winston-Salem—was ranked as the fastest-growing large law firm in the country by the *National Law Journal* and was widely recognized as one of the nation's most innovative law firms. Womble Carlyle continued to grow rapidly by any measure—number of attorneys and staff, number of offices, total firm revenue—so much so that by 1999, it was ranked the 78th-largest law firm in the country. The growth was part of a

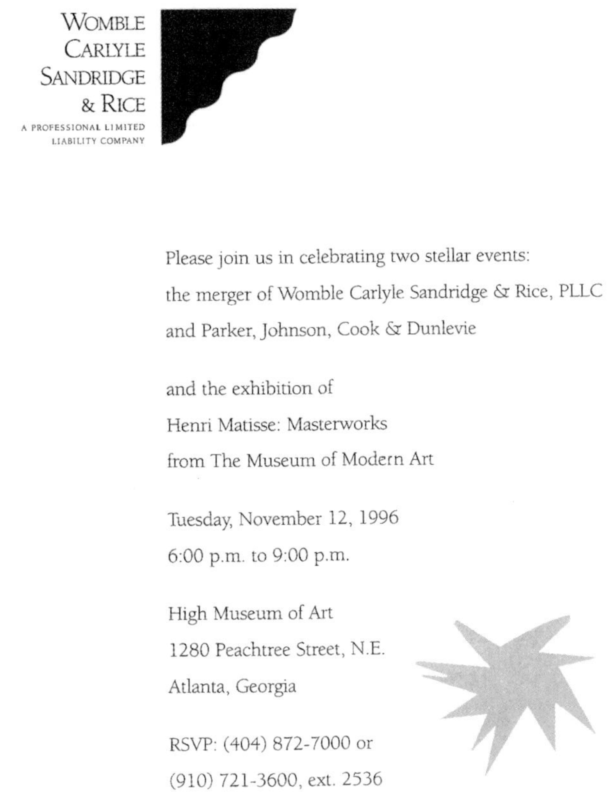
Womble Carlyle Sandridge & Rice
A Professional Limited Liability Company

Please join us in celebrating two stellar events:
the merger of Womble Carlyle Sandridge & Rice, PLLC
and Parker, Johnson, Cook & Dunlevie

and the exhibition of
Henri Matisse: Masterworks
from The Museum of Modern Art

Tuesday, November 12, 1996
6:00 p.m. to 9:00 p.m.

High Museum of Art
1280 Peachtree Street, N.E.
Atlanta, Georgia

RSVP: (404) 872-7000 or
(910) 721-3600, ext. 2536

Womble Carlyle celebrated its merger with the Parker Johnson firm with an elegant reception at Atlanta's High Museum of Art.
Womble Carlyle Collection

strategic plan to become a super-regional law firm, ready to meet the sophisticated legal needs of clients in a changing marketplace.

Although the firm had grown large and geographically dispersed by the 1990s, its employees continued to place a high priority on collegiality, fairness, and treating everyone with respect. "A lot of people feel a special pride in working for Womble Carlyle," observed Donald H. Adamick, who came with the firm in 1984. "I think that the firm does well by its people, takes care of its own in terms of benefits and working with people when they have problems and need help. There's still a sense that we're all part of the same team."

F. Keith Tedrow, who began as office manager in the Winston-Salem office in 1996, has been impressed by the degree of concern shown for employees since his interview, when he noted the placement and configuration of the employee break room on the 15th floor: "Interestingly enough, that break room was one of the things that impressed me most about the firm. It's kind of an unusual thing, and something that most people wouldn't really notice. But in a law firm, window space is extremely important and a very crucial piece of real estate. The attorneys all have window offices, so for a firm to devote that amount of space to the employee break room indicated to me that the attorneys were not just focused on themselves, but were interested in their employees' needs and concerns and preferences."

By 1995, over a decade after its founding, the Raleigh office had grown to some 30 lawyers. By the end of the decade, it housed 50 attorneys. Under the leadership of Managing Member Don Donadio, the office had developed strong corporate, commercial, real estate, government relations, and litigation practices. Donadio described the office's growth by the year 2000: "The mix of legal services that we provide here reflects the needs of the business community in this particular market. Growth in the Research Triangle has been explosive, which has given rise to our very active real estate practice. From the Raleigh office, the firm has represented developers and lenders in real estate transactions for developments from Burlington to the coast, including several major golf course developments."

The firm's Research Triangle Park office—which formally opened to the public on April 9, 1997—saw its size triple within three years. Deborah Hylton, a founding partner of the office, looked back on the whirlwind growth for the firm in the Raleigh-Durham area: "We've added lawyers in health care, land use, and litigation to our initial core of corporate and

Donald A. Donadio of the Raleigh office and John C. Cooke of the Research Triangle Park office teamed up to represent resort owners and golf-course developers in eastern North Carolina.

R. A. Flynn, Inc.

securities and intellectual property lawyers. We now service corporate clients such as GlaxoSmithKline, Inc., as well as many start-up companies, and we're close to Chapel Hill, where many of the region's venture capitalists are located."

Corporate lawyers in the Research Triangle Park office are very active in helping start-up companies raise capital, while the office's intellectual property lawyers help establish and protect trademarks and patents and address the various information technology issues of new ventures. Womble Carlyle lawyers in the office have been major supporters of one of the area's most productive incubators of high-tech enterprises, the Council for Entrepreneurial Development. Member Kenneth Carroll of the Research Triangle Park office has served on the Council for Entrepreneurial Development's Board of Directors for several years. He and other attorneys in the firm often offer seminars and chair conferences on behalf of the council.

Womble Carlyle has a long history of service to the health care industry. To meet the challenges created by dynamic changes in health care delivery systems, the firm expanded this practice in the Research Triangle Park and Raleigh offices in the late 1990s. Widely respected health care lawyers Patricia Meador, Mary Beth Johnston, and Gary Qualls joined the firm to represent a wide range of health care providers and ancillary health care companies. These organizations—hospital and large nursing home companies, pharmaceutical companies, and HMOs—have looked to the firm to guide them through the labyrinth of changing operational structures, regulatory compliance issues, and merger and acquisition opportunities.

Deborah Hylton explained the approach that she and her Research Triangle Park colleagues take to attracting and serving clients in the Raleigh-Durham area: "We want to demonstrate our ability to work with companies of all levels. We're clearly a business law firm that sees the young companies, the high-growth companies, the start-ups as the future of this area, but there are also plenty of us who've spent most of our lives working with big companies. We enjoy the challenge of the big deal, the complex transaction. And we think that it's hard to persuade somebody to let you take them there if you haven't been there already. So we're very interested in maintaining a balance of continuing to represent big companies, as well as those who are on their way to becoming big companies."

Late in 1996, the firm was involved in one of the nation's most publicized jury trials, the ABC/Food Lion case. The supermarket chain had sued ABC/Capital Cities over an undercover investigative report aired on

Mary Beth Johnston and Patricia T. Meador anchor Womble Carlyle's growing health care practice from the firm's Research Triangle Park office.

R. A. FLYNN, INC.

its *PrimeTime Live* program. The report accused the company of unsanitary food practices and labor law violations in its stores. Lawyers for Womble Carlyle (outside general counsel for the company) and the Washington firm of Akin, Gump, Strauss, Hauer & Feld, co-counsel for Food Lion, sued the network and its producers not for libel but for fraud, trespass, and breach of duty as company employees.

Andy Copenhaver and Tim Barber tried the case for Food Lion in federal District Court in Greensboro, arguing that the *PrimeTime Live* producers were "spies" who had "staged events" and engaged in "a pattern of deception." In his closing argument in the compensatory damages phase of the eight-day trial, Tim Barber asked the jurors to consider whether the producers could be loyal to both Food Lion and ABC, whether they could "serve two masters" at the same time.

In December, the jury ruled that ABC and its producers had committed fraud, trespass, and breach of loyalty in the exposé, which aired on ABC on November 5, 1992. While the jury awarded Food Lion only $1,402 in compensatory damages for the costs of training and employment, jurors awarded $5.5 million in punitive damages. Barber and Copenhaver said that the best way to stop deceitful hidden-camera reporting was for jurors to require television networks to pay hefty damages. In his closing argument in the punitive phase, Andy Copenhaver told the jury, "You twelve are now in the position of being, in effect, the policemen on the media highway." Barber added, "This is not a case of media uncovering wrongdoing. This is a case of media doing wrong."

Though the trial judge reduced the jury award to $316,000 and the Fourth Circuit Court of Appeals later dropped the damages to a mere two dollars—finding that the journalists' falsification of their credentials had caused no measurable harm to Food Lion *as an employer*—the original damage award nonetheless served as a warning to journalists, news producers, and television executives about the methods used by investigative reporters.

Timothy G. Barber and W. Andrew Copenhaver represented Food Lion, Inc., in a case against ABC/Capital Cities in 1996 and 1997.

PHOTOGRAPH BY MICHAEL J. N. BOWLES

Earlier in 1996, the firm had won a major victory in a case before the North Carolina Supreme Court. In *Maready v. City of Winston-Salem*, the court ruled that economic development incentive grants made to private corporations by the Winston-Salem Board of Aldermen and the Forsyth County commissioners during the early 1990s were constitutional. Writing for the court, Justice Willis Whichard stated, "The public advantages sought here clearly serve a public purpose, [as] they are directly aimed at furthering the general economic welfare of the communities affected. While private actors will necessarily benefit from the expenditures authorized, such benefit is merely incidental." Rod Ligon, longtime Winston-Salem city attorney, represented the city on the firm's behalf.

Womble Carlyle took great pride in July 1997 when one of its own, Betty Quick, was elected the 103rd president of the North Carolina Bar Association, the eighth of the firm's attorneys to serve in that capacity and only the second woman president in the association's history. During her term as president, Betty Quick advocated for children's rights, coordinated the association's long-term planning effort, helped organize the association's centennial celebration, and participated in the reform of Legal Services of North Carolina, the state's indigent defense umbrella organization.

"It was enjoyable and a very rewarding experience," Quick recalled, "and I would not trade it for anything. It was a big commitment, of course. During that year, I ended up spending one-half to two-thirds of my time with the bar association. It was wonderful to get involved with the bar and issues affecting the profession as a whole. And it gave me an opportunity to meet and get to know many of the wonderfully committed lawyers that we have across the state of North Carolina."

Betty Quick contributed an additional year of service to the North Carolina Bar Association through July 1999 as an ex officio member of many committees in the active role of "immediate past president."

Several months later, on November 4, 1999, the firm lost one of its most beloved senior members with the death of Charles Fogle Vance, Jr., at the age of 75. A member of Womble Carlyle for 47 years, he saw the firm grow from eight lawyers in one office to nearly 400 lawyers in seven offices. At an April 2000 ceremony at the North Carolina Bar Center honoring Charles Vance, his partner and friend William F. Womble delivered these remarks: "As we honor Charles Fogle Vance, Jr., in this way he honors us by the way he lived—setting an example of steadfast love of family; of devotion to one's church; of dedication to the law and the highest standards of the legal profession; of service to the community; of giving of oneself to help others; of the importance of music and good humor as a contribution to one's own life and the lives of others."

Womble Carlyle expanded into the highly competitive Washington, D.C., market through a merger with the 19-lawyer firm of David, Hagner & Kuney, PC, in October 1998. An impressive firm with a strong practice, a high degree of collegiality, and a fine reputation in the Washington area, the David Hagner firm was known for its commercial real estate practice, as well as for its strengths in bankruptcy, tax, and litigation. John Hagner, a senior partner in the David Hagner firm, said this about the merger:

> We must have talked to 20 other firms. Three met all of our terms, but Womble Carlyle was the unanimous choice because of the people in the firm. Womble made such a commitment of resources to the process. There were probably 15

Elizabeth L. Quick (far right) served as president of the North Carolina Bar Association in 1997 and 1998.

BUSINESS LIFE

Womble Carlyle expanded into the Washington, D. C. market through a merger with the David Hagner firm in 1998. Pictured here are John Hagner (left) and Richard David.

WOMBLE CARLYLE COLLECTION

or more people from Womble who were extensively involved in our merger discussions, and the next largest number from another firm may have been four people. It was not even close.

They held meetings for us in every one of their offices so that we could meet the attorneys and staff. In Atlanta, they brought in many of the former Parker Johnson lawyers, put us in a conference room, and encouraged us to have a full and frank discussion about their merger with Womble Carlyle. Finally, we had a meeting in Charlotte to negotiate certain business aspects of the merger, and there were some very tough financial issues to work through. Steve Dunlevie chaired the meeting in Murray Greason's absence, and Hass Parker and Deborah Hylton were there as well. But those of us who were there were just overwhelmed by the sense of fairness in the way that the Womble Carlyle attorneys approached the issues. In fact, they were quite generous in a way that a lot of firms would not have been. By the end of that session, I was convinced that these were the kind of people that I wanted to work with for the rest of my career.

"I was impressed by the quality of the people in the firm," said Paul Kaplan, a David Hagner litigator. "My perception has since been confirmed—these are people who do what they say they're going to do. They care about each other. They know that money is important, but it's not the only thing for them. And I think that many of us just enjoy their company. In terms of law-firm culture, I think that there was an enormous compatibility between our two firms. But in terms of the personal cultures of the people, they're really quite a bit different. And I think that's been an extremely enriching thing for us, and I hope for them. It adds some zest or some fun to what you do. The Womble folks are just high-quality, delightful people who have treated us well, who seem to respect us and like us. And the feeling is mutual."

That same month—October 1998—the firm continued its aggressive expansion through a merger with the Atlanta firm of Isaf, Vaughan & Kerr, a highly regarded intellectual property and patent-law boutique specializing in patent, trademark, and copyright litigation, licensing, and negotiation. The former Isaf, Vaughan & Kerr lawyers have been an important addition to the firm's burgeoning intellectual property practice.

Louis T. Isaf and James F. Vaughan, formerly of the firm of Isaf, Vaughan & Kerr. The Atlanta intellectual property firm merged with Womble Carlyle in 1998.

PHOTOGRAPH BY TIM CONWAY

In February 1999, Womble Carlyle established a presence in thriving Upstate South Carolina with an office in Greenville. A possible expansion into the Greenville area—located about halfway between the business centers of Atlanta and Charlotte—had been a key part of the firm's strategic plan for several years. Members of the Executive Committee had first approached one of Greenville's most prestigious law firms, Wyche, Burgess, Freeman & Parham, about a possible merger. But when those talks ended, Womble Carlyle was able to convince Larry D. Estridge, a senior partner at Wyche, to start the firm's Greenville office. Estridge soon recruited other attorneys, including D. Allen Grumbine, a 24-year veteran of Wyche; W. Lindsay Smith of the city's McNair law firm; and Brent O. E. Clinkscale, a partner at the Greenville-based firm of Haynsworth, Marion, McKay & Guerard.

"The firm needed to be in Greenville—it's right in the middle of our strategic development area," Larry Estridge noted. "Upstate South Carolina boasts the largest concentration of international manufacturing companies of any region in the country. Some 300 companies based in Europe and Asia have manufacturing or distribution facilities in the Upstate. These businesses have traditionally turned to firms in New York, Chicago, and Atlanta for their sophisticated legal needs. But we believe that we can offer the same services that the out-of-state firms have been providing, but with a local connection."

"Larry [Estridge] had given me some information on the firm's philosophy and culture," said Allen Grumbine. "It was very impressive. I found it hard to

Larry D. Estridge became the managing member of Womble Carlyle's Greenville, South Carolina office when it opened in 1999.

THE GREENVILLE NEWS

believe that a firm this large could have this kind of culture, but it proved to be very true when I met people from Womble and talked with them. It was a given that they would be incredibly able lawyers with an excellent practice and a superb reputation, but what I found remarkable is the way that they respect and treat each other. Our firm is just a great group of people to be with."

In February 2001, Womble Carlyle further expanded its reach into the northern Virginia technology corridor through a merger with The Jefferson Law Firm, PLC, of McLean, Virginia. The addition of the respected 13-lawyer firm allowed Womble Carlyle to complete its coverage of the southeastern technology crescent, which encompasses Atlanta, Research Triangle Park, and northern Virginia. In announcing the merger, Womble Carlyle chairman John Garrou said, "We are very excited about the many benefits this merger presents. The lawyers in The Jefferson firm have outstanding credentials and a culture very similar to our own. Several of the lawyers at both firms have known each other, personally and professionally, for a long time, so it is a very comfortable merger. The establishment of a Northern Virginia office of Womble Carlyle is obviously important to our technology and venture capital clients. But it is also vital to the long-term interests of our institutional clients, because technology is transforming the way business is conducted."

The Jefferson Law Firm was formed in 1997 by veteran lawyers Daniel R. Mackesey, W. Thomas Parrot, and Thomas J. Sawyer with the intent of building an entrepreneurial, multi-practice business law firm to serve the technology community in northern Virginia. Senior Partner Mackesey explained the reasons for the merger: "Our firm had very quickly built a solid and varied client base of technology and traditional businesses, and we were beginning to see bigger opportunities come our way. But we hadn't yet achieved the critical mass necessary to consistently capitalize on these opportunities. The technology market is consolidating and maturing, and we had reached the stage where we needed the support of a large, full-service law firm. The merger gives us the requisite depth to provide that support, particularly in the areas of intellectual property and telecommunications. Womble Carlyle is one of the most innovative and sophisticated business law firms in the nation. We couldn't be happier with the way things have worked out."

In February 2001, Womble Carlyle merged with the respected Jefferson Law Firm of McLean, Virginia.
WOMBLE CARLYLE COLLECTION

> *"The great thing about Womble Carlyle and its values is that, in any situation, you ask yourself, 'What's the right thing to do? What is the right, fair, ethical, moral thing to do?' And that's the answer. And you implement it, and you're right. So it's easy to work that way. That permeates the way that we deal with our clients, the way that we deal with our staff, the way that we're able to attract good merger candidates, because people see that."*
>
> Terry Wiley

Just as B. S. Womble had the vision to foresee that taxation would be the driving force of the business world, so the firm had the boldness to leverage its experience in employing technology to solve the complex needs of clients into an entirely new practice area of "nontraditional" or "ancillary" services. Technology was but another means of fulfilling the firm's driving principle: better service to the client.

In the latter half of the 1990s, Womble Carlyle further incorporated technology as an integral part of its legal services to clients. The firm added an intranet, secure client extranets, and virtual private networks, enabling lawyers and clients in any location to simultaneously access documents and information.

In 1996, the firm further solidified its position as a pacesetter by creating the ClientPlus Technology Services Group. Separated from the firm's Technology Department and focused solely on the needs of clients, the team of some 35 computer programmers, systems engineers, communications and applications support specialists, and trainers provided consulting services and developed software and systems solutions for client problems. Led by Marvin Chavis and Marlene Houser, ClientPlus pioneered the concept of externally focused technology support and consulting services. The consulting group soon proved to be yet another innovative way to fulfill one of the firm's core principles: solving problems and adding value for clients.

In 1998, the firm created the Ancillary Services Group, a unit consisting of nontraditional legal services (such as ClientPlus) that supported and supplemented traditional legal representation. Hass Parker, the longtime executive director of the firm, accepted the challenge of becoming the first chief executive officer of Ancillary Services.

In 1999, Managing Partner John Garrou described

Then Director of Technology Marvin Chavis (right) headed the ClientPlus Technology Services Group. Here he is shown with Steve Dunlevie, managing member of the Atlanta office.

PHOTOGRAPH BY JOHN DISNEY

his hopes for Ancillary Services: "We believe that the multidisciplinary practice represents the future. In an increasingly complex global marketplace, clients look for problem solvers, and we want to be the problem solver of choice in those areas where our expertise and talents give us an advantage."

In the late 1990s, the Settlement Administration Services unit of Ancillary Services was perhaps the most innovative, high-profile aspect of the firm's non-traditional services. After a 10-year legal fight, a $799 million settlement was reached in 1998 in the *Bailey, Patton*, and *Emory* tax cases against the state of North Carolina. Following the settlement, class counsel and the court-appointed settlement administrator invited Womble Carlyle to provide administrative support in distributing refunds to state, local government, and federal retirees. The firm faced the daunting task of contacting over 50 state and federal retirement pay agencies in order to obtain data regarding retirement benefits paid to almost 250,000 retirees subject to North Carolina taxation between 1989 and 1997. After the administration of the Bailey tax settlement had begun, Womble Carlyle was also selected to handle the administration of the Smith/Shaver intangibles-tax settlement, which refunded $440 million to some 325,000 claimants.

In August 1999, the firm was chosen to administer the North Carolina and South Carolina portions of Phase II of the National Tobacco Settlement, a $5.15 billion trust fund set aside for tobacco growers and allotment owners. By agreement, the monies in the fund were to be paid out over 12 years to help offset cuts in tobacco production due to the expected decline in smoking. The firm's Phase II Settlement Administration Group set up a processing center to handle certification forms and a call center to field inquiries from growers and quota owners.

In 1999, after 10 years of litigation on a contingent-fee basis, Womble Carlyle and several other law firms shared in the fees awarded in the $799 million final settlement of the *Bailey* case, as ordered by Superior Court judge Jack Thompson of Fayetteville. More than 100 Womble Carlyle attorneys and staff had worked on the tax cases over the course of a decade. In addition to the class counsel, Gene Boyce, and Keith Vaughan, lawyers and staff who made significant contributions to the success of the case included Sandy Sands, Bill Raper, Rob Fields, Dave Edwards, Bruce Williamson, Kim Stevenson, Larry Edgerton, Ann Kimrey, Jimmy Barnhill, Ashley Thrift, Murray Greason, Don Donadio, and Deborah Hylton. Independent of the firm, retired naval captain and aeronautical engineer Ira Schwartz, who was a member of the Bailey class, also fought tirelessly from the beginning on behalf of the retirees. Upon settlement of the case, Womble Carlyle was chosen to administer the distribution of retiree refunds. The firm hired Schwartz to head up the settlement administration group.

In his order awarding attorneys' fees in the case, Judge Thompson praised the collective work: "Never has so much been done for so many as a result of a lawsuit brought on behalf of North Carolina taxpayers. Attorneys' fees awarded and expenses reimbursed, together with all the costs of administering this settlement, result in class members paying, in effect, less than 15 cents on each dollar recovered on their behalf, and nothing for their future tax exemption."

Womble Carlyle also participated in the court-ordered $440 million settlement of the *Smith/Shaver* case over the intangibles tax, levied by the state of North Carolina on out-of-state stock during the early 1990s. The North Carolina General Assembly repealed the tax in 1995. Gene Boyce and Jack Cummings, lawyers in the firm's Raleigh office at that time, and Bill Raper of the Charlotte office played major roles in the suit.

Womble Carlyle Sandridge & Rice was commonly viewed by most outsiders as a conservative "white shoe" North Carolina law firm, averse to change and traditional in its practice. Yet it was Womble Carlyle—a firm that for decades had spurned the very notion of advertising for the law profession—that actually became one of the first firms in the region to develop an extensive marketing and advertising program.

The Marketing Committee, chaired by Karen Carey, convinced the Firm Management Committee to develop a marketing strategy to increase the firm's name recognition. A national marketing consulting firm was hired in 1995 to coordinate market research and the development of a corporate identity and positioning program, including an institutional advertising campaign. The now-familiar "wavy triangle" logo representing the firm's geographical region along the coast of the Southeast was approved by the Firm Management Committee in December 1995, as was the tag line "Our Lawyers Mean Business."

When the firm began running advertisements in publications that included the *Wall Street Journal* and *Business North Carolina* in January 1996, Womble Carlyle became the first major law firm in the state to launch an advertising campaign. Ads also appeared that year on display boards in airport concourses in Charlotte, Greensboro, Raleigh, and Atlanta.

While the firm's entire campaign proved successful, the advertisements featuring a bulldog struck an emotional chord. Consultants came up with the firm's very own bulldog, named Winston, and made him the centerpiece of a new print campaign conveying the message that Womble Carlyle was a tenacious—but approachable—advocate for its clients.

Mark Poovey, a longtime member of the Marketing Committee, summed up his colleagues' goal: "We wanted to convey the message that we are not bound by tradition; that we are a law firm that can pretty much handle your needs, whatever they are and wherever you are; that we have a strong commitment to our clients; and that we have a sense of humor. And I think that campaign has changed the image of what Womble Carlyle is."

The year 1999 was another banner one for the firm. That September, upon his retirement as chief justice of the North Carolina Supreme Court, Burley B. Mitchell, Jr., joined Womble Carlyle Sandridge & Rice to head the firm's appellate practice. A member of the state's high court for 17 years, Chief Justice Mitchell had previously served as an Appeals Court judge, as Wake County district attorney, and as secretary of the North Carolina Department of Crime Control and Public Safety in the administration of Governor James B. Hunt, Jr. Also in 1999, a member of the

Winston, the star of a popular advertising campaign, led the way for the firm.

Womble Carlyle Collection

Another award-winning shot of Winston.

WOMBLE CARLYLE COLLECTION

In 1999, Winston welcomed Burley B. Mitchell, former chief justice of the North Carolina Supreme Court, to Womble Carlyle.

WOMBLE CARLYLE COLLECTION

After guiding the firm for almost twenty years as its chief administrative officer, Hassel Parker became President and CEO of FirmLogic.

WOMBLE CARLYLE COLLECTION

FirmLogic℠

In November 2000, the firm spun off its Ancillary Services Group into a new company, FirmLogic, LP.

WOMBLE CARLYLE COLLECTION

James B. Hunt, Jr., four-term governor of North Carolina and a national leader in education, joined Womble Carlyle in February 2001.

Photograph by Jon Gardiner

firm, Michael E. Ray, served as chairman of the board of Lex Mundi, an association of over 150 leading independent law firms around the world.

In July 2000, the members voted to spin off the firm's rapidly growing Ancillary Services unit into a new company. The spin-off, called FirmLogic, would continue to offer a full range of technological and legal support services such as jury consulting, medical records analysis, and document management. As a separate entity, the new company would have greater managerial and financial flexibility and more opportunity to market these services to the largest pool of potential customers—other law firms. FirmLogic debuted as a separate company on October 1, 2000.

In January 2001, Womble Carlyle welcomed former North Carolina governor James B. Hunt, Jr., as a member of the firm. One of the nation's most experienced, innovative, and successful governors, Hunt was recognized as a national leader in the fields of educational reform, children's health, and economic development. His Smart Start early-education initiative won praise and inspired imitators across the country.

By the turn of the new millennium, the Raleigh and Research Triangle Park offices were enjoying strong growth. Taken together, the two offices had the largest practice of any law firm in the Raleigh-Durham area. Don Donadio, the managing member in the Raleigh office, joked that his job amounted to "finding more office space, filling it up with good lawyers, and letting them go to work." But, he added, "at some points in the years since 1982, it hasn't always looked like this office was headed in the right direction—that we were doing the things that we were sent here to do. But the firm has been patient, has given us time to mature, has understood that sometimes people and practices develop at different paces. And I think that the firm has been richly rewarded for its patience."

Likewise, in Atlanta, Managing Member Steve Dunlevie offered his perspective on that office's first five years: "I think what impressed us the most about Womble Carlyle was the firm's principles and values. We really felt that we were kindred spirits. From day one, our Parker Johnson lawyers have been treated like they've always been a part of Womble Carlyle. It's been a wonderful, wonderful marriage. Now, some five years later, instead of 25 lawyers, we have 75 in Atlanta. Part of that is due to the dynamic growth of Atlanta. But much is attributable to Womble Carlyle generally and the great reputation that the firm has. The first five years have been remarkable, and we look for greater things."

In the spring of 2002, the firm will return to the historic old courthouse square of Winston-Salem when it joins Wachovia Bank as anchor tenant of One West Fourth Street, a state-of-the-art office and retail complex to be completed in the city's downtown area. The new 13-story facility will underscore the firm's innovative technologies and include such features as fiber optics, wireless communications, and a videoconferencing center linking lawyers and clients in remote locations.

"Our firm was founded at the height of the Industrial Revolution, and is now at the forefront of the Technology Revolution, which is transforming the practice of law," said Managing Partner John Garrou in a statement announcing the planned relocation. "While we continue to offer clients a full array of traditional legal services, we are using technology more and more to provide innovative solutions to clients' problems. This new facility will enable us to wire innovation into the very infrastructure of the building."

Just as Womble Carlyle showed leadership in moving its offices to One Triad Park (now BB&T Financial Center) in 1987, the move to One West Fourth Street demonstrates the firm's commitment to Winston-Salem and to the city's efforts to revitalize its downtown core. The move will also give BB&T, an important client, valuable space to expand.

The year the firm was founded—1876—was also the year of Custer's Last Stand. The massacre of the troops of the Seventh Cavalry at the Battle of the Little Bighorn exemplified the hazards of life on the Western frontier. At that time, the family of a soldier injured or killed in battle had no benefits. By custom, the regiment literally passed the hat to collect money for the widow and children. But after the Little Bighorn, there was no regiment left to pass the hat, since Custer and all of his men had been killed. The army went to Congress, which voted down a bill to help the troops' families. So some army officers—among them General Philip Sheridan and Major Abner Doubleday—got together and formed a mutual-aid association to "aid the families of the deceased members in a prompt, simple and substantial manner," in the words of the association's charter. Later converted to an insurance company, it is now known as the Army and Air Force Mutual Aid Association, a major American insurance company, a major real-estate investor in the Washington, D.C., area, and a client of the firm and one of its predecessors, the David Hagner firm, for 25 years.

The Winston-Salem office returns to its roots.
In 2002, the firm's offices will return to Fourth Street opposite the old courthouse square, the site of the offices of Glenn & Glenn in the 1880s.

FORSYTH COUNTY PUBLIC LIBRARY PHOTOGRAPH COLLECTION AND MAGNOLIA PROPERTIES

Since 1876, Womble Carlyle Sandridge & Rice has been privileged to serve many of the region's leading businesses, governmental bodies, and educational and health-care institutions. Today, the firm provides a full range of legal services to regional, national, and international clients in industries that include financial services, commercial real estate, information technology, health care, manufacturing, and telecommunications. It also serves educational institutions and governmental bodies and agencies.

Womble Carlyle's dynamic growth has mirrored that of the Southeast. From its roots in Winston-Salem, the firm has expanded in tandem with its clients and other businesses drawn to the region by its economic and lifestyle advantages. At the dawn of a new era, Womble Carlyle is helping clients thrive in the vibrant economy of Greenville and Upstate South Carolina; connect with capital in Charlotte and Atlanta; grow emerging technology in Research Triangle Park and northern Virginia; and influence state and federal policymakers in Raleigh and Washington, D.C.

By the turn of the millennium, the firm's practice rivaled any in the country for sheer scope and quality. Womble Carlyle's corporate and tax lawyers handle multimillion-dollar transactions and high-tech start-ups. Firm labor and employment lawyers help companies cope with the complexities of the workplace environment. Womble Carlyle patent lawyers protect clients' inventions and other intellectual property, while the firm's litigators handle some of the most complex and demanding cases in the country. And the firm's banking and commercial real estate attorneys advise lenders and developers responsible for premier projects in the Southeast and the Mid-Atlantic region.

As Chairman John Garrou said at a firm retreat in October 2000, "Womble Carlyle has a long and proud legacy to uphold, and we have the foundation in place for continued success. We have great people of skill and good will, both lawyers and staff; we are in great and expanding markets; we have a wonderful reputation; our core values are strong and bind us together. We look to the future with hope and excitement."

Appendix A
FirmLogic, LP

A new kind of practice support service, FirmLogic, LP, debuted on November 1, 2000. It was a spin-off of the pioneering and highly successful Ancillary Services Group of Womble Carlyle Sandridge & Rice. FirmLogic acquired a combination of other industry leaders, including HSV Legal Consulting Services of Atlanta, Enhanced Systems and Solutions of Houston, and Legal Application Holding Company (DataTrends Technology Company and Client Profiles).

Upon its launching, FirmLogic partnered with law firms and corporate legal departments, offering them a competitive advantage through a comprehensive selection of critical support services and customized, integrated software products. The company's full range of support services was designed to free lawyers from administrative tasks and allow them to focus on strategic matters for clients.

"Law firms and corporate legal departments need help to leverage their business in the current marketplace," said FirmLogic president and chief executive officer Hassel L. Parker in a press release announcing the start of the company. "FirmLogic offers the legal community the most extensive resources and industry expertise, helping them feel secure and confident while making them heroes in the eyes of their clients."

The company offers a full range of integrated software products and critical support services, including medical issue analysis, imaging systems, settlement administration, trial consulting, practice management, litigation document management, management and technology consulting, custom software development, application hosting, Web development, infrastructure management, integration services, and information security services. The company's "one-stop shop" offers a variety of leading-edge products and services heretofore available only to large firms with great financial resources.

FirmLogic's multidisciplinary team includes nurses, medical transcriptionists, psychologists, consulting attorneys, paralegals, CPAs, technology and security experts, trainers, and other support personnel. The company also has a research-and-development group dedicated to building new products and services to meet the needs of the legal industry. L. Donald Holland, one of the nation's leading legal-industry consultants, heads the company's research-and-development efforts as president of the FirmLogic Technology Group. "Our executive team has more than 150 years of combined experience working with law firms and corporate general counsels," said Parker. "Our unique understanding of their practice support needs fuels our research-and-development efforts."

FirmLogic is based in Winston-Salem, North Carolina, and has offices in Atlanta, Raleigh, and Houston. As of the spring of 2001, the company's 300-plus employees served more than 2,000 clients in Europe and the Americas.

Appendix B
WOMBLE CARLYLE DISTINGUISHED SERVICE AWARD WINNERS

In October 1996, Womble Carlyle initiated the practice of honoring the exemplary lives and singular achievements of selected attorneys and staff with Distinguished Service Awards, presented at the firm's biennial retreat. The awards are intended to recognize those who have exemplified selfless devotion to the firm or to the profession. Award winners are presented with an engraved silver bowl at a formal dinner on the final evening of the retreat.

William F. Womble Award for Service to the Bar

Dewey W. Wells 1996
Elizabeth L. Quick 1998
Patricia T. Meador 2000
Diane J. Fuchs 2000

Irving Carlyle Pro Bono Publico *Award*

Reid Cal Adams, Jr. 1996
Bonnie Kay Donahue 1998
John D. Hagner 2000

W. P. Sandridge, Sr., Award for Service to the Firm

Murray C. Greason, Jr. 1996
H. Grady Barnhill, Jr. 1998
Hassel L. Parker 2000

Leon L. Rice, Jr., Award for Service to the Community

William A. Davis II 1996
R. Michael Leonard 1998
Larry D. Estridge 2000

H. Grady Barnhill, Jr., Award for Service to Clients

G. Donald Johnson 1996
Martin L. Holton III 1998
Roddey M. Ligon, Jr. 2000

Appendix C

PREDECESSOR NAMES OF WOMBLE CARLYLE SANDRIDGE & RICE

Watson & Glenn 1876-1885

Glenn & Glenn 1885-1891

Glenn & Manly 1891-1898

Glenn, Manly & Hendren 1898-1905

Manly & Hendren 1905-1911

Manly, Hendren & Womble 1911-1942

Womble, Carlyle, Martin & Sandridge 1942-1954

Womble Carlyle Sandridge & Rice 1954-

BIBLIOGRAPHY

A starting point for any study of Womble Carlyle Sandridge & Rice is a short unpublished history of the firm written by Kathy Warden Manning in 1979. Based on newspaper research and several interviews with firm attorneys, Ms. Manning's history provides an outline of significant personages and events during the firm's first 100 years.

William F. Womble graciously consented to a number of conversations with the author and provided copies of previous interviews. Mr. Womble also supplied a copy of the memoirs of his father, B. S. Womble, and shared articles and news stories from his extensive personal files on the history of the firm.

Leon L. Rice, Jr.'s, memoir, *Living, Loving and Lawyering,* was a key source of information on the growth and development of the firm since World War II. The Irving Edward Carlyle Papers at the Wake Forest University Library contained several files of material relating to Mr. Carlyle's law practice. Minutes of the Firm Management Committee from the late 1970s to the present were another important source of statistical information and key dates in the recent history of Womble Carlyle.

Interviews supplied information on the history of the firm unavailable anywhere else. The attorneys who contributed to this project included William F. Womble, John L. W. Garrou, H. Grady Barnhill, Jr., Allan R. Gitter, Calder W. Womble, Murray C. Greason, Jr., Leslie E. Browder, Linwood L. Davis, William A. Davis II, Kenneth A. Moser, Jimmy H. Barnhill, Roddey M. Ligon, Jr., William F. Womble, Jr., David A. Irvin, Mark N. Poovey, Elizabeth L. Quick, Keith W. Vaughan, Donald A. Donadio, Deborah J. Hylton, Kenneth G. Carroll, G. Michael Barnhill, Lesley G. Powell, William C. Raper, Larry D. Estridge, Steven S. Dunlevie, Robert F. Cook, Paul A. Kaplan, John D. Hagner, and W. Andrew Copenhaver.

Staff members interviewed for this project included Hassel L. Parker, Terry M. Wiley, Keith Tedrow, Patricia A. Kight, Donald H. Adamick, Cavelle L. Lund, Betty P. Stephenson, Claudia G. Lyda, Marie S. Rodden, Anita L. Brannan, Frances P. Couch, Beth B. Keiger, Lynn C. Hester, Hazel Levin, Barbara Sims, John T. Boyer, and Susan F. DeVore.

Much of the material in the book is based on extensive research in secondary sources available in North Carolina libraries. The author scanned decades of issues of Winston-Salem newspapers, including the *Union Republican* and the *Sentinel*, while Robin Jackson laboriously photocopied dozens of articles from the Salem *People's Press* and the *Journal*. City directories for Winston, Salem, and Winston-Salem at the Forsyth County Public Library and the North Carolina Collection at UNC-Chapel Hill provided valuable information, particularly for the 19th century. Moravian records collected by Bishop Edward Rondthaler in *The Memorabilia of Fifty Years, 1877 to 1927* conveyed a sense of the texture of daily life in Winston and Salem. The *Proceedings* of the North Carolina Bar Association contained essential background information on the history of the legal profession in the Tar Heel State.

Important historical works consulted included the following: *Forsyth: The History of a County on the March* by Adelaide Fries, Stuart T. Wright, and J. Edwin Hendricks; the special bicentennial edition of the *Winston-Salem Journal and Sentinel*; *Winston-Salem in History*, published by Historic Winston; *Descriptive Sketch of Winston-Salem* by David Peter Robbins; *Souvenir of the Twin Cities of North Carolina* by Angelina V. Winkler; *Winston-Salem, "City of Industry"* by C. E. Weaver; and *Winston-Salem: Half-Century of Progress* by the Winston-Salem Chamber of Commerce.

Key sources for pictorial images of Winston-Salem included *Winston-Salem: A Pictorial History* by Fambrough L. Brownlee; *Winston-Salem: A History* by Frank V. Tursi; *100 Years of Images: Capturing the Moment* by Sue J. Hendricks; *North Carolina Illustrated, 1524-1984* by H. G. Jones; and *Images of America: Forsyth County, 1849-1999* by Cindy H. Casey.

—Lynn Roundtree

Interviews

Adamick, Donald H. Interview by the author. Tape recording. Winston-Salem, N.C., 26 June 2000.

Barnhill, G. Michael. Interview by the author. Tape recording. Charlotte, N.C., 21 September 2000.

Barnhill, H. Grady, Jr. Interview by the author. Winston-Salem, N.C., 4 August 2000.

Barnhill, Jimmy H. Interview by the author. Tape recording. Winston-Salem, N.C., 24 August 2000.

Boyer, John T. Interview by the author. Tape recording. Washington, D.C., 5 October 2000.

Brannan, Anita L. Interview by the author. Tape recording. Winston-Salem, N.C., 14 September 2000.

Browder, Leslie E. Interview by the author. Tape recording. Winston-Salem, N.C., 17 August 2000.

Carroll, Kenneth G. Interview by the author. Tape recording. Research Triangle Park, N.C., 21 September 2000.

Cook, Robert F. Interview by the author. Tape recording. Atlanta, Ga., 2 October 2000.

Copenhaver, W. Andrew. Interview by the author. Tape recording. Winston-Salem, N.C., 6 October 2000.

Couch, Frances P. Interview by the author. Tape recording. Winston-Salem, N.C., 14 September 2000.

Davis, Linwood L. Interview by the author. Tape recording. Winston-Salem, N.C., 18 August 2000.

Davis, William A., II. Interview by the author. Tape recording. Winston-Salem, N.C., 18 August 2000.

DeVore, Susan F. Interview by the author. Tape recording. Atlanta, Ga., 2 October 2000.

Donadio, Donald A. Interview by the author. Tape recording. Raleigh, N.C., 21 September 2000.

Dunlevie, Steven S. Interview by the author. Tape recording. Atlanta, Ga., 2 October 2000.

Estridge, Larry D. Interview by the author. Tape recording. Greenville, S.C., 28 September 2000.

Garrou, John L. W. Interview by the author. Tape recording. Winston-Salem, N.C., 3 August 2000.

Gitter, Allan R. Interview by the author. Tape recording. Winston-Salem, N.C., 4 August 2000.

Greason, Murray C., Jr. Interview by the author. Tape recording. Winston-Salem, N.C., 8 September 2000.

Grumbine, D. Allen. Interview by the author. Tape recording. Greenville, S.C., 28 September 2000.

Hagner, John D. Interview by the author. Tape recording. Washington, D.C., 5 October 2000.

Hester, Lynn C. Interview by the author. Tape recording. Winston-Salem, N.C., 15 September 2000.

Hylton, Deborah J. Interview by the author. Tape recording. Research Triangle Park, N.C., 21 September 2000.

Irvin, David A. Interview by the author. Tape recording. Winston-Salem, N.C., 25 August 2000.

Kaplan, Paul A. Interview by the author. Tape recording. Washington, D.C., 5 October 2000.

Keiger, Beth B. Interview by the author. Tape recording. Winston-Salem, N.C., 14 September 2000.

Kight, Patricia A. Interview by the author. Tape recording. Winston-Salem, N.C., 1 September 2000.

Levin, Hazel. Interview by the author. Tape recording. Winston-Salem, N.C., 15 September 2000.

Ligon, Roddey M., Jr. Interview by the author. Tape recording. Winston-Salem, N.C., 25 August 2000.

Lund, Cavelle A. Interview by the author. Tape recording. Winston-Salem, N.C., 7 September 2000.

Lyda, Claudia G. Interview by the author. Tape recording. Winston-Salem, N.C., 8 September 2000.

Moser, Kenneth A. Interview by the author. Tape recording. Winston-Salem, N.C., 31 August 2000.

Parker, Hassel L. Interview by the author. Tape recording. Winston-Salem, N.C., 1 September 2000.

Poovey, Mark N. Interview by the author. Tape recording.

Winston-Salem, N.C., 15 September 2000.
Powell, Lesley G. Interview by the author. Tape recording. Charlotte, N.C., 22 September 2000.
Quick, Elizabeth L. Interview by the author. Tape recording. Winston-Salem, N.C., 15 September 2000.
Raper, William C. Interview by the author. Tape recording. Charlotte, N.C., 22 September 2000.
Rodden, Marie S. Interview by the author. Tape recording. Winston-Salem, N.C., 8 September 2000.
Sims, Barbara. Interview by the author. Tape recording. Winston-Salem, N.C., 15 September 2000.
Smith, W. Lindsay. Interview by the author. Tape recording. Greenville, S.C., 28 September 2000.
Tedrow, W. Keith. Interview by the author. Tape recording. Winston-Salem, N.C., 7 September 2000.
Vaughan, Keith W. Interview by the author. Tape recording. Winston-Salem, N.C., 15 September 2000.
Wiley, Terry M. Interview by the author. Tape recording. Winston-Salem, N.C., 1 September 2000.
Womble, Calder W. Interview by the author. Tape recording. Winston-Salem, N.C., 17 August 2000.
Womble, William F. Interview by the author. Tape recording. Winston-Salem, N.C., 3 August 2000.
Womble, William F., Jr. Interview by the author. Tape recording. Winston-Salem, N.C., 25 August 2000.

Other Sources

American Red Cross, Winston-Salem Chapter. *History of the Winston-Salem Chapter of the American National Red Cross in World War II.* Winston-Salem, N.C.: Winston-Salem Chapter, 1947.
Branson's North Carolina Business Directory. Raleigh, N.C.: Levi Branson, 1877, 1884, 1890, 1896.
Brogden, Curtis H. *Message of the Governor to the General Assembly of the State of North Carolina for the Year 1876.* Raleigh, N.C.: Josiah Turner, 1877.
Brownlee, Fambrough L. *Winston-Salem: A Pictorial History.* Norfolk, Va.: Donning Company, 1977.
Carlyle, Irving Edward. Papers. Wake Forest University Library.
Casey, Cindy H. *Images of America: Forsyth County, 1849-1999.* Dover, N.H.: Arcadia Publishing, 1998.
Charles Emerson & Co.'s Winston, Salem & Greensboro, North Carolina, Directory. Raleigh, N.C.: Edwards, Broughton & Company, 1879.
Directory of Greensboro, Salem and Winston, and Gazetteer of Forsyth and Guilford Counties. Atlanta, Ga.: Interstate Directory Company, 1884.
Ellis Classified Directory of Winston-Salem, N.C. Columbia, S.C.: Ellis Classified Directory Company, 1915.
Foltz, Henry Wesley. *Winston Fifty Years Ago.* Winston-Salem, N.C.: 1926.
Forsyth County Board of Commissioners. *A Decade of Progress in Forsyth County, North Carolina.* Winston-Salem, N.C.: Board of Commissioners, 1960.
Fries, Adelaide, et al. *Forsyth: The History of a County on the March.* Chapel Hill, N.C.: University of North Carolina Press, 1976.
Gray, Robert T. Oration delivered at Salem, North Carolina, on July 4, 1876. Unpublished typescript.
Heer, Clarence. *Winston-Salem: An Analysis of City Finances.* Winston-Salem, N.C.: *Twin City Sentinel*, 1946.
Hendricks, Sue J. *100 Years of Images: Capturing the Moment.* Winston-Salem, N.C.: *Winston-Salem Journal*, 1999.
Hill's Winston-Salem, North Carolina, City Directory. Richmond, Va.: Hill Directory Company, 1933, 1935, 1938.
Jones, H. G. *North Carolina Illustrated, 1524-1984.* Chapel Hill, N.C.: University of North Carolina Press, 1983.
MacNeill, Ben Dixon. "The Town of a Hundred Millionaires." *North American Review* (August 1931): 101-110.
Manning, Kathy Warden. "The First 100 Years of Womble Carlyle." Unpublished manuscript, 1979.
Martin, Nancy Stockton. *Changing Times: As Remembered by Nancy Stockton Martin.* Winston-Salem: 1983.
Miller's Winston-Salem, N.C., City Directory. Asheville, N.C.: Commercial Service Company, 1928-1931.
North Carolina Bar Association. *Bar Notes.* Raleigh, N.C.: North Carolina Bar Association, 1954-1972.
North Carolina Bar Association. *Proceedings of the Annual Session of the North Carolina Bar Association.* Raleigh, N.C.: North Carolina Bar Association, 1899-1948.
North Carolina Supreme Court. *North Carolina Reports: Cases Argued and Determined in the Supreme Court of North Carolina.* Raleigh, N.C.: North Carolina Supreme Court, 1876-2001.
People's Press, 1876-1892.
Pfohl, J. Kenneth. *Memorabilia of Salem Congregation, 1931-1961.* Winston-Salem, N.C.: Moravian Archives, 1993.
Rice, Leon L., Jr. *Living, Loving and Lawyering.* 1986.
Robbins, David Peter. *Descriptive Sketch of Winston-Salem.* Winston-Salem, N.C.: *Sentinel* Job Print, 1888.
Rondthaler, Edward. *The Memorabilia of Fifty Years, 1877 to 1927.* Raleigh, N.C.: Edwards & Broughton Company, 1928.

Shirley, Michael. *From Congregation Town to Industrial City: Culture and Social Change in a Southern Community.* New York: New York University Press, 1994.

Southern Business Guide. New York: United States Central Publishing Company, 1879-1886.

Turner's North Carolina Almanac. Raleigh, N.C.: James H. Enniss, 1876-1877.

Turner's Winston and Salem City Directory. Yonkers, N.Y.: Turner & Company, 1891-1894.

Tursi, Frank V. *Winston-Salem: A History.* Winston-Salem, N.C.: John F. Blair, Publisher, 1994.

Twin-City Club. *Directory.* Winston-Salem, N.C.: Twin-City Club, 1935-1937.

Twin-City Daily Sentinel, 1886-1916.

Union Republican, 1874-1944.

Walsh's Winston-Salem, North Carolina, City Directory. Charleston, S.C.: Walsh Directory Company, 1906, 1908.

Waters, D. P. *Matters of Interest and Importance Concerning Winston-Salem, North Carolina.* Winston-Salem, N.C.: Board of Trade, 1909.

Weaver, C. E. *Winston-Salem, "City of Industry": Illustrated, Historical, Biographical Facts and Figures.* Winston-Salem, N.C.: Winston Printing Company, 1919.

Western Sentinel, 1887-1926.

Winkler, Angelina V. *Souvenir of the Twin Cities of North Carolina, Winston-Salem, Forsyth County.* Salem, N.C.: Blum's Steam Power Press Print, 1890.

Winston-Salem Board of Trade. *Souvenir of Winston-Salem, N.C.: Photogravures.* Brooklyn, N.Y.: Albertype Company, 1909.

Winston-Salem Chamber of Commerce. *Winston-Salem: Half-Century of Progress, 1885-1935.* Winston-Salem, N.C.: Chamber of Commerce, 1935.

Winston-Salem in History. Winston-Salem, N.C.: Historic Winston, 1966-1977.

Winston-Salem Journal, January 1900-April 2001.

Winston-Salem Journal and Sentinel, bicentennial edition, 1966.

Winston-Salem, N.C., City Directory. Asheville, N.C.: Piedmont Directory Company, 1910-1926.

Womble, Bunyan Snipes. Unpublished memoirs.

Womble Carlyle Sandridge & Rice Partnership Management Committee. Minutes, 1979-2001.

Young, Terrell. *Brief History of West End Development Company and Hotel Zinzendorf.* Winston-Salem, N.C.: 1977.

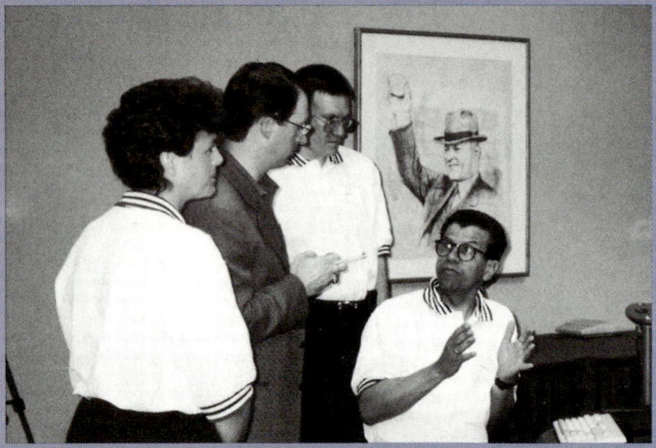

W C S R

INDEX

ABC/Capital Cities, 168–69
ABC/Food Lion case, 168–69
Academy of Music, 44
Adamick, Donald H., 142, 166, 168
Adams, Reid Cal, Jr., 185
ADEA (Title IX and the Age Discrimination in Employment Act), 134
advertising, by lawyers, 17, 18, 27, 80, 95, 177
Aetna Life and Casualty, 122
African-Americans
  admission to North Carolina Bar Association, 121–22
  B. S. Womble and Duke University policy toward, 113
  Brown v. Board of Education of Topeka, Kansas, 105
  employment of, 77
  General Assembly and, 115
  Glenn as governor and, 44, 46
  Glenn & Glenn cases involving, 21
  integration issues and, 115, 116, 117, 121
  labor issues and, 90, 91, 100, 102, 116
  lawyers hired by Womble Carlyle, 139
  lynching cases, 21, 46
  Manly, Hendren & Womble cases involving, 61
  Manly support for, 28
  segregation in Winston and, 52
  Slater Industrial and Normal School and, 36
"Against th' Law" (song), 102
Akin, Gump, Strauss, Hauer & Feld, 169
Allen, Oliver, Judge, 63
Allied Aviation Corporation of Baltimore, 86
Alspaugh, John W., Colonel, 10
Alspaugh & Buxton, Attorneys-at-Law and Insurance, 10
American Bar Association, 70, 114
American Bar Association General Council, 79
American College of Trial Lawyers, 116
American Express Company, 78
American Law Institute, 114
American Tobacco Company, 31, 51, 90, 108
AmLaw Tech, 160, 162
AMP, 119
Ancillary Services Group, 175–76, 183
Anglin, Jean, 142
antitrust law practice, 90, 110, 129, 149
appellate practice, 177
Arbor Acres, 113
Arista Mills Company, 102
Arista Mills Company, Textile Workers Union of America, CIO v., 102
Army and Air Force Mutual Aid Association, 180
Arnold v. Eastern Airlines, 135
Associated Aviation Underwriters, 134
Associated Family and Child Service Agency, 114
associates, of Womble Carlyle Sandridge & Rice, 133, 138, 148, 152
Atkins, Simon Green, 36
Atlanta office, of Womble Carlyle, 159
  celebration of opening, 167
  consideration of forming, 149
  growth of, 180
  opening of, 155–56, 163, 165–66
Austin, Frances, 124
aviation litigation, 128
Aycock, Charles B., 44

Bailey, James H. Pou, Judge, 159
Bailey, Josiah, 110
Bailey case, 159, 176
Baldwin, Garza, III, 138, 152
"Ball for British Relief," 86
Bancshares, Inc., 166
banking and finance practice, 122
bankruptcy practice, 158–59
Banks, J. C., 28, 36
Barber, Timothy G., 159, 169
Barnhardt, Zeb E., Jr., 127
Barnhill, G. Michael, 159
Barnhill, H. Grady, Jr., 129, 156
  as assistant to I. Carlyle, 114, 123
  awards of, 185
  becomes member of firm, 107, 111
  cases of, 135
  as head of Litigation Section, 149
  Irvin as associate to, 126
  litigation practice of, 135, 137
  on Partnership Management Committee, 134, 144
  Piedmont Aviation case and, 124–25
  on pro bono program, 160
  smoking and health litigation and, 150
Barnhill, Jimmy H., 124, 126–27, 129, 157, 176
baseball, 21, 39
Basic Pension and Profit-Sharing Plans (Rice and Schlaudt), 114–15
Bassick-Sack, 107
BB&T Financial Center, 180
Beasley, J. W., 37
Belews Lake facility of Duke Power, 122
Bell, J. Spencer, Judge, 115
Bellamy, Emmett, 85
Belo, Edward, 12
Belo v. Commissioners of Forsyth County, 12
Berrier, Robert, 21
Berry, R. Russell, 166
Bethel, C. A., 99
Biggs, James Crawford, 31
blacks. *See* African-Americans
Blair, David H., 39, 52, 55, 91
Blair, W. A., Colonel, 8
Board of Aldermen, 47, 70
Board of Commissioners of Winston v. Taylor, 20
Board of Education of Topeka, Kansas, Brown v., 105
Board of Elders, Home Moravian Church, 114
Board of Governors, Temple Emanuel, 113
Board of Higher Education, 115
Board of Trustees, Salem College and Academy, 114
Board of Trustees, Trinity College, 55
Board of Trustees, Wake Forest College, 97
Board of Trustees of Duke University, 111
Board of Trustees of Old Salem, Inc., 100
Bonsack Machine Company v. National Cigarette & Tobacco Company, 31

Booke, Sam L., 99
Booke & Company, 114, 134
bookkeepers, 99
"Booze Line," 42
Bost, S. Fraley, 138, 160
Bowman Gray Development Center, 120
Bowman Gray School of Medicine, 122
Bowman Gray Stadium, 77
Boyce, C. Eugene, 148, 159, 160, 176
Boyer, John, 20
Boyer, Peggy, 140
Boyer v. Teague, 20
Brad Ragan, Inc., 134
Brannan, Anita, 139, 142
Brenner Companies, Inc., 122
Brenner Industries, 134
Brett, Anthony H., 138, 139, 149
Briggs, William Cyrus, 24, 31, 33, 48
Briggs Shaffner Company, 86
Brogden, Willis, Judge, 89
Brooks, George, 11
Browder, Les M., 107, 110–11, 122, 144, 163
Brown, T. J., Major, xvii, 5
Brown and Williamson, 77
Brown's Warehouse, 14, 22
Brown v. Board of Education of Topeka, Kansas, 105
Broyhill Industries, 126
Buford, A. S., Colonel, 24, 28
Bunker, Adelaide, 38–39
Bunker, C. W., 38
Bunker, Chang, 38–39
Bunker, Eng, 39
Bunker, Sarah Yates, 39
Bunker v. Bunker, 38
Bureau of Internal Revenue, 91
Burlington Mills Corporation, 110
Burroughs, Mr., 91
Business Section, 156
Buxton, Anna, 55
Buxton, J. C., Colonel
  B. S. Womble and, 54
  cases of, 20
  as lawyer in early Winston, 6, 10
  on tobacco industry, 41
  Twin-City Club and, 19
  Watson joins with, 13
Bynum, John Gray, 6

California Court of Appeals, 116
Calloway, James, Dr., 38
Camel cigarettes, 58, 59, 86, 108
Cannon, Anne, 78
Cannon, Charles, 78
Cannon Mills, 122, 126
Carey, Karen, 177
Carlyle, Dora Dunn, 68
Carlyle, Irving E., 71, 85, 123
  background of, 68
  Barnhill and, 111
  becomes member of firm, 82
  clients of, 76, 90, 91, 97, 109
  as coach, 69
  community service of, 81, 99, 114, 122, 129
  cuspidor of, 124
  death of, 129–30
  as Democrat, 116–17
  political career of, 81, 89, 102, 105
  religion and, 113
  as senior partner, 109
  as Winston-Salem attorney, 109, 127
  World War II years and, 89
Carlyle, John Bethune, 68
Carlyle, Mary Belo, 124
Carolina Aluminum Company v. Federal Power Commission, 83
Carolina Biological Supply Company, 110
Carolina Container Corporation, 129
Carolina Portland Cement Company v. Washington Mills, 72
Carroll, Kenneth, 163, 168
Carter Machine Company v. P. H. Hanes and Company, 31
Centenary United Methodist Church, 113
Cessna Aircraft, 128
Chamber of Commerce, 27, 28, 89, 103, 108, 115, 119
Chambers, Claude, 82
Chambers, Julius L., 122
Chambers et al., United States v., 82–83
charities, supported by Manly, Hendren & Womble, 59, 61
Charlotte Court House, 34
Charlotte-Mecklenburg School, Swann v., 129
Charlotte office, of Womble Carlyle, 150
  building in, 151
  lawyers and associates in, 152
  litigation section in, 159
  staff of, 152
Chatham, H. G., 72
Chatham Manufacturing Company, 42, 47, 58, 75, 86, 126, 134
Chavis, Marvin, 160, 162, 175
The Checkerboard Corridor (Hunter), 97
child labor issues, 47–48, 62
child sexual-abuse cases, 160
Cipollone v. Liggett Group, Inc., 158
Citizens' Committee on Consolidation, 58
City-County Planning Board, 97, 99, 114
City Market, 74
City of Winston-Salem, Koontz v., 129
City of Winston-Salem, Maready v., 170
City of Winston-Salem v. Forsyth County, 89
City of Winston v. Wachovia Bank and Trust, 55–56
city solicitors, 54
Civil Aeronautics Board, 89, 100
civil and criminal law, 12
class-action suits, 126
ClientPlus Technology Services Group, 175
Clinard, Keith A., 138
Clinkscale, Brent O., 173
Cloud, John R., 6
Coan, George W., Jr., 76
Cobb, Joyce, 140

Cobb, Ty, 47
Coffee Pot, 67
Commissioners, Lemly v., 13
Commissioners of Forsyth County, Belo v., 12
Committee on Pension and Profit-Sharing Plans, Taxation Section, American Bar Association, 114
Committee on Taxation, North Carolina Bar Association, 92
Community Chest, 79, 89, 103, 104
Comptek Barrister 300 System, 141, 150
Conaway, David, 152
Congregation of United Brethren of Salem, 28
Connor, Henry Groves, 48
Container Corporation of America, United States v., 129
Continental Can Company, 119
Cook, Robert F., 166
Cooke, John C., 168
Cooke, Maddrey, 114
Cooley, Jim, 159
Copenhaver, W. Andrew, 128, 135, 149, 150, 169
Corporate and Tax Section, 123, 126, 133
Cosmos Club, 47
Council for Entrepreneurial Development, 168
Court Study Committee, 115
court week, 4–5
Craige, Burton, 47
Craven, J. Braxton, Jr., Judge, 129
Crutchfield v. Railroad, 13
Cummings, Jack, 176
cycling, 24, 33, 34

Dagenhart, Hammer v., 62
Daniels, Frank A., 114
David, Hagner, Kuney, PC, 170, 171, 180
David, Richard, 171
Davidson County, 19
Davie County, 13, 19
Davis, Archie K., 82
Davis, E. Lawrence, 126, 144, 147–48
Davis, Egbert, 88, 126
Davis, Linwood L., 113, 124, 125, 126, 127
Davis, Thomas H., 88
Davis, William A., II, 126, 134, 149, 156
Davis, William A., III, 185
Deal, Roy L., 68
Declaratory Judgment Act, 97
DeHart, Martha, 100
Democratic Party
- B. S. Womble and, 55
- I. Carlyle and, 116–17
- Manly and, 35
- R. B. Glenn and, 19, 43
- Simmons and, 27
- Simmons & Manly and, 24
- W. B. Glenn and, 6–7

Descriptive Sketch of Winston-Salem (Robbins), 19
Distinguished Service Awards, 185
Donadio, Donald F., 144, 168
- *Bailey* case and, 176
- becomes member of firm, 128
- on Bill Womble, 134–35
- as head of Financial Representation & Real Estate Section, 156
- as head of Raleigh office of Womble Carlyle, 147–48, 167
- on Raleigh office growth, 180

Donahue, Bonnie Kay, 159, 163, 185
Donahue, Daniel W., 138, 150, 157
Drake, Annie, 124
Duke, J. B., 41, 51
Duke Law School, 121
Duke Power Company, 78, 90, 122
Duke University, 55, 111, 113
Duke University Alumni Association, Forsyth County, 105
Duncan, Davy Crockett, 138
Duncan, Edwin, Sr., 138
Duncan, Joyner v., 138
Dunlevie, Steven S., 165, 166, 172, 175, 180
Duplan, 107

Eastern Airlines, Arnold v., 135
Eastern Air Lines, Inc., 135
Eastern Band of the Cherokee Nation, 83
Eaton, Oscar B., 58
Edens, Hollis, 111
Edgerton, Larry, 176
Edison, Thomas A., 25, 62
Edward Bello House, 2
Edwards, Dave, 176
Eighteenth Amendment, repeal of, 82
11th District Bar Association, 81
Eller, A. H., 70
Emerson, Charles, 13
Emmons, Mary, 140
Emory case, 159, 176
employee-benefits practice, 134
Employee Retirement Income Security Act (ERISA), 134
employment discrimination cases, 149
Enhanced Systems and Solutions of Houston, 183
environmental law, 149
Episcopal Diocese of North Carolina, 72
Equitable Life Assurance Society, 78, 100, 110
ERISA (Employee Retirement Income Security Act), 134
Ernst & Young, 159
Ervin, Samuel J., Jr., 105, 129, 135, 138, 139
estate cases, 38–39, 72, 90
estate planning, 149
Estridge, Larry D., 173, 185
ethics, 70, 72
Everett, George P., 12
Executive Committee, 11th District Bar Association, 81
Executive Committee, Womble Carlyle, 152, 156
"Experiment in Self-Reliance," 115

Fairchild-Hiller Corporation, 134
Family and Child Service Agency, 102
Farmers' National Bank, 76
Federal Appeals Court, 90

Federal Building, 130
Federal Court, 67
Federal District Court, 62
Federal Fair Labor Standards Act (1938), 90
Federal Power Commission, 83
Federal Power Commission, Carolina Aluminum Company v., 83
Field, Justin, 10
Fields, Rob, 176
Finance Committee (state Senate), 69, 102
Financial Representation & Real Estate Section, 156
Firestone, Harvey, 62
FirmLogic, LP, 178, 179, 183
Firm Management Committee, 160, 163, 177
Firm Study Committee, 141, 143, 152
First Amendment lawsuits, 149
First Atlanta Corporation, 148
First National Bank of Salem, 13
First Presbyterian Church, 113
First Wachovia Corporation, 148, 156
Fleming, J. Carlton, 150
Fleming, Robinson and Bradshaw, 150
Fogle, Charles A., 15
Fogle Bros. planing mills, 13, 17
Fogle Brothers Iron Works, 24
Foil Division, R. J. Reynolds Tobacco Company, 86
Foltz, Henry W., 6
Food Lion, Inc., 152, 168–69
football, 35, 69
Ford, Henry, 62
Ford Motor Company, 134, 138
Forsyth Citizens Planning Council, 103
Forsyth Country Club, 81
Forsyth County, 12, 20, 70
Forsyth County, City of Winston-Salem v., 89
Forsyth County Bar Association, 72, 79, 81, 121
Forsyth County Committee on Public Solicitation, 102
Forsyth County Court, 68
Forsyth County Courthouse, 9, 32
Forsyth County Democratic Club, 28
Forsyth County Democratic Convention, 28
Forsyth County Democratic Party, 35
Forsyth County District Attorney's Office, 160
Forsyth County Junior Bar Association, 81, 89, 114
Forsyth County Welfare Board, 81
Forsyth Riflemen, 28, 44, 59
Forsyth Superior Court, 19, 37, 48, 72
Fourth Circuit Court of Appeals, 169
Frankel, Gusti, 113
Fries, Adelaide, 55
Fries, Henry E., 15, 57
Fries Manufacturing and Power Company, 47
Frye, Henry E., 121
Fuchs, Diane J., 185
Fuller, W. W., 72
Fulton, Pink, 36
Furr, Jeffrey L., 160

Gailor, Carole S., 148
Gallant, Wade M., Jr., 128, 144
  banking and finance work of, 122
  becomes member of firm, 107, 110
  community service of, 114, 122
  death of, 157
  on Partnership Management Committee, 134
Garrou, John L. W., 164
  on Ancillary Services Group, 175–76
  cases of, 126
  on firm's propensity for change, 165
  on Greason, 163
  on history of firm, 181
  mergers-and-acquisitions work of, 149
  on Northern Virginia office of Womble Carlyle, 174
  religion and, 113
Gaston, William, 24
General Assembly (North Carolina), 54, 160
  Manly as candidate for, 28
  R. B. Glenn as member of, 43
  W. B. Glenn as member of, 6
  W. F. Womble as member of, 115
General Litigation Section, 156
German prisoners of war, 88
GI Bill of Rights, 95–96
Gibson, Byrum, 82
"The Girls" or "Old Bun Womble had a Firm," 105
Gitter, Allan R., 133, 140
  becomes member of firm, 111
  Greason as assistant to, 123
  insurance defense and, 125, 149
  Irvin as associate to, 126, 127
  Raper as associate to, 129
  W. F. Womble, Jr. as associate to, 128
GlaxoSmithKline, Inc., 168
Glenn, Annie Dodge, 17
Glenn, Chalmers, 17
Glenn, Margaret Bynum, 6
Glenn, Nina Deaderick, 17, 44
Glenn, Robert Broadnax, 13, 71
  background of, 17
  baseball and, 39
  community service of, 19, 28
  formation of Glenn & Manly, 27
  government service of, 19, 35, 36–37, 43–46
  as governor of state, 44–46, 48, 49
  leaving Glenn, Manly & Hendren, 48
  support for consolidation of Winston and Salem, 57
  as U.S. Attorney, 28, 43
Glenn, Tyre, 6
Glenn, William Bynum, xvii, 19, 71
  background of, 6
  cases of, 21
  government service of, 6–7, 12
  health problems and death of, 21, 27
  investments of, 20
Glenn & Glenn, 187
  advertising by, 17, 18
  clients of, 19–20
  earliest description of, 19

formation of, 13, 19
Glenn & Manly, 187
advertising by, 27
clients of, 28, 31, 35
formation of, 27
Hendren joins, 35
Glenn, Manly & Hendren, 187
cases of, 36, 37–39
clients of, 47
dissolution of, 48
formation of, 35
offices of, 43, 50
Glidewell, P. W., 61
Goodyear Tire and Rubber Company, 126
Gorrell, A. B., Colonel, 15
Goslen, J. R., 51
governmental law, 20
governor, of state of North Carolina, R. B. Glenn as, 44–46, 48, 49
Graham, Frank Porter, 103
Graham, Kitty, 99
Gravely Tractor Company, 119
Gray, Bowman, Sr., 66, 81
Gray, Eugene E., 10, 34
Gray, Gordon, 81–82, 104, 115, 116
Gray, James A., Jr., 55, 100
Gray, James A., Sr., xvii, 11, 17, 19, 57, 63
Gray, Robert, 56
Graylyn, 66
Greason, Joan, 123
Greason, Murray C., Jr., 123, 126, 144
on Atlanta office, 156, 166, 172
awards of, 185
Bailey case and, 176
on Charlotte office, 159
on hiring Hass Parker, 142
on litigation versus corporate law, 157
as managing partner, 163
mergers-and-acquisitions work of, 149
on old-fashioned feel of firm, 124
on Pen Sandridge, 135
on technology investments by firm, 160
Great Depression, 76
Greenville office, of Womble Carlyle, 173–74
Growth Study Committee, 141
Grumbine, D. Allen, 173–74
Guilford County Bar Association, 163
Guion, Owen H., 24
Gulley, Needham Y., 68
Gunter, Michael D., 134, 149
Guthrie, Woody, 102

H. Grady Barnhill, Jr., Award for Service to Clients, 185
Habitat for Humanity, 163
Hagner, John D., 113, 170, 171, 185
Hammer v. Dagenhart, 62
Hammons, J. W., 48
Hanes, Gordon, 120
Hanes, John Wesley, 120
Hanes, Pleasant Henderson, 15, 17, 31, 120
Hanes Dye and Finishing Company, 77, 86, 134
Hanes Hosiery Mills Company, 107, 120
Harden, Debbie W., 159
Harrison, J. W., 37
Hart, Rand, 36
Haulsee, Hada V., 138
Hayes, Rutherford B., 3
Hayes Microcomputer Products, Inc., 166
health and medical law practice, 61, 149–50, 152, 158, 168
Heilig, Fay, 99
Hendren, Annie J. Rawley, 35
Hendren, Linville, 34
Hendren, Mary Elizabeth, 34
Hendren, William Mayhew, 71, 72
background of, 34–35
baseball and, 39
cases of, 38, 48, 61–62, 72, 82–83, 83
community service of, 35, 47, 61, 79
death of, 83
financial status of, 75
new federal court and, 67
Hennis, 107
"Herbs of Life" case, 20–21
Hicks, John, 10
Hicks boys case, 10
High, Russell, 61–62
High Museum of Art, 167
Hodges, Luther, Gov., 114, 116
Hoey, Clyde R., Senator, 105
Holland, L. Donald, 160, 183
Hollings, Ernest, Senator, 159
Holman, Libby, 78
Holton, Mark, 150
Holton, Martin L., III, 185
Home Insurance Company of New Orleans, 28
Home Moravian Church, 36, 113, 114
hospital law practice, 139, 149
House of Representatives (North Carolina)
B. S. Womble terms in, 69
L. Davis terms in, 126
Houser, Marlene, 175
HSV Legal Consulting Services of Atlanta, 183
Hughes, Charles Evans, Chief Justice, 82–83
Hughes, Will, 10
Hughes case, 10
Hunt, James B., Jr., 177, 179
Hunter, Rixie, 97
Hylton, Deborah J., 148, 163, 167–68, 172, 176

income-tax law, 59. *See also* Rice, Leon Leftwich, Jr.; Tax law
The Industrial Commission of Winston-Salem, 75
in-house counsel, 157
insurance companies, 28, 31. *See also names of specific companies*
insurance defense practice, 78, 90, 100, 110, 125, 149
Integon Corporation, 122, 126
integration issues, 115, 116, 117, 121
intellectual-property practice, 172

Internal Revenue Service, 123, 126, 138
International Bar Association Conference, 69
International Business Machines Company, 77
International Division, Wachovia Bank and Trust Company, 121
Internet website, Womble Carlyle, 160
Interstate Securities Corporation, 152
Irvin, David A., 126, 127, 128, 149
Irving Carlyle *Pro Bono Publico* Award, 185
Isaf, Louis T., 172
Isaf, Vaughan, & Kerr, 172

J. A. Jones Construction Company, 152
J. A. Vance Company, 33
J. A. Vance Iron Works, 13, 58–59
J. A. Vance Machine Shops, 24
J. C. Spach Wagon Works, 59
J. E. Mickey Tinsmith Shop, 67
The Jefferson Law Firm, PLC, 174
Jefferson Standard Life Insurance Company, 76, 78
Jim Crow laws, 46
Johnson, Cy, 150, 152
Johnson, G. Donald, 166, 185
Johnson, Ross, 158
Johnston, David, 152
Johnston, Mary Beth, 168, 169
Jones, H. G., 96
Joseph Schlitz Brewing Company, 119, 134
Joyner v. Duncan, 138
Junior Bar Association, 81, 89, 114

Kaplan, Paul, 172
Kernersville, 110, 126
Kight, Pat, 129, 135, 140, 142, 163
Kilgo, Dr., 92
Kimrey, Ann, 176
Knight, Douglas M., Dr., 113
Knollwood Baptist Church, 113
Kobre, Henry, 48
Kobre, Sam, 48
Kohlberg Kravis Roberts and Company, 158
Koontz v. City of Winston-Salem, 129
Korner, J. Gilmer, Jr., 91
Kurfees, Marshall, 97

labor and employment law practice, 100, 102, 110, 149
labor issues
  African-Americans and, 90, 91, 100, 102, 116
  child, 47–48, 62
  unionization and, 97, 100, 102
Labor Section, 126
Lash, Israel G., 13
Law Office Administrator Committee, 141
"Lawyers Nine," 21
Leach, James Madison, 8
Legal Application Holding Company (Data Trends Technology Company and Client Profiles), 183

Lemly, W. A., 13
Lemly v. Commissioners, 13
Leon, Christopher E., 156, 166
Leonard, R. Michael, 185
Leon L. Rice, Jr., Award for Service to the Community, 185
"Lexington Lynchers" case, 21
Lexington Manufacturing Company, 13
Lex Mundi, 179
Liberty Bond drive, 61
Liggett Group, Inc., Cipollone v., 158
Liggett & Myers, 90
Ligon, Roddey M., Jr., 139
  argued last case in old Post Office Building, 130
  awards of, 185
  as head of Trade, Employment, and Governmental Regulations Section, 156
  as lateral attorney, 127
  long-range planning and, 141
  religion and, 113
  as Winston-Salem city attorney, 149, 170
Lilly, James E., 156, 166
litigation, 110, 124–26, 128, 133, 135, 137, 150, 157. *See also specific cases*
Litigation Section, 148, 149, 156, 159
Living, Loving, and Lawyering (Rice), 99, 117, 139, 152–53
Lizzie Penn v. Western Union Telegraph Company, 55
Long, Bill, 83
Long, Nell, 83
Long Range Planning Committee, 159
Lowe's Companies, 123
Lumbermen's Mutual Casualty Company, 100
Lund, Cavelle, 135, 137
Lyda, Claudia, 140
lynching cases, 21, 46

Macemore, Sandra, 140
Mackesey, Daniel R., 174
Manly, Clement B., Colonel, 26, 71
  background of, 24
  baseball and, 39
  cases of, 31, 37, 48, 70, 72
  community service of, 28, 35, 47
  death of, 72–73
  formation of Glenn & Manly, 27
  formation of Simmons & Manly, 24
  income-tax law and, 59
  on last hours of R. J. Reynolds, 63
  professional service of, 42–43
  religion and, 113
  support for consolidation of Winston and Salem, 57
  tributes to, 72, 73
Manly, Emily Buford, 24
Manly, Matthias E., 24
Manly, Sarah Simpson, 24
Manly & Hendren, 38, 47–48, 187
Manly, Hendren & Womble, 187
  cases of, 55–56, 61–62, 78–79
  changes in law and, 67–68

clients of, 55–56, 61, 70, 76, 77, 78, 81, 89–90
community service of, 61
location of, 54
name change of, 90–91
World War I years and, 59, 61
World War II years and, 88–93
Maready v. City of Winston-Salem, 170
Marketing Committee, 177
marketing program, of Womble Carlyle, 177
Marshall, Nina, 99
Martin, Eva Hendren, 68
Martin, Frank A., 68
Martin, James, 17
Martin, Linville Kerr "Hip," 71, 104
background of, 68
"Ball for British Relief" and, 86
becomes member of firm, 82
clients of, 70
community service of, 80–81
death of, 103
health of, 99
real estate and trial work of, 80
war service of, 88–89
Martin, Mrs. Linville Kerr "Hip," 104
Mary Reynolds Babcock Foundation, 100, 113
Mast, Daniel P., 6, 10
Masten, Joe, 6
Mast & Gray, 10
Maxwell, Jo, 99, 113
Maynard, W. L., 116, 143
McDowell, Mary Bynum, 6
McLean, Malcolm, 86
McLean Trucking Company, 86, 88, 100, 101, 107, 110
McLendon, L. P., 79
McNames, Dennis W., 128
Meador, Patricia T., 168, 169, 185
medical malpractice cases, 61. *See also* Health and medical law practice
The Memorabilia, 3, 15, 33
Merchants' Bank and Trust Company, 76
mergers-and-acquisitions practice, 149
Metropolitan Life Insurance Company, 78, 81, 110
Michael, Ken, 113
Mickey, Julius, 67
Mickey, Samuel, 67
Miller Airport, 77
Miller family, 13
Mitchell, Burley B., Jr., 177, 178
Mitchell, Eddie C., 124
Mitchell, W. G. Champion, 129, 139, 150
Modern Chevrolet, 96
Montgomery Ward & Company, 78
Moon, Owen, 77
Moore, William, 148
Moravian Brethren, xvii
Moravian Church, 124
Moravians, 28
Morganton, 110
Morrell, S. J., 20–21
Morrison, Cameron, 81
Moser, Kenneth A., 126, 134
municipal-law practice, 110, 139
murder cases, 48, 78–79

Nantahala Power and Light Company, 83
National Carbon Company, 86, 96
National Christian Charitable Foundation, 113
National Cigarette & Tobacco Company, Bonsack Machine Company v., 31
National Highway Auto Tour, 47
National Labor Relations Board, 100, 126
The National Law Journal, 166
National Prohibition Act, 82–83
National Tobacco Settlement, Phase II, 176
negligence practice, 149
Newcomen Award, 113
New York Bowery Fire Insurance Company, 28
Niagara Fire Insurance Company, 28
Ninth Judicial District, 19
Nissen Building, 66, 89, 122
Nixon, Richard M., 127
North Carolina Bankers Association, 80
North Carolina Baptist Hospital, 66, 67, 122
North Carolina Bar Association
African-Americans admitted to, 121–22
B. S. Womble as president of, 79–80, 121
C. Manly as president of, 43, 73, 121
Elizabeth L. Quick as president of, 170
ethical standards of, 70
formation of, 35
I. Carlyle as president of, 89, 121
Linville K. Martin as president of, 121
W. F. Womble as president of, 121
W. M. Hendren as president of, 69, 121
North Carolina Bar Association Committee on Legal Aid, 79
North Carolina Board of Public Welfare, 103
North Carolina Committee to End the War in Indochina, 130
North Carolina County Commissioners Association, 126
North Carolina Department of Crime Control and Public Safety, 177
North Carolina Department of Revenue, 123, 126
North Carolina Eye Bank, 113
North Carolina Fund, 115
North Carolina League of Municipalities, 126, 149
North Carolina Supreme Court
Boyer v. Teague, 20
Briggs case, 48
City of Winston-Salem v. Forsyth County, 89
City of Winston v. Wachovia Bank and Trust, 55–56
Joyner v. Duncan, 138
Koontz v. City of Winston-Salem, 129
Lizzie Penn v. Western Union Telegraph Company, 55
Maready v. City of Winston-Salem, 170
Rolin case, 47–48
Valk case, 61
Wachovia Bank and Trust Company v. Ogburn, 72
Wilson case, 37
Northern Virginia office, of Womble Carlyle, 174
Northside Shopping Center, 108
Northwestern North Carolina Railroad, 19, 24, 28

Ogburn, Wachovia Bank and Trust Company v., 72
O'Hanlon Building, 66
Oldham, Edward A., 17
Old Joe (camel), 59
Old Salem Restoration Fund Campaign, 100
Old Town Club, 113
Olivia Raney Library, 44
One Triad Park, 154, 155, 180
One West Fourth Street, 180
Owens-Illinois Glass Company, 119

P. H. Hanes and Company, 15
P. H. Hanes and Company, Carter Machine Company v., 31
P. H. Hanes Knitting Company, 42, 47, 77, 86, 107, 120
paralegals, 139, 140, 150
Parker, E. S., 69
Parker, Hassel L.
  Atlanta office and, 172
  awards of, 185
  expansion of firm and focus of, 152, 166
  on firm's sense of community, 133
  as head of Ancillary Services Group, 175
  as head of FirmLogic, 178, 183
  hired as firm administrator, 141–42
  on pivotal events for Womble Carlyle, 145
  on smoking and health litigation discussions, 150
Parker, John J., Judge, 83, 102
Parker, Johnson, Cook & Dunlevie, 163, 165–66
Parker, Raymond G., Judge, 68
Parker, Terrill A., 113, 166
Parkway Plaza, 108
Parrish & Deal, 70
Parrot, W. Thomas, 174
Partnership Agreement, 127
Partnership Management Committee, 127, 134, 144, 145, 152, 156, 159
patent infringement cases, 31
Patrons' Group for the Arts Council Follies, 102
Patterson, Lindsay, 72
Patton case, 159, 176
Pearson, Richmond, Judge, 6, 7, 17, 19
Peebles, R. B., Judge, 48
pension and profit-sharing practice, 99–100
People's National Bank, 47, 76
Perkins, C. E., 97
personal injury and negligence claims, 47–48, 78, 90
Pfohl, E. A., 6
Pfohl and Stockton, 5
"Philosophy of Life," credo of W. M. Hendren, 83
Philpott, H. Cloyd, 114
Pickford, Mary, 115
Piedmont Aviation, Inc., 100, 101, 122, 124–25, 126, 134
Piedmont Federal Savings and Loan, 122
Piedmont Natural Gas Company, 134
Piedmont Publishing Company, 81, 115–16, 124, 134
Piedmont Publishing Company v. Rogers, 115–16
Pilot Freight Company, 100, 107, 110
Pilot Life Insurance Company, 78, 90
Pilot Mountain case, 37
Planters Tobacco Warehouse, 86
Pohl, Kenneth, Rev., 76
Poovey, Mark, 150, 177
possum hunts, 55
Powell, Lesley, 143, 152
PPLC (professional limited liability company), Womble Carlyle as, 159
predecessors, of Womble Carlyle Sandridge & Rice, xvii, 187. *See also* *specific firm names*
Premier Bank, 166
Presbyterian Church, 48
Price Waterhouse, 124, 141, 150, 152
Prince Albert pipe tobacco, 59, 108
pro bono legal work, 113, 160, 185
product-liability practice, 138, 149, 157
professional limited liability company (PPLC), Womble Carlyle as, 159
Prohibition, 46, 82
Prudential Insurance Company, 78
Purrington, Al, III, 100, 147
Purrington, Al, Jr., 100, 146, 147
Purrington & Purrington, 143

Qualls, Gary, 168
Quick, Elizabeth L., 171
  awards of, 185
  becomes member of firm, 128
  estate planning work of, 149
  on *Joyner v. Duncan* case, 138
  as partner, 139
  as president of North Carolina Bar Association, 170
Quick, Robert, 128

R. J. Reynolds Auditorium, 69
R. J. Reynolds Tobacco Company
  buildings of, 64, 66, 118
  as client of Manly, Hendren & Womble, 61, 77, 90
  as client of Womble, Carlyle, Martin & Sandridge, 100, 102, 107, 109, 122, 126
  growth of, 51, 75, 76, 120
  insurer for, 78
  products of, 58, 59, 108, 120, 149
  Rolin case and, 47–48
  smoking and health litigation against, 149–50
  Winston-Salem and success of, 148
  World War I and, 59
  World War II and, 86, 88
racial issues, 61–62. *See also* African-Americans
Ragland, George A., 138
Railroad, Crutchfield v., 13
railroads, 5, 10, 28, 42, 78
Raleigh office, of Womble Carlyle
  associates hired in, 148
  building for, 147
  focus of, 147, 159
  growth of, 167, 179–80

office technology in, 150
staff of, 152
Womble Carlyle expansion to, 143, 145, 147
Raper, William C.
Bailey case and, 176
becomes member of firm, 129
Charlotte office and, 159
as co-head of General Litigation, 156
on Sandridge, 135
Smith/Shaver class action suit and, 160
on smoking and health project, 150
Ray, Michael E., 138, 179
Rayle, Bartlett Y., 10
real-estate practice, 70, 80, 108, 110–11, 122, 156
receptionists, 99
Reconstruction, end of, 4
Recorder's Court, 54
Red Cross, 61, 81, 86, 102, 103
RegO Company, 157
Reliance Trust Company, 166
Republican Party, 6
Research Triangle Park office, of Womble Carlyle, 163, 167–68, 179–80
retirement planning practice, 149
Revenue Act (1942), 92
Reynolda, 78
Reynolda Manor, 108
Reynolds, Katharine, 63, 78
Reynolds, Richard Joshua, 11, 33, 78, 100
B. S. Womble and, 54
death of, 63
early years in Winston, 6
epitaph of, 73
formation of Winston Board of Trade and, 15, 17
possum hunts and, 55
wealth of, 40, 41
Reynolds, Richard Joshua, Jr., 96
Reynolds, William N., 41, 79
Reynolds, Z. Smith, 63, 78–79
Rice, Leon Leftwich, Jr., 126, 136, 157
B. S. Womble hiring of, 92
on B. S. Womble, 128
clients of, 110
community service of, 100, 102, 113
death of, 153
Elizabeth Quick on, 128
on firm's sense of community, 155
on *Joyner v. Duncan* case, 138
Living, Loving and Lawyering, 99, 117, 139, 152–53
on Nixon, 127
on paralegals, 139
Partnership Agreement and, 127
pension and profit-sharing work of, 99–100
religion and, 113
retirement of, 152–53
as senior partner, 109, 134, 135
taxation work of, 110, 114–15, 123
on work, 117, 133–34
Rice, Richard T., 138, 160
Richmond & Danville Railroad, 12–13
Riley, Elizabeth, 148
RJR Foods, 120
RJR Nabisco, 149, 155, 156, 157–58
Robbins, David Peter, 19
Robert E. Lee Hotel, 66
Rochester Lyceum Bureau, 48
Rockingham County, 19
Rodden, Marie, 140
Rogers, Buddy, 115
Rogers, Piedmont Publishing Company v., 115–16
Rolin, Willie, 47–48
Rondthaler, Edward, Bishop, 3, 13, 15, 33, 59
Rotary Club, 130–31
Royal Indemnity Company, 100
Royall, Kenneth C., 91
"Rule Against Perpetuities," 138
Rules Committee (state senate), 102
Russell, Daniel, 28

Safe Bus Company, Washington v., 90, 91
Salem
in 1876, 4
consolidation with Winston, 56–58
Salem Boys School, 58
Salem College and Academy, 124
Salem College and Academy Board of Trustees, 114
Sandridge, William Pendleton, Jr., 111, 133, 141, 163
Sandridge, William Pendleton, Sr., 126, 128, 129, 136
awards of, 116
becomes member of firm, 82
cases of, 115–16, 122–23, 124–25
clients of, 81, 100, 102, 110
community service of, 89, 102, 103, 113
death of, 143
on expansion of firm into new markets, 143
religion and, 113
as senior partner, 109, 134, 135
World War II years of, 89
year joined firm, 80
Sands, Alexander "Sandy," 159, 176
Sawyer, Thomas J., 174
Schlaudt, Edward M., 114
Schwartz, Ira, 176
scrap-metal drives, 88
Sears Roebuck and Company, 96
secretaries
Beth Keiger, 140–41
Claudia Lyda, 140
Fay Heilig, 99
Kitty Graham, 99
Pat Wilson, 94
Security Life and Trust Company, 66, 68, 77, 79, 100, 110, 122
segregation, 52
Senate (State of North Carolina)
B. S. Womble terms in, 69–70
C. B. Watson terms in, 8
I. Carlyle terms in, 89, 102–3
L. Davis terms in, 126

R. B Glenn terms in, 35, 43
W. B. Glenn terms in, 12
W. M. Hendren terms in, 79
Senate (U. S.)
R. B Glenn runs for, 37
Simmons terms in, 27
Watson terms in, 37
Settle, Thomas, Judge, 6
Settlement Administration Services unit, of Ancillary Services, 176
7,405.3 Acres of Land in Macon, Clay, and Swain Counties, N. C., et al., United States v., 83
Sherman Antitrust Act, 90, 129
Sherrod, Slade v., 61
Sherrod, W. J., 61
Sherwood Plaza, 108
S & H Green Stamp people, 38
Shreve, Lamb & Harmon, 66
Simmons, Furnifold M., 24, 27, 43, 59, 73
Simmons & Manly, 24, 27
Sims, Barbara, 109, 124
Slade, West, 61
Slade v. Sherrod, 61
Slater Industrial and Normal School, 36
smallpox epidemic, 35–36
Smith, James Howell, 75
Smith, W. Lindsay, 173
Smith, Willis, 103
Smith Reynolds Airport, 88
Smith/Shaver class action suit, 159–60, 176
smoking and health litigation, 149–50, 152
Sorrell, Al, 163
Southern Bell, 66
Southern Public Utilities Company, 78
Southern Railway Company, as client of firm, 28, 35, 47, 61, 70, 78, 81, 90, 100, 108
Souvenir of the Twin Cities (Winkler), 23
Special Committee on Cooperation Between Lawyers and Corporation Trust Companies, 79–80
Special Task Force, 152
Sperry and Hutchinson Company, 38
Spray Cotton Mills, 102, 110
St. Leo's Catholic Church, 113
St. Mark Presbyterian House, 113
Stacy, C. J., Justice, 89
Stacy, Walter P., Justice, 97
staff, office, 99, 139–41, 152
Stakeman, Kurt, 160
Standard Oil Company of New Jersey, 78
Standing Committees on Fires, 12
Stanly County, 12
Starbuck, D. H., 6, 12
Starbuck, H. R., 27
Starbuck & Field, 12
State Advisory Budget Commission, 102
State Board of Law Examiners, 81, 89, 102
State Democratic Executive Committee, 28, 35
State Life Underwriters Association, 92
Stephenson, Betty, 140
Stevenson, Adlai, 103
Stevenson, Gilbert, 70
Stevenson, Kim, 176
Stewart, Sallie, 48
stock-market crash (1929), 76
Stockton, Paul, 37
Stokes County, 12, 19, 72
Sullivan, Bill, 158–59
Sunny Side Club, 27, 28
Surry County, 19
Swann v. Charlotte-Mecklenburg School, 129

Tanglewood Manor House, 142
Taxation Section, American Bar Association, 114
tax law, 59
B. S. Womble and, 91–92
Corporate and Tax Section, 123, 126, 133
Rice and, 110, 114–15, 123
Taylor, Board of Commissioners of Winston v., 20
Taylor Brothers, 77
Teague, Boyer v., 20
Teague, M. E., 20
Technology Department, 175
Tedrow, F. Keith, 168
Temple Emanuel, 113
textile companies, 102, 110
Textile Workers Union of America, CIO v. Arista Mills Company, 102
Thomas, Max, 114
Thomas, William Holland "White Chief of the Cherokee," 82, 83
Thomas Built Buses, Inc., 122, 134
Thomasville Furniture Industries, 110, 123, 134
Thompson, Jack, Judge, 176
Thrift, Ashley O., 159, 176
Thruway Shopping Center, 108
Tilden, Samuel J., 3
Timberlake, Edward, 68
Tise, J. Cicero, 72
Title VII of the Civil Rights Act (1964), 126
Title IX and the Age Discrimination in Employment Act (ADEA), 134
tobacco
early industry in Winston, 5–6, 14, 41
growth of industry in Winston, 33, 51, 52
tobacco companies, cases against, 47–48, 90, 149–50, 152, 158. *See also names of individual companies*
"Tobacco Nine," 21
Tobacco Workers Union, 100
Trade, Employment, and Governmental Regulations Section, 156
"trade day," 52
Transcontinental Gas Pipe Line Corporation, 110, 124
Transit Group, 166
Triad United Methodist Home, 113
"The Trial of Christ From a Judicial Standpoint" (Manly), 36
Triangle Broadcasting Corporation, 115
Trinity College Alumni Association, 55
Trinity College Board of Trustees, 55
Trinity College School of Law, 55
Truman, Harry S., 98
Trustees of Wake Forest College, Z. Smith Reynolds Foundation v., 97
Tursi, Frank V., 58

Twenty-first Amendment, 82
Twin-City Club, 19, 44, 55, 69, 81
Twin-City Hospital, 39
Twin-City Sentinel, 81, 93

Umstead, William B., 105, 114
Union Guano Company, 47
Union Indemnity Company, 78
unionization, 97, 100, 102
United Fund, 103, 111
United States Army Air Force's Office of Flying Safety, 88, 89
United States Court for the Western District of North Carolina, 35
United States Court of Appeals for the Fourth Circuit, 82, 83, 102
United States v. 7,405.3 Acres of Land in Macon, Clay, and Swain Counties, N. C., et al., 83
United States v. Chambers et al., 82–83
United States v. Container Corporation of America, 129
U.S. Court of Appeals for the Third Circuit, 158
U.S. Supreme Court
- *Brown v. Board of Education of Topeka, Kansas,* 105
- *Cipollone v. Liggett Group, Inc.,* 158
- *Hammer v. Dagenhart,* 62
- *Smith/Shaver* class action suit, 159–60
- *Swann v. Charlotte-Mecklenburg School,* 129
- *United States v. Chambers et al.,* 82–83
- *United States v. Container Corporation of America,* 129

Vade Mecum Springs, 72
Valk, A. de T., Dr., 61
Vance, Charles Fogle, Jr., 126, 128, 144, 146
- becomes member of firm, 99, 107
- cases of, 122, 149
- clients of, 124
- community service of, 114
- death of, 170
- litigation work of, 110, 135
- on Partnership Management Committee, 134
- RegO Company and, 157
- religion and, 113
- as senior partner, 109

Vance, Zebulon B., 6
Vaughan, James F., 172
Vaughan, Keith W., 129, 150, 160, 176
Vaughn, R. C., Jr., 143
veterans of World War II, law practice and, 95–96
Vulcan Materials Company, 122–23, 124, 126

W. B. Taylor & Bros., 20
W. P. Sandridge, Sr., Award for Service to the Firm, 185
Wachovia Bank and Trust, City of Winston v., 55–56
Wachovia Bank Company, 24
Wachovia Bank and Trust Company
- building and financial resources of, 121
- *City of Winston v. Wachovia Bank and Trust,* 55–56
- class-action suits against, 126
- as client of Womble Carlyle and predecessors, 47, 61, 75, 77, 81, 100, 107, 109, 124, 134
- ethics and, 70, 72
- First Atlanta Corporation and, 148–49
- Merchants' Bank receivership and, 78
- runs on, 76
- Tise case and, 72

Wachovia Bank and Trust Company v. Ogburn, 72
Wachovia Historical Museum, 58
Wachovia Loan and Trust Company, 51
Wachovia Mortgage Company, 134
Wachovia National Bank, 35, 42, 51
Wachovia Realty Investments, 134
Wake Forest College, 97, 98
Wake Forest College Board of Trustees, 97
Wake Forest University, 122
Walker, Albert "Ab," 78
War Advisory Board, 61
Ward, Hiram H., Judge, 130
War Revenue Act (1917), 59
Washington, D.C., office of Womble Carlyle, 159, 170, 171, 172
Washington, Leonard E., 90
Washington Mills, 72
Washington Mills, Carolina Portland Cement Company v., 72
Washington v. Safe Bus Company, 90, 91
Watson, Cyrus Barksdale, xvii, 19, 24, 71
- background of, 7–8
- government service of, 8, 26
- leaving Watson & Glenn, 13, 17
- military service of, 6
- support for consolidation of Winston and Salem, 57
- Teague case and, 20

Watson, John, 7
Watson, Marie Folger, 7
Watson & Buxton, 17, 54
Watson & Glenn, xvii, 10, 187
- cases of, 10, 12, 13
- corporate clients of, 12–13
- government clients of, 12, 13
- location of, 10
- termination of practice of, 13, 17

Wells, Dewey W., 185
Wells-Whitehead Tobacco Company, 48
West End Hotel and Land Company, 31
West End Land and Improvement Company, 27
West End Methodist Church, 103
Western Electric Company, 96–97, 107, 110
Western Union Telegraph Company, 35, 55, 61, 78
Western Union Telegraph Company, Lizzie Penn v., 55
Whichard, Willis, Judge, 170
Whitaker, W. A., 17
Whitaker Park, 108
White, John, 10
"White Chief of the Cherokee," 82, 83
"Why I Am a Democrat" (Carlyle), 116
Wiley, Calvin H., 17
Wiley, Terry M., 142, 160, 161, 175
Wilkes County Superior Court, 138
Wilkes Superior Court, 61
Williamson, Bruce, 176

William Womble Award for Service to the Bar, 185
Wilson, Pat, 94
Wilson, Richard, 37
Wilson, Thomas J., Judge, 6, 37
Winkler, Angelina, 23
Winston
in 1876, xv–xvii, 3–6
consolidation with Salem, 56–58
early legal scene in, 6, 10, 12
in early 1900s, 41–42, 51–52
legal cases involving, 55–56
in 1880s, 13, 15
in 1890s, 23–24, 33–34
segregation in, 52
town hall of, 57
Winston Board of Aldermen, 38
Winston Board of Trade (Chamber of Commerce), 17, 19
Winston (bulldog), advertising campaign and, 177, 178
Winston Cigarette Machine Company, 48
Winston Graded School, 13, 16, 17
Winston-Salem
bicentennial celebration, 132
in early 1920s, 65–67
Fourth Street, 120
Great Depression and, 76
I. Carlyle as attorney for, 109, 114
post-World War II, 95–99, 106
in 1930s, 75–77
in 1950s-1960s, 107–8
in 1960s-1970s, 119–21
success of R. J. Reynolds Tobacco Company and, 148
World War II and, 85–88
Winston-Salem: A History (Tursi), 58
Winston-Salem Arts Council, 114
Winston-Salem Athletic Association, 39
Winston-Salem Board of Trade, 47
Winston-Salem Chamber of Commerce, 27, 28, 89, 103, 108, 115, 119
Winston-Salem City School Board, 79
Winston-Salem Civic Ventures, 155
Winston-Salem/Forsyth County Board of Education, 126, 129
Winston-Salem Foundation, 72, 113
Winston-Salem Hospital Commission, 113
Winston-Salem Journal, 81
Winston-Salem National Guard Armory case, 129
Winston-Salem Power Company, 47
Winston-Salem Railway and Electric Company, 25, 37
Winston-Salem Rotary Club, 55
Winston-Salem School Board, 114
Winston-Salem State University, 36
Winston-Salem Teachers' College, 36
Woman's Club of Winston-Salem, 76
Womble, Bunyan Snipes, 53, 62, 71, 112, 157
background of, 52, 54–55
Barnhill and, 111
Browder on, 111
Carlyle's cuspidor and, 124
cases of, 55, 90
clients of, 55
community service of, 55, 89, 102, 111, 113
death of, 130–31
53rd year party for, 113
financial status of, 75
knack for innovation, stories about, 92
Manly's funeral and, 72–73
religion and, 113
as senior partner, 109
tax law and, 91–92
on W. M. Hendren, 83
Womble, Calder W., 112, 128, 146
banking and finance work of, 122
becomes member of firm, 99
clients of, 134
community service of, 103, 111, 114, 155
Donadio on, 134–35
expansion of firm to Raleigh and, 147
long-range planning and, 141
as managing partner, 156
on Partnership Management Committee, 134, 144, 145
religion and, 113
as senior partner, 109
war service of, 88
Womble, Edith, 80
Womble, Olivia Snipes, 52
Womble, William Fletcher, 52
Womble, William Fletcher, Jr., 128, 134–35, 149, 156, 157, 170
Womble, William Fletcher, Sr., 112, 127, 128, 144, 145
on advertising by lawyers, 95
African-Americans and North Carolina Bar Association, 121–22
as assistant to I. Carlyle, 114
clients of, 89
community service of, 103, 111, 115
desegregation cases of, 126
on firm location changes, 119
government service of, 115
as managing partner, 109
narrative of firm history, 107
religion and, 113
as senior partner, 134
war service of, 88
Womble, Carlyle, Martin & Sandridge, 187
air conditioners installed, 108
associates of, 126
budgets and, 108
changes in law and, 91
clients of, 97, 100, 102, 107–8, 109–10, 122, 123, 124
community service of attorneys in, 113–14 (*see also* "Community service of" *under names of individual attorneys*)
government service of, 114
growth of, 109, 119, 125, 126
location changes of, 117, 119
name change of, 90–91, 127
religious ties in community, 113
Womble Carlyle Sandridge & Rice
associates of, 133, 138, 148, 152
budget of, 139–40
cases of, 168–70, 176 (*see also specific cases*)
change in location of, 154, 180, 181
clients of, 134, 149–50 (*see also names of specific clients*)

community service of, 160, 163
expansion into other markets by, 141 (*see also* Atlanta office, of Womble Carlyle; Charlotte office, of Womble Carlyle; Greenville office, of Womble Carlyle; Northern Virginia office, of Womble Carlyle; Raleigh office, of Womble Carlyle; Research Triangle Park office, of Womble Carlyle; Washington, D.C. office, of Womble Carlyle)
firm retreats, 142–43
growth rate of, 133, 134, 138, 149, 150, 152, 155, 166–67
long-range planning of, 141–42
marketing program of, 177
mergers with other law firms, 100, 146, 150, 152, 156, 163, 172
name change of, 127
paralegals of, 139, 140, 150
partners' retreats, 141
practice groups of, 156
predecessors of, xvii, 187 (*see also specific firm names*)
as professional limited liability company, 159
smoking and health litigation, 149–50, 152
staff of, 99, 139–41, 152
technology and, 141, 150, 160, 175
women lawyers, in firm, 128–29. *See also names of individual lawyers*
Works Progress Administration (WPA), 77
World War I, 58–59, 60, 62
World War II, 85–93
WPA (Works Progress Administration), 77
WSJS radio station, 77, 81
WSJS-TV, 115
Wyche, Burgess, Freeman & Parham, 173

Yadkin County, 13, 19
Yeagy, Stephen A., 138
YMCA, 28, 35, 81
Young Men's Democratic Club, 55
Yurka, Blanche, 78

Z. Smith Reynolds Foundation, 79, 97
Z. Smith Reynolds Foundation v. Trustees of Wake Forest College, 97
Zinzendorf Hotel, 24, 29, 30, 42
Zinzendorf Hotel fire case, 31
Zoning Board of Adjustment, 114
zoning ordinance, 97, 99